Celebrate
the
Wonder

Celebrate the Wonder

A FAMILY CHRISTMAS TREASURY

Kristin M. Tucker and
Rebecca Lowe Warren

A Ballantine/Epiphany Book
Ballantine Books • New York

To our families—

Roger and Holly Warren
Tom, Nicole, and Michael Tucker

And to the eternal spirit of Christmas.

BRITTLE COOKIES

From Bonnie Cohen and
Chronicle recipe archives

- **40 saltine crackers**
- **1 cup butter**
- **1 cup brown sugar**
- **1 (6-ounce) package
  chocolate chips**
- **1 cup chopped nuts**

- Preheat oven to 350
degrees.
- Place a layer of foil on a
rimmed baking sheet. Spread
crackers over foil.
- In a saucepan, combine
butter and brown sugar and
bring to a boil. Boil 3 minutes.
Pour over crackers.
- Bake for 5 minutes or until
crackers "float."
- Remove pan from oven and
sprinkle chocolate chips over
top of crackers. When melted,
spread evenly over the
crackers, then top with nuts.
- Cut into bars. Allow to
cool, then serve. These taste
amazingly like toffee bars.

CONTENTS

PREFACE

Christmas brings to mind intertwining images of the humble crèche, boughs of holly, and merry ol' St. Nick. Around the world, dramas, feasts, decorations, and gifts mark Christmas celebrations. Yet today, the richness of these traditions is often overshadowed by holiday stress, and our celebrations no longer befit the birthday of the Prince of Peace.

In *Celebrate the Wonder*, we honor Christmas as an event shrouded in mystery and rich in meaning. As Christians and concerned parents, we affirm the importance of tradition and seek to return to the simple joys of the first Christmas. Here you will find tools for setting holiday goals, and guidelines to help you evaluate, plan, and prepare your Advent and Christmas celebrations. We have also included a carefully chosen sampling of traditional, historical, and contemporary Christmas celebrations which we hope will add a richness to your holiday plans.

Throughout these four chapters we advocate creative occasions, flexible attitudes, and simple fares:

Chapter 1—"Bringing Christmas Home" helps you evaluate previous Christmas celebrations and plan for the upcoming Christmas season.

Chapter 2—"Gift Giving" develops a philosophy of giving and receiving gifts, and offers history, traditions, and suggestions.

Chapter 3—"Tinsel and Treasures" discusses Christmas decorations as a personal and home-centered expression of holiday greetings to friends and strangers.

Chapter 4—"Where Two or More Are Gathered . . ." presents entertaining as an enjoyable experience for hosts and guests. Included are guides for fourteen holiday celebrations, each depicting entertaining as a wonderful opportunity to share time, food, and self.

ACKNOWLEDGMENTS

We offer our heartfelt thanks to:

Toni Simmons, our gracious and enthusiastic editor at Ballantine/Epiphany;

Our church families at Montavilla United Methodist Church (Portland, Oregon) and Twin Falls (Idaho) United Methodist Church;

The many friends who helped us develop and test the ideas in *Celebrate the Wonder*;

And especially our families, whose love, laughter, and faith brought life to this dream of ours. It is to them—and the spirit of Christmas—that we dedicate this book.

Let us go over to Bethlehem and see this thing that
has happened, which the Lord has made known to us.
—Luke 2:15

Celebrate the Wonder

CHAPTER 1
Bringing Christmas Home

C hristmas is evergreens, red bows, candles, and carolers . . . grinning elves on Christmas cards, Santa visits, and presents hidden under beds or nestled in attic trunks. Crèche figures emerge from their tissue paper cocoons and a Christmas pageant transforms Dad's robe into the regal garb of a Wise Man.

The first Christmas was a creative experience: God performed the unexpected. A baby was born in a rustic stable in Bethlehem. No real cause for celebration—babies were born every day. But this birth was different. In the midst of the squalor angels sang, astonished shepherds left their flocks, and Wise Men far to the east of Bethlehem began their journey to the stable. The spirit of this first Christmas was joy, astonishment, and wonder.

Two thousand years later, our Christmas celebrations are filled with traditions. We seek the spirit of the first Christmas but may experience weariness and pressures instead. Everyday realities, including limitations of time, money, and energy, pull us from those pleasant images of Christmas. Yet we still believe that the spirit of Christmas lives despite our humble and harried attempts to celebrate the birthday of the Prince of Peace.

Christmas needs to be brought home. Our celebrations must touch us at the center of our lives and respond to our immediate needs and hopes. As celebrants we must:

• Examine our concerns and set priorities.
• Share our honest and heartfelt expectations with family and friends.
• Create celebrations reflecting these personal concerns and expectations.
• Look beyond traditional holiday images and explore unfamiliar traditions—the Saint Lucia festivities in Scandinavia, Las Posadas in Mexico, and Epiphany in England and South America.

Christianity is a frontier, too. It must ever be a challenge or it no longer will serve its Founder's purpose.
—John E. Baur
Christmas on the American Frontier

We are not finished with Christmas. To "serve its Founder's purpose," our celebrations must challenge us to explore, to share, and to enjoy our faith.

CHRISTMAS PRAYER

O God, our loving Father,
help us rightly to remember the birth of Jesus,
that we may share in the song of the angels,
the gladness of the shepherds
and the worship of the wise men . . .
May the Christmas morning make us happy
to be thy children
and the Christmas evening bring us to our beds
with grateful thoughts,
forgiving and forgiven, for Jesus' sake.
Amen.

—Robert Louis Stevenson

SETTING THE STAGE

With the determination to personalize Christmas—to bring the Christmas message home—comes the opportunity for prayerful and careful planning with family members.

PRAYERFUL PLANNING is an attitude of caring about the Christmas story, of feeling its significance for the twentieth century, and of being sensitive to how this is shared with family and friends. Prayerful planning:

• Guides celebrants in searching for the true meaning of Christmas. Just as the Wise Men returned home by a different route after seeing Jesus (Matthew 2:12), our annual journeys to Bethlehem can guide us back to our jobs, schools, and homes along different routes than we previously traveled. Christmas becomes a time of renewal.

• Sensitizes one to the feelings and thoughts of family members and friends.

• Enhances traditional images with personal ones.

• Keeps participants "on track" so commercialism does not dominate the holiday.

CAREFUL PLANNING involves the specifics—the who, what, when, where, and how of the ideas generated during sharing sessions. Careful planning:

• Contributes to a more relaxed and orderly experience. It allows for more time to plan and organize the event.

• Allows for the sharing of responsibilities. Usually the planning and follow-through of family events fall to one or two members. Careful planning distributes the responsibilities more equitably.

• Reduces tension, since a timetable can be worked out together. Participants can decide what jobs (i.e., baking, cleaning, decorating . . .) can be done in advance to avoid hectic schedules and tense holidays.

• Creates the feeling that the celebration is a joint venture, a common experience.

Throughout prayerful and careful planning, keep in mind that sharing beliefs and ideas is not always easy. Listen, compromise, and try to include everyone.

SELECTING THE CAST

Traditionally, Christmas is seen as family-centered, but celebrating with relatives may be impossible or even undesirable. Being with family is important but not essential for joyous celebrations. As you begin planning, determine which of the following "cast" possibilities applies to you.

Your Family

Discuss the role of the immediate family (those living under the same roof and sharing daily with each other) and the extended family (grandparents, in-laws, cousins, aunts, uncles, married siblings, and single family members who have established their own homes) in the upcoming Christmas. It is not necessary to invite the same people each year, nor is it essential to include them in the same way. Aunt Harriet may be a caroler at a Christmas party one year and be invited to your Christmas Eve gathering the next. Be flexible, imaginative, and considerate.

Consider how family circumstances may change from one Christmas to another.

• AGE: The children are a year older. Santa Claus visits may no longer be appropriate, but attending Christmas plays may be. All "cast" members are a year older as well and may have needs and new circumstances deserving consideration.

• LOCATION: Moving to a new town or neighborhood with new friends, or no friends, presents concerns but also possibilities. Exploring these can be an adventure. Moving closer to family or friends suggests changes as well.

• MARRIAGE: Weddings bring new in-laws and traditions (and perhaps a stepparent and stepchildren).

• DIVORCE or SEPARATION: Breaking up a family may separate loved ones, change incomes, and create animosities.

• ILLNESS: Sickness or hospitalization may strain the family budget and add extra tension to the holidays.

• DEATH: Fond memories and grief accompany recollections of a deceased family member. Share these concerns and empathize with each other. Be as open as you can about these sensitive feelings. Decide if you want to include your memories of this person in the holiday plans through a special gift, a celebration, or a memorial.

• JOB CHANGES: Unemployment or a new job usually changes salaries and schedules. Perhaps both parents are working this year in contrast to one last year. This may reduce the time the family has to share with each other or with friends, but increase the money available for gifts, outings, contributions, and decorations.

One year never duplicates another. Each Christmas offers the chance to create a meaningful celebration from different circumstances.

When sharing and planning together as a family, encourage full participation. Everyone's suggestions are valuable. The family becomes a forum for ideas and feelings—a communications center generating concern and creativity.

Your Friends

Both "tried and true" and "fairly new" friends may be included in your Christmas. Invite them to occasional gatherings in December and January. Or select a "Christmas Family" with whom you plan to share most of the holiday. This might be another family or just friends who live together, work together, or won't be going home for the holidays.

Age, mobility, marital status, and health affect the lives of friends as well as family members. Consider these circumstances as you plan to include your friends in your holiday celebrations.

Yourself

For all of us, Christmas can be a grueling, tension-filled holiday. You can reverse this trend by:

• Appraising your personal expectations for Christmas.

• Sharing your expectations and feelings with those with whom you will be sharing Christmas.

• Acknowledging the need for a growing personal faith and acting to fulfill that need. Daily devotions, journal keeping, sharing groups, or inspiring workshops are worthy possibilities.

In setting the stage or selecting the cast, there will be traditions, creative ideas, and practical matters to consider. Meshing these and celebrating Christmas with people we value are paramount in bringing Christmas home.

Whichever (traditions) you choose for your family, the most important element should be sharing the holiday. Christmas is represented to us as a time for giving, and there are no greater gifts we can give each other as families than our time and our care.

—Portland Family Calendar
December 1980

PLANNING TOGETHER

As the family plans and prepares for the holiday season together, it is embracing the essence of Christmas. Talking with one another, listening to each other, and working together as a family are gifts worth exchanging. These gifts not only contribute to a more meaningful holiday but may continue beyond Christmas to improve a family's life together.

To help you plan together, we suggest five family celebrations. These will direct the planning while providing opportunities to improve communication skills and explore creative possibilities as a family unit.

This process is not without problems. Families include different personalities who may find interacting and planning quite a challenge. The cynic must work with the romantic, the bug collector with the gourmet, and the bookkeeper with the musician. But there is reason to hope. Diversity can be cause to celebrate: it can infuse a holiday with new energy and potential. The Apostle Paul, in his letter to the church at Corinth, explained the harmony inherent in diversity.

> But as it is, God arranged the organs in the body, each one of them, as he chose. If all were a single organ, where would the body be? As it is, there are many parts, yet one body. . . . If one member suffers, all suffer together; if one member is honored, all rejoice together.
>
> —1 Corinthians 12:18–20, 26

Paul's message applies to families as well. Sometime when your family is together, talk about how each member is different. What is unique? What skills are enjoyed? What interests? What idiosyncracies? Brainstorm about your family's potential in light of these individual strengths.

Attitudes and feelings sometimes impede planning. A family member fearful of change may refrain from evaluating traditions or creating new ones. Or a college student, enthused with new ideas, may criticize the limited scope of the family's plans. Doubting the importance of his or her ideas, a child may remain silent or make inappropriate comments. Anger, depression, and exhaustion affect one's ability to communicate well.

In working with this diversity of personalities and ever-changing attitudes and feelings, we encourage an atmosphere of acceptance. Such acceptance can lead to a holiday celebration that expresses your family's interests and fulfills its needs.

Beginning on page 13 are FIVE FAMILY CELEBRATIONS. These are provided as a guide for families as they prayerfully and carefully plan for the holidays. If you become concerned with the direction the family is headed during these celebrations, ask yourself:

• Are we achieving the purpose of the celebration?

- Is everyone sharing?
- Is everyone listening?
- Is everyone having a good time?

If the answer to any of these questions is no, try to define the problem and search for solutions.

- If the group appears tired and unenthusiastic, a break may be appropriate. Take a walk together, fix a snack, tell jokes, or just "take five."
- If you are not making progress in a certain area, move on to something else. Return to the problem later.
- If a stalemate occurs, encourage compromise.
- If some individuals feel alienated, "strength bombardment" may help. It is easy to forget or even be too self-conscious to tell family members what we like and admire about them. These exercises "bombard" participants with affirmations that confirm each individual's value to the family. You can write down the affirmations or say them aloud.

Writing Down Affirmations

Sit in a circle. Distribute pens and paper to everyone. Individual names go at the top of these "strength sheets." Pass these sheets around so other family members can jot down what they most appreciate and admire about the person whose name appears at the top of the sheet. Everyone should write something for each person. It can be one remark or several: there's no limit to compliments!

When every strength sheet has gone around the circle, it's time to share. Participants read the information about themselves aloud and respond. This response should be brief—"Thank you," "This makes me feel good," "Oh, WOW!" or "I had no idea." It is important to affirm what is written and not deny it. Avoid saying, "This is all wrong" or "You have got to be kidding!" Denying someone's compliment ignores the sincerity of what was shared.

Encourage all participants to keep their strength sheets for an attitude boost any time.

Saying Them Aloud

Form a circle. Take turns standing in the center—the complimentary hot seat! Select someone to begin. The person in the center always faces the speaker giving the compliments and graciously accepts the positive comments.

The problems encountered in the FIVE FAMILY CELE-BRATIONS may not be solved during these four months: some solutions require more time. However, the sharing, planning, and working together will reap benefits—new activities, more time together with loved ones, and pleasant memories. Families may even adopt new and more effective communication patterns. Like the Magi, we can return to our homes by a different path: we are changed people after our four-month journey together.

FIVE FAMILY CELEBRATIONS

The activities and time estimates that follow have been carefully selected to make Christmas planning successful and enjoyable. If you believe the celebrations are valuable in their entirety but would be too much for your family at one time, hold two, three, or four shorter get-togethers in September and October. You may see other ways the agenda can be changed to make it more appropriate and meaningful. Feel free to do this, keeping in mind the purpose of the suggestions.

"On Your Mark"
The First of Five Family Celebrations

Thinking about Christmas in September may seem extreme, but if considerations include research, reservations, and travel, months of lead time are necessary. Families can explore different options and discuss ideas thoroughly. They can examine previous holidays in greater detail and spend more time in a relaxed atmosphere affirming and creating traditions.

In late August, set a date and time for the September celebration. Your family may prefer meeting prior to Labor Day, when schedules and work routines are more relaxed. Determine this date together and encourage full participation. Select one or two family members to chair the September meeting. Responsibilities include:

• Reading through the first two celebrations.
• Distributing Questionnaire A (begins on page 22) one week before the get-together.
• Reminding family members about the event.
• Reenforcing its importance and purpose.
• Obtaining necessary supplies (i.e., pencils, pens, paper).
• Preparing the setting—cleaning off the dining room table, picnic table, sofa, floor.
• Creating a Christmas mood at the get-together—for example, play holiday music, sing carols, serve a Christmas dessert, read Luke 2:1–10, or show photographs or slides of previous Christmases.
• Leading (but not monopolizing) the discussion.

While preparing and experiencing this celebration, keep its purpose in mind.

• To recall memories of past Christmases ("Remembering Together," page 15).
• To discuss concerns and ideas ("Sharing Together," page 15).
• To brainstorm about the Christmas to come ("Dreaming Together," page 15).
• To begin moving from dreams to reality through planning ("Planning and Assigning," page 20).
• To keep before you the true meaning of Christmas.
• To enjoy being together.

REMEMBERING TOGETHER

Time: 10–20 minutes
Necessary supplies: paper and crayons for everyone
   Draw a picture of a scene from a previous Christmas. Take turns sharing the answers to these questions.

- Who is in your picture?
- What are they doing?
- What was happening?
- How were you feeling?
- How were the others feeling?
- Why did you choose this particular scene?

SHARING TOGETHER

Time: 10–20 minutes
Necessary supplies: completed Questionnaire A
   Questionnaire A begins on page 22. Make copies of these pages for each family member. Distribute them to the family one week before the September celebration. THEY ARE TO COMPLETE THE QUESTIONNAIRE AND BRING IT TO THIS GET-TOGETHER.
   Parents and older siblings can work with the younger children. Before sharing, you may want to take a few minutes individually to review and update your questionnaire. Then move from one question to the next. In sharing, encourage family members to accept all answers. Criticism and ridicule are not constructive responses, they stifle sharing.
   Keep these completed questionnaires to refer to when working on Questionnaire B (begins on page 23).

DREAMING TOGETHER

Time: 20 minutes
Necessary supplies: crayons and paper for everyone
   Each person is to take ten minutes to describe a fantasy Christmas. Assume you have unlimited resources of time, money, and energy. Be as specific as you like and include

TOUR OF DECORATED HOMES

SINGING CHRISTMAS TREE PROGRAM

A NEIGHBORHOOD CHRISTMAS PARTY

DISNEYLAND

HANDEL'S MESSIAH

SLEIGH RIDE

MAKING DECORATIONS FOR A LOCAL HOSPITAL OR HOME

FAMILY SCRAPBOOK OF ADVENT

people, places, and experiences. After ten minutes, participants should share their creations. When everyone has shared, talk about any common themes in the fantasies. Are there similar activities, people, places?

A REMINDER! In the brainstorming that follows, don't limit celebrations to December 24, 25, and 31. All of December and January are yours to plan!

Keeping the fantasies in mind, brainstorm about family activities that might take place during the holidays. Then list the names of people your family would like to spend time with during the holidays.

Take time to share your lists with each other, as well as the reasons for your selections.

THINKING IT THROUGH

Time: 30 minutes
Necessary supplies: pencils and Questionnaire B (not filled in yet, and just one copy!)

Moving from "Dreaming Together" to "Thinking It Through" allows realism to enter the picture. Brainstorming may yield ideas never considered before, but these innovative suggestions require evaluation. Geography, community, health, and finances impose limitations. Acknowledging these limitations and discovering alternatives will reduce frustrations.

• GEOGRAPHY: What does your community look like in December? Is there snow nearby? Sunshine? Mountains? Deserts? How do climate and terrain affect your Christmas? What activities are possible in your area this time of year (skiing, hiking, sailing . . .)?

Where would you like to spend Christmas? Can you get there? Do you have access to woods where you could cut your own tree? What are some alternatives to your plans?

• COMMUNITY: What's happening during the holidays? Are religious services, holiday exhibits, concerts, plays scheduled locally? Are reservations necessary? How about cost?

What social obligations do you have? Is it necessary to go? Does your family want to create or organize a Christmas event? Would there be friends who might want to help you plan a Christmas musical program, puppet or magic shows, a story-telling session with music or sound effects?

Could you present your program at local detention facilities, nursing homes, service clubs, churches . . . ?

• HEALTH: Physical, Mental, and Emotional

During the holiday season, be sensitive to waning energy and enthusiasm and revise plans accordingly. Signs of exhaustion may include

—temper tantrums
—sibling rivalry and family squabbles
—children becoming too loud, overactive, or "out-of control" (applicable to adults as well!)
—illness
—withdrawal, depression, lethargy

• FINANCES:

$ $ $ $ $ $

Let's face it: Christmas may have been invented by Christians, but it has long since fallen into the hands of the moneychangers.
                    —"How to Beat Those Christmas Blues"
                    Ebony, December 1980

$ $ $ $ $ $

In 1985 alone, $25 billion was spent in the United States for Christmas. (Fifteen billion dollars of that total was "on credit.") Americans seem to forget that Christmas can be more than a commercialized sharing. Creative giving complements the Christmas spirit more than breakable plastic wonders, elaborate crèches, and expensive parties. We encourage you not to become financially strapped by Christmas. Credit card payments, interest rates, and finance charges can be hazardous to our health, and end up making Scrooges of us all.

> Out upon merry Christmas! What's Christmas time to you but a time for paying bills without money; a time for finding yourself a year older, but not an hour richer; a time for balancing your books and having every item in 'em through a round dozen of months presented dead against you?
>
> —(Ebenezer Scrooge)
> Charles Dickens
> *A Christmas Carol*

Some suggestions—

• Keep in mind that generosity at Christmas involves more than money. Our time, energy, enthusiasm, and caring can be thoughtful gifts as well.

• Make finances a family matter. Determine how much money is available for entertaining, giving, and decorating. Set priorities and contract to stay within these limits. If expensive gifts for relatives and friends have become the norm, feel free to break with tradition. Recipients may appreciate your creative gifts more and be inspired to follow suit. Perhaps they have wanted a change for years but lacked the courage to initiate it.

• Encourage the renovation of broken or worn-out toys as a way of sharing.

• Raise extra funds for special projects or gifts with family fund-raisers: garage sales, boutiques, paper routes, etc. This money could be spent on the family or donated to a community project or special offering.

• Discuss where your family can cut corners financially.

• Avoid last-minute and impulse purchases.

• Give gifts of money for after-Christmas shopping.

• Postpone some purchases until after Christmas, when prices are reduced for toys, appliances, clothing, and bedding.

• Begin a "Christmas fund" savings account and make regular deposits. Buying on credit and borrowing funds are not the only options!

$ $ $ $ $ $

The first piggy banks were part of European children's preparations for Christmas. The children were taught to save their coins in earthenware "feast pigs," which were to be opened as a part of the Christmas Day celebrations. A modern version of this tradition could encourage the family to save money for Christmas. The collected coins might be used for a special Christmas offering or sharing project. Rinsed-out bleach bottles or papier-mâché layered over an inflated balloon, can be transformed into great feast pigs. Adding cork legs and decorating with acrylic paints or scraps of felt or calico will give each pig its own personality!

$ $ $ $ $ $

Turn to Questionnaire B (page 23). Select a secretary to record ideas and decisions. (This activity can be done as a family or by parents, if children are too young or uninterested. Parents can report back to the entire family in a few days so enthusiasm and continuity won't be lost.)

Encourage everyone to participate.
Keep limitations in mind.   Listen to each other.
Be open to creative ideas.   Be flexible.
Compromise.   Try to decide by consensus.

Some ideas may be inappropriate for the holidays but great as spring or summer activities, for weekends or vacations. A suggestion or two might be perfect several Christmases from now, when the babies are older or the savings account larger.
Continue to fill out Questionnaire B.

• Record traditions (column 1).
• Turn to ideas (column 2) and discuss how important

each category (activities, gifts, cards, and decorations) is to your celebration of Christmas.

• Refer to the family summary sheet and brainstorming lists. Decide if any of the suggestions changes your feelings toward some of the categories. For example, working on a community project as a family might alter one's attitude toward giving; new outdoor decorations might stir more enthusiasm for decorating.

• Complete the time and money sections (columns 3 and 4). If it looks like you have more ideas and traditions than you have time and money, ask these questions:

—What do we want to do this Christmas?

—Which suggestions are more in line with these wishes?

—Which suggestions are worthy of our time, money, and energy?

—How do we want to feel during the holidays, and how does this suggestion compare with these feelings?

• Complete as much of Questionnaire B as possible. Feel free to leave some gaps, but any suggestion requiring research or extensive work should be accepted, adapted, or discarded now.

SKI TRIP

XMAS SHIPS

NEW YORK CITY

GARDEN SHOW

PLANNING AND ASSIGNING

Time: 20 minutes

Decide which suggestions require immediate research or planning. Discuss resources (libraries, Chambers of Commerce, park bureaus . . .). One responsibility can be to consult with the post office and package carriers. Regulations change periodically, and being informed may save time and rewrapping later. Don't let the family assume that the people who have handled similar plans in the past will continue in that role. The sharing of assignments helps Christmas become more of a family experience.

Decide upon the value of Family Workshop Nights, when

the family would gather once a week to prepare for Christmas. In this setting, making decorations, writing cards, and wrapping presents become family tasks, not individual ones. Serve simple suppers or go out to eat on these days. Jot down your plans and assignments in column 5 of Questionnaire B. Set a date and time for the October get-together. Select a person to organize this event. (Refer to page 14 for responsibilities.) Between now and October we encourage each family member to look through *Celebrate the Wonder* and select ideas appropriate to your family's needs and preferences.

Close with a prayer—perhaps a sentence prayer to which every family member contributes.

QUESTIONNAIRE A

Your responses to this informal questionnaire can help other family members learn about your past, your preferences, and your values. When answering the questions, think of the time frame for celebrating Christmas as more than Christmas Eve and Christmas Day. All of December and January offer opportunities to celebrate with friends and family.

1. What is your earliest Christmas memory?
2. What are your favorite Advent and Christmas traditions?
3. Is Advent special to you? Why? Is Christmas special to you? Why?
4. What do you want yourself, your spouse, your children, and your grandchildren to remember and value the most about Advent and Christmas?
5. How would you celebrate Christmas if you had no money to spend on gifts?
6. How do you think Jesus would want his birthday celebrated?
7. How will this year's holiday season be different from other years (e.g., age changes, finances, marriages, deaths in the family, community or church responsibilities)?
8. How would you like this year's holiday celebration to differ from last year's?
9. What are your friends and other relatives going to be doing during the holidays?
10. Whom would you like to spend time with during this year's holiday season?

QUESTIONNAIRE B

Yuletide is here again, the Yuletide is here again, We'll dance and celebrate till Easter.
Then when it's Easter-time, Yes when it's Easter-time, We'll dance and celebrate till Christmas.

—Swedish dance carol

How important is each of these categories to your celebration of Christmas?

	1. TRADITIONS* (What have we done in the past?)	2. IDEAS (What do we want to consider doing?)	3. TIME (How much time do we want to devote to this?)	4. MONEY (How much do we want to spend on this?)	5. PLANS & ASSIGNMENTS (What are we going to do, and who is doing what?)
ACTIVITIES with family & friends List persons you want to spend time with during the holidays.					
GIFTS For family and friends, teachers, employers, employees, the mail carrier, and other community acquaintances . . .					
CARDS To whom? Purchased or homemade? What are the alternatives?					
DECORATIONS Outdoor, indoor . . . At work, school, in the community, for service organizations . . .					

* If you have changed some traditions that affect other family members or friends, decide how and when to share these changes with them.

23

"Get Set"
The Second of Five Family Celebrations

If your October calendar seems full, consider the tasks that faced a rural Norwegian family at the turn of the century:

> butcher the stock
> cure meat
> make sausage
> dip candles
> clean house
> bake a year's supply of flat *bröd*
> chop wood for two-week Yule celebration . . .

These household tasks had to be completed by December 21, St. Thomas Day. If they were not, St. Thomas would steal the ax, and the holiday festivities to come would be plagued with mishaps!

Begin this family celebration by listening to the lyrics of one of your favorite Christmas carols. Reflect on the words together. What ideas was the writer trying to share? What do you think the writer was feeling? What feelings do you have as you listen to the lyrics? What images come to mind?

BACK TO B (BASICS)

Time: 20–30 minutes

Return to Questionnaire B. Family members who received assignments in September can report their findings. Share ideas discovered while browsing through *Celebrate the Wonder*. DISCUSS how these ideas affect the proposed plans. DETERMINE what remains to be done. Assign more responsibilities, and set DEADLINES. You'll need a "date checker," who scans newspapers, churches, park bureaus, colleges, service organizations, and public service announcements for potentially interesting family activities. This person can give a report at the next get-together in early November.

Children might enjoy special assignments through Christmas, such as being appointed song leader, fire builder, kitchen helper, or devotional leader.

THINGS TO THINK ABOUT

Time: 15 minutes

How do the following words relate to your plans so far? Mark a + by those that are included and a − by those that are absent. Make this a family poll, with each member putting a mark by each word. Discuss the results. Do some plans need to be changed? Eliminated? Added?

joy	spiritual	new
spontaneous	hope	old
creative	promise	expensive
stress	closeness	alone
relax	together	organized
tradition	sharing	unusual
adventure	friendship	peace
excitement	fun	wonder

Set a date and time for the family's next get-together in early November. Select an organizer for this event. (See page 14 for responsibilities.) Close by sharing this thought:

But I am sure I have always thought of Christmas time when it has come round—apart from the veneration due to its sacred name and origin, if anything belonging to it can be apart from that—as a good time: a kind, forgiving, charitable, pleasant time: the only time I know of, in the long calendar of the year, when men and women seem by one consent to open their shut-up hearts freely, and to think of people below them as if they really were fellow-passengers to the grave, and not another race of creatures bound on other journeys. And therefore, uncle, though it has never put a scrap of gold or silver in my pocket, I

believe that it has done me good, and will do me good;
and I say,
God bless it!

—(Fred, Uncle Scrooge's nephew)
Charles Dickens
A Christmas Carol

"Go"
The Third of Five Family Celebrations

There is a thread winding through all the events of
Christmas, the winter solstice, and the return of the
light, that returns us to the awe of the child, the reverence and joy that is part of our nature.

—Barbara and Nadia Rosenthal
*Christmas—New Ideas for an
Old-Fashioned Celebration*

HOLIDAY CHEER

Time: 15 minutes

Begin this celebration by creating a family rhythm band,
reading a children's Christmas story, or preparing a package
of holiday gifts.

• To create a family rhythm band, just play and sing
Christmas carols together using such symphonic instruments
as spoons, pots, pans, lids, or dried beans in a cardboard
cylinder.

• The Christmas story could be read by a youngster. That
would be a treat for everyone!

• The parcel of gifts might be to a foreign friend, a relative, or a mission project—foreign or local. Before sending
gifts to missions, try to find out what is needed most: clothing,
bedding, hygienic or medical supplies, money, food, toys.
Relief organizations and churches are possible sources of such
information.

Do not overlook *Give But Give Wisely*, a quarterly from the Better Business Bureau's Philanthropic Advisory Service. This valuable resource lists charitable, educational, and religious organizations whose practices agree with and differ from the BBB's voluntary standards of public disclosure, financial accountability, fund-raising practices, and so forth. For a copy, write: Philanthropic Advisory Service, Council of Better Business Bureaus, Inc., 1515 Wilson Blvd., Arlington, VA 22209.

Ancient legends depicted the Christ Child as a beggar wandering the earth on Christmas Eve in search of food and shelter. If a household refused to help a needy passerby on December 24, they might be rejecting Jesus himself. Christians in the Middle Ages continued to aid and even revere the poor, who were considered akin to the penniless Jesus. Mercy shown to the needy reflected the donor's love for Christ.

REVIEW

Time: 30 minutes

• Post the summary sheet and have the brainstorm lists from "Dreaming Together" available.

• Share information learned since October.

• Talk about what remains to be discussed and decided. Try to tie up loose ends, but leave room for spontaneity.

• Turn to Questionnaire C (begins on page 28), select a secretary, and together, answer question 1. Share dates for school productions, gift exchanges, and office parties. Hear from the date checker, who may have discovered interesting and inexpensive Christmas programs. Family members should jot down these dates in their personal calendars as well. You may want to set shopping schedules with each child or schedule time to be spent with children individually.

• Answer question 2. Your family may want to put together an annual Advent scrapbook with family photographs, drawings, special Christmas cards, etc. Or you may want to create a family Christmas scrapbook to which holiday me-

QUESTIONNAIRE C
LOOKING AHEAD TO CHRISTMAS . . . AND BEYOND

	Before Thanksgiving	First Week of Advent	Second Week of Advent	Third Week of Advent	Fourth Week of Advent	Christmas Eve	Christmas Day	Epiphany
1. What do we have planned? What are the expectations for church, school, job, community responsibilities?								
2. What would I like to do?								
3. How would I like to feel?								

mentos and photos can be added each year. If the family enjoys creative writing, consider an anthology of your own Advent and Christmas poems, short stories, and drawings. For these projects, questions about themes and who will be in charge must be resolved now.

• Turn to question 3. Ask yourselves:

—How do you feel about the plans so far?
—Are they too much? Too little? Too structured? Too materialistic?
—Is there some event you can realistically look forward to?

• Set the date and time for the family celebration during Thanksgiving weekend. Select an organizer.

FROM ATTIC TO BASEMENT

Time: 10 minutes

Holiday preparations, activities, and house guests may make it difficult to complete household projects and home repairs. Take a few minutes to list those jobs which must be done before December 25. Arrange them in order of priority, and then cross off half the list. Put them out of your mind (hold a burning ceremony if that would help) and deal with the remaining half. Who's to say you won't cross off half of those as well?

TOASTS TO ONE AND ALL

Time: 5–10 minutes

Close by serving beverages and cookies. While enjoying the treats, toast Christmas. Share what you want the holidays to be for the family, for a specific family member, or for yourself.

May you be the first house in the parish to welcome
St. Nicholas.

—an Irish toast

"A Time of Thanksgiving"
The Fourth of Five Family Celebrations

Between turkey servings and pumpkin pie slices, find time this Thanksgiving weekend to say thanks together.

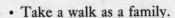

- Take a walk as a family.
- Build a fire in the fireplace and share a simple supper.
- Enjoy a noncompetitive activity together: complete a puzzle, tell stories, feed the birds . . .
- Make a Thanksgiving wreath or spray for the family.

To do this, you'll need small sheets of paper, greens, ribbon, wire, and other decorative items. Have each family member write an expression of thanks on separate sheets of paper. Arrange greens to form a wreath or spray, and use wire to hold the greens together; attach the notes of thanksgiving with ribbon; decorate; and hang for all to see!

- As you make plans to set up the crèche, consider placing only the shepherds around the manger. Put the Wise Men in a far corner of the house, and daily move them closer to the crib. They will arrive at the stable on Epiphany, January 6.
- Read John 1:1–18 together and personalize the Apostle's message.
- Close by singing "O Come All Ye Faithful."

Between this Thanksgiving Family Celebration and the fifth family celebration scheduled for January 6, you will experience Advent and Christmas as planned. Suggestions for making Advent wreaths and calendars begin on page 131 in Chapter 3.

Chapter 3 includes five devotional celebrations that your family may enjoy during the four weeks of Advent and on Christmas Eve. Below is the Family Christmas Calendar, that begins December 1 and continues through Epiphany. The suggested activities are short (two to twenty minutes) and are designed to bring families together daily to share the simple joys of Christmas.

THE FAMILY CHRISTMAS CALENDAR
❄ DECEMBER ❄

1	2	3	4	5	6	7
Take a short walk.	Read Mark 1:4–8.	Tell jokes.	Imagine a Christmas without any expenses.	Feed the birds.	Give a secret gift.	Dress up for a meal.
8	**9**	**10**	**11**	**12**	**13**	**14**
Whistle a Christmas carol.	Phone or write a distant relative.	Talk about the Christmas present you most enjoyed giving in the past	Pay someone a compliment.	Make Christmas table decorations.	Sing carols.	Recycle your newspapers.
15	**16**	**17**	**18**	**19**	**20**	**21**
Read a children's Christmas story.	Create a red and green snack.	Fingerpaint with chocolate pudding.	Imagine that you are spending Christmas in another country.	Smile at a neighbor.	Go window-shopping.	Clean up the kitchen.
22	**23**	**24**	**25**	**26**	**27**	**28**
Hug each other.	Finish a project.	Hang the stockings.	Say a prayer.	Draw pictures.	Surprise a friend with a gift.	Plan a summer family outing.
29	**30**	**31**				
Read John 3:16–21.	Visit a neighbor.	Look through the family scrapbook.				

❄ JANUARY ❄

			1 Play hide-and-seek.	2 Make sundaes.	3 Sit and watch people—smile at everyone you see.	4 Leave notes to each other.
5 Recall a previous Christmas together.	6 Read Matthew 2:1–12.	7	8	9	10	11
12	13	14	15	16	17	18
19	20	21	22	23	24	25
26	27	28	29	30	31	

Advent became a widely celebrated season eight centuries after Christ's birth. It was not until the fourth century that Christians even celebrated Christ's birth or "The Feast of the Nativity of Our Lord Jesus Christ." In A.D. 354 the Roman Church selected December 25 for Christmas.

Why December 25? St. Chrysostom, a fifth-century Bishop of Constantinople, suggests that the church chose this date so Christians could celebrate Christ's birthday undisturbed while "the heathen were busy with their profane ceremonies." The heathen were ending the Saturnalia (eight days of feasting, gambling, and animal sacrifice to Saturn, the god of harvests) by honoring Mithras, a prophet and founder of a sun-worshipping cult. This was the Birthday of the Unconquered Sun and December 25!

Later, forty preliminary days of fasting and prayer were introduced. In the sixth century Pope Gregory the Great shortened this season to just the four weeks before Christmas. This change prevails in the West, with each week of Advent enjoying a special significance:

> Advent symbolized all possible comings of the Lord and some of these were attached to the different weeks. The first spoke of His appearance from heaven in great humility, the second of His rebirth in the soul of every believer, the third of His coming at the death of every man, and the fourth of his final manifestation in glorious majesty at the great judgment day.
> —William Auld
> *Christmas Traditions*

Since the ninth century, Advent customs have included making Advent wreaths and writing letters to Jesus telling him what children want for Christmas. In southern Germany, every Thursday in Advent was *Klopfelnachte* (Knocking Night). Children went house to house singing hymns and knocking on doors with little hammers, or throwing peas and lentils against windows.

And bounce and beate at every doore,
   with blowes and lustie snaps,

and crie, the Advent of the Lorde not
    borne as yet perhaps
and wishing to the neighbours all,
    that in the houses dwell
a happie yeare, and every thing
    to spring and prosper well; . . .

—Thomas Naogeorgus
Sixteenth century

The Latin word *adventus* means coming. Each day of Advent brings us closer to the coming of the Christ Child. Prior to his arrival, Christians around the globe are visited by other special guests honored for their Christ-like charity and faith. Throughout Europe, St. Nicholas, the patron saint of children, bestows gifts on December 5, the eve of St. Nicholas Day. On December 13, Sweden welcomes the Lucia Queen, who symbolizes the promise of light and plenty. In the past, St. Thomas Day (December 21) involved "Thomassing"— going from house to house to collect gifts of wheat or flour for Christmas breads and cakes; the poor received enough supplies to sustain them through the winter. These special days reflect an expectancy and a sharing with one another— both important aspects of Advent.

Custom Inspection

Christmas is a holiday shared by Christians around the world, and Christmas celebrations vary from country to country. Throughout *Celebrate the Wonder*, Custom Inspections highlight some of these delightful and inspiring celebrations. Look for the "Custom Inspection" stamp, and perhaps weave some of these traditions into your own holiday celebrations.

Colombia

December 16 marks the official beginning of the Christmas season. Evening devotions, carols, and prayers are followed by dancing and parties.

Greece

Preparing for Christmas involves forty days of fasting to purify the soul through prayer and penitence. Baking is done the last week before Christmas.

Spain

Christmas celebrations begin on December 8, which also marks the Feast of the Immaculate Conception and Mother's Day.

The name *Christmas* first appeared in A.D. 1038. It derives from *Christes Maess* or *Christes-Messe* for the Mass of Christ held at midnight on Christmas Eve. Introduced in Rome around A.D. 400, the Mass was offered at the hour Christ was believed born.

> When the midnight, dark and still,
> Wrapped in silence vale and hill:
> God the Son, through Virgin's birth,
> Following the Father's will,
> Started life as Man on earth.
> —fourth-century Latin hymn

"The Family Epiphany Experience" The Fifth of Five Family Celebrations

Just as the Magi journeyed to discover the meaning of the bright star in the heavens, Epiphany reminds us we should continue our personal journey to the Christ Child. We have learned of God's gift and must now approach The Word Incarnate as adorers and bearers of gifts.

Chasing demons and witches away with lighted torches and homemade noisemakers was common during the Twelve Days after the Roman Saturnalia. January 6, or Twelfth Night, was the concluding day.

As Christian customs meshed with pagan rites, Twelfth

Night became Epiphany, meaning "manifestation" or "appearance" in Greek. When the Eastern Church observes Epiphany, it celebrates Christ's baptism and his miracle at Cana. For the Western Church, Epiphany commemorates the visit of the three Wise Men to the Christ Child. To celebrate the visit of the Magi, churches hold special services and priests bestow blessings upon parishioners' homes. The initials of Gaspar, Melchior, and Baltasar are written in white chalk on the inside of the door, framed by the year and connected by cross signs.

Since the Wise Men presented gifts to Jesus, Epiphany is a gift-giving time. Children write letters to the Christ Child listing the gifts they want. In most countries, Epiphany signals the close of the holiday season.

> Noel is leaving us,
> Sad 'tis to tell,
> But he will come again,
> Adieu, Noel.
>
> His wife and his children
> Weep as they go:
> On a grey horse
> They ride thro' the snow.
> The Kings ride away
> In the snow and the rain,
> After twelve months
> We shall see them again.

—French Epiphany chanson

The Family Epiphany Experience brings Christmas to an official close. The format for this experience is not as explicit as previous celebrations. Suggestions include some entertaining Twelfth Night activities and a "wrap-up" to the planning process used during these family celebrations. Select the ideas appropriate for your family, but don't omit "Sharing Together" (page 15), which will help you evaluate this year's celebrations and look ahead to next year.

AN EPIPHANY CEREMONY

If you have been moving the Wise Men closer to the stable each day, have them arrive today. This is cause to celebrate— sing "We Three Kings," read Matthew 2:1–12, or share the first stanza from Henry Wadsworth Longfellow's "The Three Kings":

> Three Kings came riding from far away,
> Melchior and Gaspar and Baltasar;
> Three Wise Men out of the East were they,
> And they traveled by night and they slept by day,
> For their guide was a beautiful, wonderful star.

A TWELFTH NIGHT PARTY

> Now, now the mirth comes
> With the cake full of plums,
> Where bean's the king of the sport here;
> Besides we must know,
> the pea also
> Must revel as queen in the court here.
> —Robert Herrick

Le Gateau des Rois (the Kings' Cake) originated at the Mont-Saint-Michel Monastery in the thirteenth century. There, the finder of the bean baked in the cake became the Epiphany King. Why a bean? In ancient times beans were considered sacred vegetables!

Adopt this idea for your family's celebration. Perhaps the first person to find a bean becomes the Lord of Misrule for the evening. A descendant of the Roman King of Games and the King of Winepots during the Saturnalia, this master of revelry declared a state of "topsy turvydown." Masters exchanged places with servants. In the family, parents can switch places with children!

Or bake a Kings' Cake (the Grand Finale cake on page 312—Chapter 4—is ideal for this occasion) and add to the batter symbolic items that hold significance for the New Year. These objects can include:

button or ring: faithfulness
dime: wealth
beans and peas: wisdom
thimble: patience
paper heart: devotion
clove: being a fool or court jester

Select other items, assign them special meanings, and eat the cake carefully!

As for ENTERTAINMENT . . . frolicsome mirth was the rule at English Twelfth Night parties. Dice games degenerated into the throwing of eggshells brimming with rosewater, while refreshments included pies filled with live frogs.

• Try "Jump the Candle": The nursery rhyme "Jack be nimble, Jack be quick" comes to mind as, one by one, jumpers leap over a lighted candle twelve consecutive times. If the flame is not snuffed out, good luck will follow for the next twelve months.

• Read *Twelfth Night* together. William Shakespeare wrote this play specifically for this holiday.

A FAMILY FAREWELL—NOEL IS LEAVING US

Down with the Rosemary, and
Down with the Baies and mistletoe;
Down with the Holly, Ivie, all
    wherewith ye drest the Christmas Hall.
        —Robert Herrick
          "Ceremony Upon Candlemas Eve"

If the Christmas tree is still up, light it for the last time before removing the decorations. Enjoy a fire in the fireplace or gather candles and light them in one spot. Legend admonishes you to burn the mistletoe or the berries will change into imps who bedevil the family during the year. As you pack away the decorations, put items needing repair in a special place. Select another spot to store cones, pods, dried flowers, and so forth, that you collect during the year. Then, next year, when it is time to create decorations, your materials will be in one place.

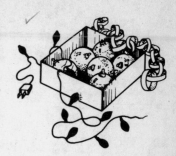

SHARING TOGETHER

Share an item you have personally enjoyed this holiday, or a symbol of something that has been personally meaningful to you—a snapshot, a recording, a memory . . .

Do some informal sharing and evaluating about the holiday season.

- What did you like the most? The least?
- What changes do you wish you had made?
- How are you feeling as the holiday comes to a close? Inspired, refreshed, relieved?
- What would you like to repeat next year?
- What would you like to do differently?

Take the answers and attach them to the September page of your family calendar, or put them inside this book.

If planning, sharing, and working together as a family has been fun, why stop even though Christmas is over? Plan family get-togethers for the year—vacations, weekend outings, or midweek activities. Your family may want to set aside an evening each week to do something together.

Custom Inspection

Puerto Rico

January 6 is Three Kings' Day, when children receive gifts and goodies. Families and friends exchange greetings and visit one another on this church holiday.

Argentina

On Epiphany Eve, children place their shoes by the bed, hoping they will be gift-laden in the morning.

Ecuador

On the Sunday before Christmas, church school children honor the Magi by delivering baskets of food to shut-ins and the elderly.

Syria

Epiphany Eve is "The Night of Destiny." The devout experience unusual and awesome events (such as food supplies increasing mysteriously). At midnight trees bow down in reverence to the Christ Child or the visiting Wise Men. The bent trees may also serve as guideposts for the Magi on their return voyage home or for the Holy Family in their flight to Egypt.

England

Celebrants call Epiphany "Old Christmas Day" because January 6 was December 25 prior to 1752, when the Gregorian Calendar was adopted.

Spain

The Wise Men pass through Spain each year as they travel to Bethlehem to pay homage to the Christ Child. En route, they leave gifts of toys and sweets for the good children.

Austria

Some villages enjoy parades with marchers representing monsters, shepherds, clowns, and musicians. The forces of good struggle with sinister powers, and good always triumphs.

Christmas is a tender holiday—as tender as a newborn babe— yet as powerful as the love of God. It is a season of surprises (a King in a manger?) underlined by the promise of abundant life. It is our chance to reflect, renew, and rejoice with one another.

"Bringing Christmas Home" means making Christmas come alive for you. Though the traditions and celebrations last only a few weeks, it is a holiday that is truly timeless. The Christmas spirit is ours to enjoy all year.

CHAPTER 2
Gift Giving

T he first Christmas gifts were selected for their value and significance, brought long distances, and presented in person.

When they saw the star, they rejoiced exceedingly with great joy; and going into the house they saw the child with Mary his mother, and they fell down and worshipped him. Then, opening their treasures, they offered him gifts, gold and frankincense and myrrh.

—Matthew 2:10–11

Two thousand years later, billions of dollars are spent on gifts each Christmas. For many, the pursuit of the "perfect gift for that special someone" becomes an all-consuming passion. Straining for any hints (obvious or subtle), scanning the ads, and promising to be more creative and more organized next Christmas, shoppers hope the final choice is something the recipient will enjoy and value, evoking a response as enthusiastic as Will Rogers's:

The whole Christmas thing started in a fine spirit. It was to give happiness to the young, and another holiday to the old, so it was relished by practically everybody. It was a great day, the presents were inexpensive and received with much joy and gratification. . . . The merest little toy was a boon to their young lives, and what a kick it was to the parents to have them rush back up to the bedroom to show you "what Santa brought."

—*The Autobiography of Will Rogers*

? ? ? ? ? ? ?

Think back to some favorite gift you have received. Who gave it to you? Why do you think that person chose that particular item? How have you used it? Why is it so special to you?

? ? ? ? ? ? ?

Selecting a gift is an opportunity to express our appreciation to those who bring meaning into our lives, and to look anew at the personality and preferences of the recipient. We try to give something that will enrich the life of that person and bring joy whenever the gift is used, seen, and remembered.

Our quest for meaning, simplicity, and wonder at Christmas leads us to give gifts. Giving is a statement of caring for another person, a creative expression by the giver, and an important part of Christmas celebrations. Through giving, our gifts sustain the spirit of Christmas beyond the holiday.

Selecting gifts requires imagination and common sense. Throughout this chapter you will find specific ideas for a wide variety of gifts, including clever purchases, unique crafts, and suggestions for sharing your time and yourself.

? ? ? ? ? ? ?

List all the people you expect to give a gift to this Christmas. As you write each name, visualize that person. Remember his or her home and hobbies, how the person dresses, the luxuries he or she treasures, and gifts you have received from that person in the past. Make some brief notes next to each name.

? ? ? ? ? ? ?

At its best, the tradition of exchanging gifts is a response to the generosity and compassion of our Creator. Remembering the simple birth in a rustic stable, we give thanks for the miracle of life. As we read of Jesus' ministry of caring, we glimpse a life of fulfillment. We rejoice at the Resurrection and are awestruck at the gift of eternal life.

God answered our deepest needs through Jesus Christ. Each gift that we give renews the miracle, hope, and wonder that Jesus made real through his life and death. Like the Magi, we give our best to express our caring for another person, and our gifts symbolize the real Christmas gift for us all—the gift of a Savior.

A HISTORY OF GIFT GIVERS

Pre-Christian winter festivals included gift exchanges that were markedly different from contemporary giving. As the days shortened, celebrations in Sumeria, Persia, Rome, and Northern Europe included sacrificial giving to ensure the sun's return and the productivity of the earth. The Roman calends marked the election of new officials, calling for the offering of presents to the emperor and his consul. It became the custom to make gifts for friends and neighbors: "honied things that the year of the recipient might be sweeter, lamps that it might be full of light, silver and gold that wealth might attend them."[1]

As the Christian church developed its reverence for Christ's birthday, religious celebrations gradually intertwined with pagan festivities. Today's Christmas celebrations include traditions of giving that have been adapted to the twentieth century. The Three Kings, an old woman, a saint on horseback, even the Christ Child himself have become celebrated gift givers.

A new star in the heavens called the Wise Men to begin a journey still celebrated. Their pursuit for "he who has been born king of the Jews" (Matthew 2:2) was one of faith and foolishness; their guide was a star, and their purpose was to worship the newly born Messiah.

Only Matthew's gospel refers to the "wise men from the east"; there is no other biblical reference to these legendary travelers. Historians believe the wise men were not "three

[1] Alfred Carl Hottes, *1001 Christmas Facts and Fancies* (New York: A. T. De La Mare Co., Inc., 1937), p. 65.

kings from the Orient," but Babylonian astrologers who had studied the Scriptures and the stars.

The story of their journey has been embellished through centuries of retelling. The three gifts—gold, frankincense, and myrrh—led to the assumption that there were three travelers. The value of these gifts indicated that the travelers were kings. In the nineteenth century, John Hopkins gave details to the story in a Christmas hymn, and we glimpse the star's promise each time we sing

> O star of wonder, star of night,
> Star with royal beauty bright,
> Westward leading, still proceeding,
> Guide us to thy perfect light.

The Magi chose to bring their best as gifts to the King. Gold was as valuable and regal then as it is now. Frankincense was a fragrance important in establishing a proper atmosphere for worship. Myrrh was a precious substance used in embalming. The gifts the Magi brought were all of royal quality, but each had an added significance. It was as though the Wise Men knew of this baby's life and mission—of his royalty, his priesthood, even his death.

The Magi are now honored as Epiphany gift bearers in most Spanish-speaking countries. *The Child's Gifts: A Twelfth-Night Tale* is a Puerto Rican account of the Wise Men. In word and song Tomás Blanco tells of their journey and discovery:

> Returning from their visit to the manger, the Three were asked, "At least answer these questions: What have you brought back with you? What did you set out to find? And what did you receive in return for your gifts?"
>
> It fell to Balthasar, as the eldest, to make reply:
>
> "It is plain that we set out to seek nothing. We wished only to enter the presence of the Prince of Peace. We did not go to seek anything. On the contrary, we wanted to give—as well you know—the best we had. We bring back nothing but a gentle rejoicing.

The mighty Hierarch we sought was a new-born babe
who smiled in his dreams. . . .''

In other countries, the legend of the Magi took on different forms. According to Italian tradition, the traveling Wise Men asked an old woman for shelter and nourishment. Refusing to serve them and later declining to join their quest, she was left behind. Within a few hours she had changed her mind, but by then the Magi had disappeared. The old woman still searches for the Christ Child, and is remembered as *La Befana*, meaning Epiphany. Depicted in different ways—as a fairy queen, a misshapen old woman, even a witch—she visits Italian homes each Epiphany to bring gifts, confections and a threat of punishment. On the Eve of Epiphany, Italian children listen for the bell that tells them they must hurry off to bed before La Befana's arrival.

Like La Befana, Russia's *Babushka* (or *Babouschka*) is charged with misdirecting the Magi and refusing hospitality to the Holy Family. In repentance for her selfishness, she distributes Christmas Eve gifts to children and seeks the Holy Child she once turned away.

The Magi, La Befana and Babushka all bear gifts as part of their quest for the Christ Child. Searching for a new type of monarch, they bring happiness to children in tangible forms.

Legends and history crossed to create the beloved character of St. Nicholas. For generations, St. Nicholas has acted as examiner, judge, and benefactor as he has worked to prepare young hearts for the coming Christ Child. Nicholas was born in the fourth century in what is now Turkey. He became bishop of Myra and earned a reputation as a man of compassion and conscience—a church leader who was willing to stand up against the injustices of his time.

After his death in A.D. 343, stories of his generosity grew into legends abounding with miracle and magic. Providing abundant grain during a famine, bringing a donkey back to life, saving a sinking ship, and sailing stormy seas in his hat are but a few of the tales, which change with every telling.

Some of Nicholas's remains are today kept in a museum in Antalya, placed near a somber portrait of this great man. Our images of "Jolly Ol' Saint Nicholas" are certainly a far cry from the stern figure portrayed there.

St. Nicholas is honored as patron saint of merchants, mariners, and bakers, and of numerous cities and countries. He is best known as a patron saint of children, and several stories tell of Nicholas rescuing children from disaster.

December 6 is his saint's day and the anniversary of his death. During the thirteenth century, nuns celebrated the eve of St. Nicholas Day by leaving presents at the homes of the poor. That simple task may have been the origin of today's St. Nicholas Day celebrations: children around the world now eagerly anticipate his arrival each year on December 5, as well as his questions, rewards, and penalties.

The incredible one-day job of delivering gifts to all expectant and deserving children became too much even for the magical St. Nicholas. He enlisted many helpers, as well as a few unusual and frightening companions.

In some Middle European countries, the sack of gifts is carried by Knight Rupprecht, or Rupert. Dressed in simple skins and straw, Rupprecht has a fierce appearance and is responsible for punishing naughty children.

Schmutzli, the Black One, is a demonic figure who travels with St. Nicholas in Switzerland. A Moorish servant, Zwarte Piet (Black Pete), accompanies St. Nicholas in parades and on visits in Holland. Saint Peter and the angel Gabriel assist in some areas.

Shaggy monsters of various names may also accompany St. Nicholas. Known as Klaubauf, Krampus, Grampus, and Bartel, they make hideous faces and horrible noises that frighten children. St. Nicholas demands that these creatures wait outside while he distributes the gifts, and parents will often take wine out to appease the noisy characters.

In high alpine areas, two frightening creatures chastise sinners, warning them of the imminent arrival of St. Nicholas: a man with the head of a goat, and a demonic-looking being with masks and horns. They are accompanied by two "ghosts of the field" who clear the way for the entire entourage by snapping heavy whips all around.

These and other beastly characters frighten children into good behavior and assume responsibility for administering any necessary punishments, thereby freeing the saint to assume his more loving and generous roles.

Custom Inspection

Belgium

Belgian children line the parade route for St. Nicholas's arrival on December 5. Astride a white horse, the saint distributes small gifts and sweets to the crowds. The children

must wait for their larger gifts until St. Nicholas comes down the chimneys of their homes later that night.

Germany

St. Nicholas has traditionally been assisted by Knight Rupprecht on the eve of St. Nicholas Day. Rupprecht, a thin, dark man, carries a sack to put bad children into. Santa Claus now shares the responsibilities of filling stockings with rewards for good behavior.

Netherlands

A jubilant reception greets St. Nicholas in Holland on December 5. This gives him just enough time to check up on each child before St. Nicholas Day. He is accompanied by Black Peter, his Moorish helper, dressed in sixteenth century Spanish breeches. The oft-repeated stories have prepared children for his questions—and the ensuing rewards and punishments.

Look, there is the steamer arriving from Spain.
It brings us St. Nicholas, he still looks the same.
His horse is a-prancing the deck, up and down
The banners are waving in village and town.

He rides through the city, in splendid array,
Beside him Black Peter, so jolly and gay,
His bag filled with toys for the poor and the rich
A good child gets candy, a bad one—the switch!

—old Dutch melody

The processions and questions by the long-awaited saint leave children filled with the highest hopes for what he will bring. Before going to bed, wooden shoes are carefully filled with hay and sugar for St. Nicholas's horse. The shoes, placed near the fireplace or window, signal to St. Nicholas that all are now asleep and that he may return to fill the shoes with toys and treasures.

Sinterklaas, you good old man,
Come and see me if you can.
Fill my booties and my shoe.
Many, many thanks to you.

—old Dutch melody

The gifts left in the shoes are just a few of those exchanged on St. Nicholas Day. Christmas Day is free of gift exchanges and is reserved for religious celebrations and visiting.

The Dutch held fast to their St. Nicholas in spite of the Reformation's attempts to eliminate veneration of all saints. Dutch settlers in America in the seventeenth century were visited by the faithful St. Nicholas, who arrived from Holland in time for the December 6 celebrations, to issue his stern judgments and generous rewards. He became patron saint of the colony and was known as Sinterklaas by the Dutch, St. Klaas or Sancta Claas by the English and French. The festivities of the season and the tangle of many other traditions were gradually assumed by Santa Claus. In 1809, Washington Irving's portrayal of Santa Claus was as a fat and jolly fellow who rode in a sleigh pulled by reindeer—quite a change from the severe and solemn St. Nicholas first introduced to America!

Just a few nights before Christmas in 1822, a professor of

divinity recited a charming Christmas poem to his children and friends. "'Twas the night before Christmas," he began—and kept his audience spellbound with a descriptive and rhythmic account of St. Nick's activities. One member of the audience copied his words down and sent the poem anonymously to the *Troy Sentinel*, where "A Visit from St. Nicholas" was printed on December 23, 1823. The *Sentinel*'s editor explained, "We know not to whom we are indebted for the description of that unwearied patron of children, but from whomever it may have come, we give thanks for it."

Dr. Clement Clarke Moore considered the ballad unworthy of his name, in spite of the enthusiastic response it received from the *Sentinel*'s readers. He refused to claim "A Visit from St. Nicholas" until it was included in an 1844 volume of his poetry. Although referring to St. Nicholas, the verses depict the cheery and round fellow we have come to love as Santa Claus.

> He was chubby and plump, a right jolly old elf,
> And I laughed when I saw him, in spite of myself.
> A wink of his eye and a twist of his head
> Soon gave me to know I had nothing to dread.
>   —"A Visit from St. Nicholas"

A sprig of holly in Santa's hat, a twinkle in his eye, and an embrace for every child—Thomas Nast drew life into the descriptions of Santa Claus. An artist for *Harper's Weekly* in the middle of the nineteenth century, Nast, in his pictures of Santa Claus, emphasized Santa's love for children and proficiency as a gift giver. A picture in the December 29, 1866, issue of *Harper's Weekly* displays eight episodes in Santa's preparations for Christmas, with each scene detailing Santa's hard work at a job he obviously cherishes.

The magical generosity of Santa Claus is only part of his appeal. Santa always listens, radiates his love and concern for each child, and knows just what to bring. Appearing faithfully once—and only once—each year, he maintains a closeness to and distance from everyone. He is Somebody Special.

"'Twas the night before Christmas, and all through the house
Not a creature was stirring, not even a mouse."

He doesn't care if you're rich or poor
    for he loves you just the same.
Santa knows that we're God's children
    that makes everything right.
Fill your hearts with Christmas cheer,
    'Cause Santa Claus comes tonight!
                    —Gene Autrey and Oakley Haldeman
                    "Here Comes Santa Claus"

Many of Santa's annual activities parallel traditions that
are older than Santa himself. Flying through the winter in a

chariot filled with gifts, he travels much the same way as an ages-old Norse goddess named Freya. Instead of the eight flying reindeer, Freya's chariot was led by a team of cats.

Santa climbs down the chimney, an entry that is only used at Christmastime. Centuries ago the German hearth goddess, Hertha, discovered the mystique of the fireplace and chose a similar route for her arrival at the winter solstice.

"The stockings were hung by the chimney with care" is a tradition related to one of the many legends about St. Nicholas. Learning of three sisters who remained unmarried for lack of dowries, Nicholas secretly tossed gold coins down their chimney. Stockings, hanging at the fireplace to dry, caught the falling coins.

Following the Reformation, Protestants in Germany, Switzerland, France, and Alsace turned to the Christ Child as gift giver. Expecting the arrival of the gift-laden Christ Child on Christmas morning, eager children hung stockings on December 24.

German immigrants to the New World brought this tradition with them, and his name and identity gradually evolved from *Christkindlein* (little Christ Child) to Christ Kindel, Kriss Kindle, and Kriss Kringle. To some, he was the Christ Child; others saw Christkindlein as the Christ Child's messenger, who personified the spirit of gift giving. In 1842, *Kriss Kringle's Book* depicted this gift giver as generous and jolly, with a striking resemblance to Santa Claus. He was brought up-to-date in 1947 as Kris Kringle in Valentine Davies's movie and book, *Miracle on 34th Street*, assuring audiences that Kris was still active at his wonderful work.

Following the Reformation, a menacing, fur-clad *Pelznickol* often accompanied the Christ Child in his annual visits. Pelznickol became known for his merciless questions and frightening presence. Dressed in scraps of fur and a long robe, his appearance seemed to mimic St. Nicholas as it intimidated the children.

The tradition came to America with German settlers and, with time, softened to become part of the annual festivities. Pelsnickol or Belsnickle made annual visits to friends and

neighbors, and his inquisitions became ridiculous threats interspersed with equally silly treats.

The hilarity of the custom grew with its popularity. Eventually groups of costumed party-goers enjoyed "belsnickling" from house to house, sampling Christmas goodies as they entertained with spoofs and skits created for the occasion.

Custom Inspection

Finland

Pre-Christmas advertising includes a plea for many "Father Christmases.'" Those chosen to fill the role bring the Christmas spirit to homes for a small fee. Neighborhood taverns often provide ⌐ ⌐st stop for the weary "Fathers," giving them a chance to share the cheer of the holiday over a cup or two of brew.

France

Yuletide gifts are exchanged from December 6 to January 6. Parts of rural France celebrate St. Nicholas Day, and many children throughout France set out shoes, not stockings, to be filled by *Le Petit Nöel* on Christmas Eve. Rooted in the calends celebrations of the Roman Empire, New Year's gifts are given with wishes for the coming year and blessings for the Yuletide season. Remembering the journey of the Wise Men, some French children journey to their village churches on January 5 to leave gifts for the Bethlehem-bound Magi to deliver.

Hungary

When communism took hold of Hungary, the new leaders introduced Father Winter to replace the revered Christ Child as the central character in Christmas festivities. Most Hungarians ignored this challenge to their Yuletide customs and, instead, strengthened their celebrations. Today the Christ Child still brings Christmas to most of Hungary.

Poland

A few days before Christmas, Polish children leave their wishful Christmas letters for the Wise Men. Christmas Eve's formal meal is followed by a visit from the Star Man (often impersonated by the village priest), who arrives to hear the children's catechism. Later that evening, the three Wise Men come bringing gifts.

Russia

As Holy Night becomes Christmas Day, St. Nicholas or Kolya travels through parts of the Russian countryside delivering small wheat cakes to the homes.

> Kolya, Kolya,
> On Christmas Eve, when all is still
> He puts his cakes on the windowsill.

> Kolya, Kolya,
> Come this Holy Night, we pray,
> Come and bring us Christmas day!
> —a Russian carol

Switzerland

A sleigh pulled by six reindeer carries the Christ Child through the countryside. En route he shares a bounty of gifts, trees, decorations, and sweets. In other parts of Switzerland, jovial Father Christmas and his wife Lucy distribute gifts together.

Syria

Syria's gifts arrive on a little camel. Legend tells of the small animal's inclusion in the Wise Men's caravan to Bethlehem. With the larger animals setting a fast pace, the little camel soon became tired, yet pressed on to see the new Messiah. At the manger he collapsed in exhaustion. Jesus was so moved by the camel's devotion that the animal was blessed with immortality and given the honor of bringing gifts to Syrian children.

HELPING CHILDREN UNDERSTAND GIVING AND RECEIVING

In the Western world, descriptions of Santa's fact-finding abilities have replaced St. Nicholas' stern examinations. Santa knows who has been "naughty or nice," and lumps of coal are promised to those who don't deserve better. Seeing all and knowing all, he brings gifts only to good boys and girls—or so the story goes.

The significance of gift giving is destroyed when a gift is offered as a reward or bribe. If we believe that our gifts represent what God has given us, there can be no preconditions. The gifts of forgiveness, love, and new life come to us regardless of who we are and what we have done.

Children are able to understand a good deal about the practicalities of giving without destroying their fantasies. A child's image of Santa rests greatly on the wonder of being remembered, the mysteries of his work, and the surprises he brings. Even small children can comprehend that Santa—and Grandma—can't bring everything. Helping family members limit their lists reduces the chances of disappointment and cynicism.

Children eventually grow up, and the magic of Santa may become harder for them to believe and accept. In 1897, an eight-year-old girl recorded her skepticism in a letter addressed to the editor of the *New York Sun*. The answer became famous, and Santa Claus was immortalized as the essence of Christmas:

> Yes, Virginia, there is a Santa Claus. He exists as certainly as love and generosity and devotion exist, and you know they abound and give to your life its highest beauty and joy. Alas, how dreary would be the world if there were no Santa Claus. . . .
>
> Thank God! he lives, and he lives for ever. A thou-

sand years from now, he will continue to make glad
the heart of childhood.
                    —Francis P. Church
                    the *New York Sun*, September 21, 1897

Recognizing the Santa in each of us is part of learning the
art of giving. Santa is not "God in a red flannel suit," nor is
he an arm of the devil. His unfinished work becomes our
responsibility. We must spread the glad anticipation and generous spirit that Santa personifies.

Santa can be a child's key to seeing the giving side of gift
exchanges. As our example of a giver, he demonstrates the
"love and generosity and devotion" that parents try to instill
in their children. The countless variations of the "Santas" that
appear each December are a visible reminder that Santa Claus
enlists many helpers in his work. Convincing children that
Santa needs *their* help can lead to fun activities and a new
perspective on the holiday.

If you are a parent:

Listen carefully when your children say what they want
for Christmas. Don't be surprised if their lists change daily.

Help your children arrange their gift lists in order of priority. (You may want to leave out this step if the list includes
a Great Dane—or some other out-of-the-question wish!)

Feel free to tell your children that Santa only brings one
(or a few) gifts to each child.

Plan to experience Christmas in many ways with your children. Consider their interests and attention span: attending
a parade, window shopping, hosting an informal party, and
sharing Christmas cookies may be fun possibilities for a young
family.

Help your child make a list of people to give to this Christmas. Include family, close friends, neighbors, Scout leaders,
teachers, and others who have been important in the child's
life recently. With your child, think about each person listed.
Remember together some time shared with that person. Imagine what he or she might be doing today and how that friend
might be spending Christmas. Make notes or draw simple
pictures to help you and your child remember your discussion.

Talk with your child about Santa Claus. What makes his gifts so special?

Help your child "play Santa" and give a gift secretly—to a friend, a family member, an acquaintance, or through a charitable organization to someone you don't know.

It takes some thinking and imagination to choose the right gift—one that says, "I care about you and I want to help make your Christmas special." The Buy It—Make It—Become It—Redirect It section beginning on page 68 may help you and your child begin to make some decisions. Some children will be able and willing to make their own creative and practical choices, but may need an adult's guidance in exploring the options.

Check the ideas below—you may find some new "just-right" ideas to suggest!

• *Personalized greetings* can take many forms. These all are a type of gift.

—a taped message (include the family singing Christmas carols, a talking letter, family discussions, parts of a Christmas program . . .).

—a telephone call just to say, "Merry Christmas! I am thinking of you!"

—a handmade card (see page 74).

—a poster greeting: enlarge a photo, make a Christmas mural, decorate a window—OR—assemble drawings, photos, and writings into a collage of greetings.

• *A gift from the whole family* may be appropriate for some persons on your child's list. Take care to include your child in making the choice, and in preparing and delivering these gifts.

—Prepare a basket of freshly baked bread or some of your family's favorite cookies.

—Offer to help with some job (yard work, decorating, shopping . . .).

—Make a donation to a Christmas charity in the name of your friend. Many cities have a group that rehabilitates toys, collects foods, and plays Santa to people who need some extra Christmas cheer.

• *Artwork by children* is especially appreciated by grandparents and other special people.

—Compile drawings, current photos, letters, and a self-portrait in a booklet—or make a calendar with each month featuring some special touches by your child.

—Turn a child's drawings into a set of note cards (with or without matching envelopes). A single design, made camera-ready with black ink on white paper, can be copied (and reduced or enlarged) by most photocopy shops. Check on the shop's variety of papers and run a sample through before placing your order. Pages may be cut and folded as desired; then tie the completed stationery neatly with a ribbon and place in a box.

—Boxes, cans with lids, and small jars are fun to decorate. Use colored adhesive tapes, acrylic paints, dry pasta, sequins, sewing scraps, string, ribbon and yarn, dried flowers, fancy labels, and so forth.

—Check the ideas for "Homemade Gifts" (beginning on page 84) for many more ideas. Keep in mind whom you are working with, and for whom you are working. Try not to overestimate or underestimate competence or time.

• *Current photos* of the children (or the whole family) are great additions to any gifts mailed to relatives and friends whose homes are far from yours. Plan accordingly! Snapshots would make a great tag for a gift (write the message on the back of the photo) or they could be enlarged for a poster or calendar.

Shopping trips with children can be an adventure—or a disaster. For best results:

—Shop individually with each child.

—Plan your shopping excursions. Consider the age, endurance, and decision-making abilities of your child or children, and plan where you will shop, how you will help your child choose and purchase, and so on.

—If lists are long or attention spans are short, don't try to get everything done in a single shopping trip. Several short shopping excursions (and perhaps some catalog shopping; see "There's More to Mail Order," beginning on p. 79) may make this more enjoyable for everyone.

—Include some "just for fun" activities on every shopping trip. Take time to look at displays, visit Santa, enjoy a snack, watch people, and window-shop.

Getting the Most for a Kid's Money

import store   magazine counters   delicatessens
special soaps, candles, bubble bath, sponges
road maps   seashells   hair ribbons
camping gear   stationery   wool socks
spiced teas   a new variety of seeds   jump ropes
yo-yos   nuts in the shell   sewing notions
wooden spoons, cheese graters, cookie cutters, nutcrackers
hand tools, paintbrushes, measuring tapes, flashlights

GET INTO THE ACT

• Help a neighbor clean up a yard, rake leaves, shovel snow, or decorate for Christmas.

• Go caroling in the neighborhood (a nice way to deliver gifts, too!).

• Care for neighbors' pets and plants during their Christmas travels.

• Keep a contagiously joyous and thankful attitude!

As a child I spent much time with my grandmother, who had been a slave. From her I learned that "Christmas Gif'" was a surprise game played by the slaves on Christmas Day. Two people, meeting for the first time that day, would compete to be the first to call out, "Christmas Gif'!" The loser happily paid a forfeit for a simple present—maybe a Christmas tea cake or a handful of nuts. Truly, there was more pleasure in being "caught," and having to give a present—the giving, though comically protested, was heartwarming to a people who had so little they could with dignity share with others.

—Charlemae Rollins
Christmas Gif'

PRESENTS AND PACKAGES

? ? ? ? ? ? ?

Find the personalized gift list you worked on while reading page 65. What would you like to say to each of these "Special Someones"? For each person on your list, think of a short message you would like your gift to express—perhaps "Thanks for being such a great friend" or "Congratulations" . . . "Remember the good ol' days," or "I'm glad you are part of our family" . . .

Write the messages on a card to enclose with the gift— or let your gift speak for itself.

? ? ? ? ? ? ?

It's not easy to choose a perfect gift—even if you have your list of Special Someones *and* your notes about each person's needs and preferences *and* the message cards that will accompany each gift. As a gift giver, you are in search of a gift that is a statement of caring . . . a creative expression . . . an important part of Christmas celebrations.

There are some wonderful gifts to be found in the shopping places around the world and in your own community. Some of the best gifts in the world are things only you can

make. And then there are the gifts that you become—special things you do, time you spend on something for someone, ways you share yourself.

You have so many choices! But how do you decide? Should you buy it? Make it? Become it?

The outline below will help you think it through and will give you some insight into what you will need in order to buy, make, or become a gift. Most presents and packages require *some* purchasing, *some* assembly, and *some* personalizing, so don't limit your thinking to any one set of possibilities.

On the following pages are other tips to help you with the what, where, when, and how of gift giving—plus suggestions for redirecting your gift intentions in new ways. As you look at these ideas, let your gift list and your imagination work together while you select those perfect gifts for your Special Someones.

Thinking it Through

What will you need to . . .

BUY IT?

Knowledge of the recipient's tastes, needs, and dreams.
Time and energy to enjoy shopping.
Awareness of your Christmas budget.
Information about where to shop.
A shopping list with possible/probable purchases.

MAKE IT?

Knowledge of the recipient's tastes, needs, and dreams.
An idea:
    —something you'll enjoy creating
    —something the recipient will enjoy receiving
A process:
    —necessary instructions and equipment

—materials that are available and affordable
—time and patience necessary for the project
—skill and talent necessary for the project
—a "cushion" of time and money
A plan for wrapping, mailing, and/or delivery of your gift.

BECOME IT?

Knowledge of the recipient's tastes, needs, and dreams.
Necessary time and money in the future.
An idea: something you and the recipient will enjoy doing together OR something you are able to do and will enjoy doing *for* the recipient.
A specific agenda or a flexible plan that's explicit and possible.
A strategy for announcing, explaining, and/or delivering your gift.

REDIRECT IT?

Several groups have worked recently to examine gift-giving traditions and to explore new customs. A Virginia-based group, for example, was organized in reaction to the extremely commercial tone of many adult gift exchanges. Calling itself SCROOGE (Society to Curtail Ridiculous and Ostentatious Gift Exchanges), the group discouraged purchasing gifts for adults, replacing these exchanges with personal visits or donations to charities.

The Alternative Celebrations Society stresses the importance of fellowship and celebration while opposing overconsumption, meaningless tradition, and holiday stress. Their "Christmas Organizing Packet" is designed for families, churches, and communities who are committed to rejuvenating the holiday (Alternatives, P.O. Box 1707, Forest Park, GA 30051).

Evaluate your own gift-giving plans. Do your personal values and priorities align with your plans? Are there ways you can redirect your giving?

Here are some suggestions:

Shorten your list of "I wants."

Plan to make a Christmas contribution to someone less fortunate than yourself.

Select gifts that are made or sold to help others: handmade items, cultural handicrafts, gifts purchased through a non-profit organization, and so forth.

Have a "gift-giving celebration": Share an evening (or afternoon or weekend) with friends, and make your time together a statement of caring, a creative expression, and an important part of Christmas celebrations! For example—

• Host a "make it and take it" party: share ideas and expertise in creating cards and gifts.

• Carol at a hospital, a neighborhood, or in your living room.

• Collect gifts for others. Ask each guest to bring something to add to a gift basket for a shut-in, hospital patient, or prison inmate.

• Share a potluck meal, then attend a free concert.

• Sponsor a garage sale or craft bazaar to raise money for world hunger, Christmas toys for handicapped children, or your favorite charitable organization.

Cards and Letters as Gifts

Long before airmail and boxes of colorful greeting cards made it so easy, sending a special Christmas greeting to distant friends was seen as a way of sharing the Yuletide spirit. Now a multimillion-dollar industry, Christmas cards are still a favorite way to send good wishes during the holidays. In fact, Christmas cards and letters can be a very special form of giving.

For centuries, letters of Christmas news, blessings, and cheer have been an inspiration to travelers, prisoners, isolated families, and remote explorers. British art students in the early nineteenth century added an artistic dimension to the tradition when they annually prepared elaborate scrolls of Christmas greetings, each displaying handwriting, artwork, and composition skills.

During the 1840s, one of Queen Victoria's printers, W. C. Dobson, enjoyed sending seasonal cards of Christmas cheer to his friends. The idea caught the attention of the Queen, who soon commissioned the Royal Academician, John Horsley, to design a Christmas greeting card. Horsley's creation was professionally lithographed and hand-tinted. A thousand copies were sold the first Christmas they were available.

Louis Prang introduced printed cards to Boston in 1875. A native of Breslau, Germany, Prang decorated his cards with Killarney roses, geraniums, and other flowers. A few years later, snow scenes, fir trees, and eventually Santa Claus appeared in Prang's Christmas cards. The Christmas scenery overwhelmed Prang; in 1890 he became disgusted with the gaudy and cheap cards sold locally, and terminated his more expensive, artistic card production in protest.

First known Christmas card, 1843, by John Calcott Horsley. Hallmark Historical Collection, Hallmark Cards, Inc.

A MERRY CHRISTMAS AND A HAPPY NEW YEAR TO YOU

Published at Summerlys Home Treasury Office.
12 Old Bond Street London.

From

Today's well-publicized postal timetables, the long lines at the post office, and the increased staffing in the mail room indicate the incredible volume of Christmas mail. Sending Christmas cards has obviously become one of our most popular Christmas traditions.

As givers, we view Christmas cards as a way to share Christmas across the miles. Our cards communicate our sentiments and represent our caring for the recipient—and our enthusiasm for the Christmas season.

?   ?   ?   ?   ?   ?   ?

Why do you send Christmas cards?

To express warm Christmas wishes?
To share the gospel message of Christ's birth?
To let others know what you/your family are/is doing?
To enjoy a Christmas tradition that is especially meaningful to you?
To fulfill expectations that you/others have for Christmas?
To affirm and strengthen relationships?
To thank others for their role in your life, business, and so forth?

?   ?   ?   ?   ?   ?   ?

As you compile an up-to-date Christmas card list, check your reasons for sending each card. Maybe this is the year to shorten your list, to try some new greeting idea, or to postpone your "annual letters" until a less chaotic time. Try to make this tradition as personal, meaningful, and enjoyable as possible.

Below are some suggestions for evaluating your Christmas card list, plus some ideas for new ways to extend holiday greetings. Remember to include other family members in your plans—and keep in mind that your Christmas cards and greetings don't all need to be identical!

1. Look at each entry on your card list lovingly but critically. If it includes . . .

The business community, coworkers, piano teachers, the mail carrier, and the PTA: be creative with these greetings. Instead of a traditional printed card, try something new: an ad in the newspaper, a billboard, the office bulletin board, a decorated window . . . *or* convey your greetings by hosting an open house or caroling from door to door.

College roommates, childhood friends, and other across-the-continent acquaintances: ask yourself if this is the best time and method for keeping in touch. You might send a quick card in December and a follow-up letter a month later. Maybe you will want to extend your greetings over the telephone or place a "Merry Christmas" ad in their local newspaper. Or how about recording your Christmas letter on a cassette: include a greeting from each member of the family—plus family news, holiday music, etc.

Friends and acquaintances in town: your cheerful Christmas attitude is a Yuletide greeting in itself! Share it liberally— at the grocery store, in church, at work, on the bus. . . . If you decide a special Christmas greeting is important, a telephone call, a cookie party, or a handwritten note may be just the thing.

Everyone who has ever sent you a card: is "everyone" dictating your Christmas agenda?

2. Look again at page 23 in Chapter 1 to review how cards fit in with the rest of your Christmas plans. Assess your decisions.

How many to send? Consider the costs—including postage, cards, envelopes, and so forth—and the time required to prepare these greetings.

Who is responsible for choosing, designing, creating, sending? Can this be a "we" project, with several family members taking part of the responsibility?

When must cards be completed and sent? Allow six weeks for overseas cards, two weeks for cards for this country.

3. Consider some alternatives to traditional greetings.

Send cards only to those you won't see during the holidays. Be sure to include a personal letter.

Send Christmas postcards.

Have a bulletin board at work, at school, or at church where each person can post one Christmas card to all. Encourage contributing the savings to a hunger appeal or a Christmas charity.

Skip the envelopes whenever possible. Fold your letters, staple them, and put the address on a blank side.

Make your own cards. Choose a format that you will enjoy making and a design that is "you." It might be fun to make several styles, or only a few cards. Remember—your cards don't all need to be the same!

HANDMADE CARDS—some tips and ideas:

• When you choose your *paper*, consider the weight, color, how well it folds, and, if you need to trim it, how well it can be cut. How about envelopes? Can you buy them, make them, skip them? (Consult the post office for size and weight regulations.)

• *Colored cellophane tape* makes wonderful linear designs. Embellish with *colored markers, ink*, and so on.

• *Block-print* or *stencil* a favorite design.

• Place *fingerprint paper* or *aluminum foil* on a *heating tray* set on the lowest setting. Use *crayons* to draw the design— they will melt to make smooth, bold drawings. Cut the foil into pieces that fit onto card-sized paper. Glue in place.

• Make a *tissue paper* collage with contrasting or complimentary colors of tissue. Plan your design so some layers overlap. Affix with *spray-on adhesive*.

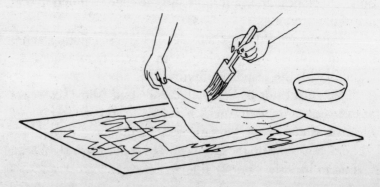

• Use *iron-on polyamide web* (available with interfacings at fabric stores) to hold *fabric scraps* onto cards. (Be sure your paper is heavy enough to stand up to the weight of the fabric.) Trim fabric and webbing into desired shapes. Put in place on the paper, with web between the fabric and the paper. Cover with a *pressing cloth*; *iron*, using wool setting and steam, for ten seconds without moving the iron. Let it cool, then turn and press the card from the other side.

• Use *colored markers* to decorate your cards. Draw an elaborate design or a simple pattern. Outline in black after you have used other colors.

• Make a *yarn* picture on your cards. Choose a *heavyweight paper*. Draw a design onto the paper—something that will be enhanced by the texture of the yarn. Trace the outline of your picture with a thin stream of *glue*. Let the glue set for a few minutes, then firmly but gently press yarn around the outer edges of the design. The glue should not saturate the yarn. Fill in the rest of the picture with more yarn, using the same procedure and ending in the center.

• *Photos, newspaper articles, children's artwork*, and other *mementos* can be collected all year to be included in your cards. Or just write your Christmas greeting on the back of each page you have collected.

For more card ideas, look at the suggestions for personalized greetings from children (page 65) and the section on gift wrappings (beginning on page 89).

4. What are you going to do with all the beautiful Christmas cards you receive? Be sure to savor each greeting, share

the news, check the addresses, save the stamps,* and put the cards in a visible place to add to your home's decor. And plan to read the cards again in a few months.

Buy it Smart!

The retail industry has the Christmas shopper figured out! Those glamorous ads, the eye-catching displays, and the enticing sales are the results of years of psychological study paid for by merchandisers. As a wise shopper, plan ahead, and keep your eyes open for surprises. And before you head for the shopping center, THINK—

> *WHOM* are you shopping for?
> *WHAT* are you looking for?
> *WHERE* should you look?
> *WHEN* will you shop?

Don't forget the wrappings!

Take inventory of your wrappings before you shop. What size boxes do you have? Do your ribbons match your papers? (Look ahead at the ideas for wrappings beginning on page 89.)

Remember your responsibilities as a gift shopper.

1. Use the same (or better) standards for selecting a gift as you do when purchasing for yourself.

2. Expect to *get* what you *pay* for, and to *pay* for what you *get*.

3. For each item, consider safety, price, quality, artistry,

---

* Commemorative stamps are collected around the world. If you aren't a stamp collector yourself, save canceled stamps for those who are. Many nonprofit organizations (especially churches) sell the stamps to distributors and collectors, with the profits going to world hunger organizations. Check with churches in your area—it's an easy way to help.

craftsmanship, foreign/domestic origin, ease of return, and general appearance.

After each shopping trip:

1. Examine every purchase. Check again for missing parts, quality and appearance of the merchandise.

2. Be organized. Put tags and sales slips in an envelope, filed with current bills, or in another safe spot you'll remember.

3. Be sure all sacks are empty before you throw them away.

4. Tag your purchases (using a code if you want). Check boxes and wrappings, noting if you need to purchase, find, or create anything to prepare each gift for delivery.

5. Store stocking stuffers in one sack or box.

WHAT TO BUY?

Fad items and hard-to-fit clothing (like blazers and pants) are some of the riskiest purchases. "Easy to enjoy," "versatile," and "timeless quality" are phrases that might describe a great gift to take to an anonymous gift exchange, or to send to a distant relative or new friend. "Practical luxuries" are usually good choices: think of things that are usable and fun to have, but which are not likely to be bought by your Special Someone for his/her own use.

SOME READY-MADE POSSIBILITIES

A picnic basket filled with deli items
A toolbox, partly equipped
A healthy potted plant (with instructions for care)
A gift certificate for food, flowers, fun . . .
A magazine rack filled with current issues
Your favorite cookbook—
with a few notes next to some favorite recipes!
The book you borrowed long ago—
with another by the same author
A set of mugs and a pound of fresh coffee beans

A box of stationery and a dozen stamps
A fruit bowl filled with fresh fruit
A recipe with the essential ingredients and/or gadget
(perhaps a favorite cheesecake recipe & a springform pan
OR Christmas cookie cutters and a recipe)
A tackle box equipped with fish line, hooks, lures.

LITTLE GIFTS AND STOCKING STUFFERS

An alarm clock, barrettes, batteries, bubble bath, a calculator, candles, cassette tapes, a chamois, chocolates, chopsticks, cocktail forks, a collapsible cup, colorful napkins, cookie cutters, corkscrews, crayons, a deck of cards, decorated toothpicks, earphones, earrings, an egg timer, engraved napkin rings, an embroidered handkerchief, emery boards, erasers, film, fish lures, flashbulbs, a flashlight, florist's tape, golf balls, a harmonica, herbal shampoo, ice tongs, jacks, a kazoo, lollipops, magnets, a magnifying glass, massage oil, mini screwdrivers, a mirror, a nail brush, nail polish, note cards, nut picks, oranges, a paring knife with blade cover, pencils, place cards, pocketbooks, pocket scissors, purse-sized containers, sachets, scratch pads, shoe laces, shoe polish, silk flowers, a silk scarf, specialty teas, sponges, stationery, a stopwatch, tape measures, thumbtacks, tiny bottles of liqueur, a tire gauge, traveler's sewing kit, travel games, tweezers, underwear, a whisk, wool socks . . . and a candy cane!

ALL READY-MADE GIFTS AREN'T FOUND IN SHOPPING MALLS!

If you know what you are looking for, check listings in the yellow pages of your local telephone book. You may be surprised to discover factories, warehouses, and sample shops that you have never heard of! If you would like to buy from a producer or wholesaler, use your telephone first. Ask for permission to buy, find out what is available, and check on the cost and location.

Many cities have a local shopping directory; check at a

nearby bookstore or library to find one for your community. You will enjoy learning about your town while taking advantage of its shopping opportunities.

A liquidation company sells odd lots, damaged merchandise, outdated stock, and various other treasures. It's a great place to start or finish up your shopping. Check your telephone directory for locations and hours.

Some used merchandise makes good gifts. Almost new appliances, linens, small furniture, tools, and antiques are a few of the possibilities. When shopping at garage sales, thrift stores, and other outlets for secondhand goods, scrutinize all interesting items. Double-check the quality. Look at the construction, the age, and the wear and tear the item has endured. A few hours and some creative labor can turn junk into a masterpiece! Paint, tape, embroidery, and new hardware can help, too! Remember there is usually no guarantee or warranty on these purchases, and owners' manuals and replacement parts may be difficult to obtain.

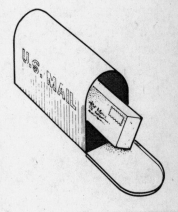

THERE'S MORE TO MAIL ORDER

The convenience of shopping by mail is hard to beat. From your mailbox you can order almost anything and have it shipped directly to Aunt Harriet in Otherstate. A good mail-order company may offer high-quality items, local handicrafts, or personalized gifts—with fast delivery and a full guarantee. There's a bounty of catalogs, brochures, and offers surrounding us all!

Some Places to Look
• The shopping guide section of a favorite magazine, often found in the back of each issue. The products are of particular interest to the readers of that magazine, and the advertisements are usually short and descriptive.
• The card catalog of your library, under "mail-order business," "catalogs, commercial," or a specific topic. Try looking under specialty cookware, solar energy, music, bicycling, travel, jellies, books, photography, music . . .

• Museum stores, outdoor clothing shops, factory outlets, and craft shops. And don't forget department stores and specialty stores: many have catalog service or make store-to-door deliveries.

• The yellow pages of the telephone book, under "Mail Order and Catalogs." You may need to do some research to find out what each of these listings has to offer (you may be surprised!)—as well as the guarantees, prices, etc.

• And of course the back of the cereal box, the insert in the Sunday paper, and the advertiser addressed to "OCCU-PANT" . . .

With a stack of catalogs in front of you, it's time to let your fingers do the walking. Keep your gift list (and your budget) in mind, but let your imagination go!

Here are some tips for ordering.

1. Read the catalog/brochure carefully. Be sure the catalog is current. Evaluate photos, descriptions, dimensions, and promises. Don't assume anything.

2. Check the cost, including postage and handling charges. Is it worth the price? Would you buy it if you found it in a store? Is there an expiration date on the offer?

3. Check for guarantees: The brochure should state a policy of prompt and complete refund if you are not fully satisfied.

4. If you have any doubts about the authenticity of the offer or the reliability of the company, check with the Better Business Bureau.

5. Place your order at least six weeks before you need to receive the items. The law requires that merchandise be shipped (not delivered) within thirty days after receiving a properly completed order, unless the catalog clearly states otherwise. If the merchandise arrives later than promised, you may refuse the merchandise and expect a full refund.

If there is a delay in shipping your order, the company must provide you with a free way to reply—even to cancel your order with a full refund.

These regulations do not apply to C.O.D. orders, magazines, photo finishing, seeds, growing plants, or record and tape club orders.

6. Fill out the ordering information carefully and clearly. You may request that your name not be rented, traded, or given to any person or organization. Include a check or money order to cover all costs, including shipping and taxes. NEVER SEND CASH. Keep the catalog or brochure, the company address, and the date you placed your order.

7. When you receive the product, immediately check it over. Get out the catalog and compare. Does it meet your expectations? Are there any broken or missing pieces? If there is any problem, DO NOT return the package C.O.D., but notify the company at once.

A carefully written *letter* will provide you with documentation of your complaint: Keep a copy! Be sure to specify the date you ordered, the invoice or order number, and your exact complaint.

OR *telephone* the company. Although this is the quickest way to get a response, it provides you with no record of your action. Before making the call, be sure to have the package, brochure, and all information in front of you. And follow your telephone conversation with a written note to the company, noting the date, time, and complaints discussed over the telephone, the person(s) with whom you spoke, and the decisions (if any) that were made.

8. If you are having the product mailed to someone else, you may wish to send a card just before you expect the product to arrive. Ask the recipient to write or phone you when the gift is received. At that time it is your responsibility to make sure the product is satisfactory; any complaints should be pursued by the purchaser!

THOSE "HAVE TO" GIFTS

Gift exchanges in the classroom, gifts for business associates and fellow employees, and gift swaps at the Garden Club . . . the list of "have to" gifts grows annually. These gifts tend to be impersonal and forgotten soon after they are given—yet the expense of several "little somethings" adds up. It can be a frustrating tradition. Still we may feel it is important to share the significance of gift giving with our everyday associates.

Here are some tips for extending the meaning of these traditions.

• Pool resources with others who want to give to one person (such as the boss or homeroom teacher), and buy one nice gift together. Or give money to the recipient's favorite charity.

• Instead of drawing names for the office gift exchange, have a money tree at the office Christmas party. Elect a "charity of the year" to receive the contributions.

• Call a hospital, hospice organization, care center, or correctional facility to find out if it could use gifts for the patients or inmates. Ask party-goers to bring a wrapped (and possibly labeled) gift to send to the chosen institution.

• Avoid cologne, liquor, neckties, and other traditional gifts. Instead, try almost-anyone-can-use-it gifts: a nice comb, dinner napkins, a notepad and pen, travel aids, household tools, and so forth.

HOSPITALITY GIFTS

The custom of giving small gifts to the host or hostess reciprocates some of the generosity extended to the guests. Some fresh flowers for the table or a warm loaf of bread say, "I'm glad to be here! Thanks for inviting me." These versatile gifts are equally capable of saying, "Welcome to our neighborhood!" "Congratulations!" or "Thanks for the help!"

During the Christmas season, it is handy to have one or two wrapped presents on hand, ready to give as hospitality gifts, to share with drop-in guests, or to take to an almost forgotten gift exchange. Inexpensive but useful items with a "homey" touch express our appreciation for the friendship of the recipient. For example:

—small plants wrapped with Christmas foil and a ribbon
—Christmas tableware or decorations

—a holiday candle in a holder

—sachets or pomanders

—spice mixes in small apothecary jars, or beverage mixes in mugs

—homemade jams and jellies in glasses or goblets

A bow, a sprig of holly, and a note card would be all the wrapping most of these gifts need.

Most hospitality gifts are easy to make in quantities. Give identical gifts to several people; keep some on hand for later or negotiate a trade with a creative friend!

GOOD BUYS ALL YEAR

When would you prefer to shop for Christmas gifts? December offers the greatest variety of traditional Christmas items—and carolers, holiday decorations, and visits by Santa, elves, and reindeer add a note of Christmas nostalgia to the shopping experiences. But our enthusiasm may be diffused by the crowds, the commercialism, and the time pressures of rapidly approaching gift exchanges.

A year-round approach to Christmas shopping may offer a new perspective. You can wait for seasonal sales on whatever you are buying, and spread out the expense of purchasing your gifts. You may especially enjoy giving more time to each gift selection—starting to purchase and make your gifts long before the "Christmas rush." Birthdays may serve as reminders for you: purchase Christmas gifts during the birthday month of each person on your gift list.

Whenever you shop, plan to enjoy the experience. Take time to say "Thank you" and "Merry Christmas," and to smile at the other shoppers. Use all of your senses to appreciate your surroundings: Listen to the chatter. Try some perfumes. Notice the colors. Feel the texture of fabrics.

There are good buys every month!

JANUARY   FEBRUARY

Post-Christmas sales: decorations, cards, toys. Year-End Inventory Sales: bedding, tableware, housewares, small appliances.

MARCH   APRIL   MAY

Spring and Summer things: garden equipment, camping gear, yard furniture, fabrics.

JUNE   JULY

Mid-Year Inventory Sales: bedding, towels, linens, table-cloths, sports equipment, small appliances.

AUGUST   SEPTEMBER   OCTOBER

County Fairs! A panorama of gadgets, handicrafts, and ideas! Back-to-School sales on children's clothing and school supplies.

NOVEMBER   DECEMBER

Fabrics and blankets. Party supplies. Holiday boutiques and bazaars.

Homemade Gifts

It's a popular myth that making every gift you give will bring you a holiday of joy. The first creative project you make will teach you that perfection has its price and that artistry is at the fingertips of a few! Creating for others requires time, talent, a place to work, and an odd assortment of resources—and the only reward may be frustration! Still, we admire displays at bazaars and boutiques, and think, "I could make it at half the price," and "It can't really be that difficult."

There is no shortage of ideas for homemade gifts. But between the idea and the finished product are hours of careful planning and hard work. The result is a gift that represents the personality as well as the labor of the giver. True, it's a risky option—there are no guarantees about the results of a craft or art project. But the made-to-order quality and character of what we have crafted is an unparalleled testament to our caring.

Look again at the "Buy It—Make It—Become It—Redirect It" chart beginning on page 68. Read over your gift list once again. Think about some of the options on the next few pages, in magazines, Christmas books, and elsewhere. Is this the year to "Make It"? Then get to work, but keep these tips in mind:

Read *all* the directions *completely* several times before you begin.

—What will it look like when completed?
—What do you need?
—How long will it take?
—Are the instructions complete? Do you need to check another source for more information?
—Where can you go for extra help—the library, a neighbor or friend, a professional service? (Sometimes it's helpful to look at finished projects at boutiques, shops, displays, etc.)

Start early. Make some "in case" plans: allow for extra time, extra materials, and extra patience. Tricky projects may require a backup plan in case the *whole thing* is a disaster!

Make it with love! While you work, think about the recipient . . . whistle a carol . . . listen to Christmas music . . . relive your Christmas memories . . . pray for your neighbors.

HOMEMADE PRESENTS AND PACKAGES: SOME IDEAS

A *Personalized Calendar*

1. Select a theme: family history, photographs, travel, recipes, inspiration . . .

2. Determine the layout: horizontal or vertical, abstract or linear . . .

3. Choose suitable paper, binding, ink, printing . . .

4. Cut, paste, draw, write . . . Be *accurate* as you write in the months and dates!

5. Add holidays, days to remember, and bits of whimsy . . .

A Book by You

Bind your book in a ring binder or homemade binding. (Use staples, string, yarn, or heavy-duty thread.) Or purchase a blank book, available in a wide variety of sizes and designs—even holiday styles—at book stores and stationery shops.

- Collect jokes, tongue twisters, or crossword puzzles.
- Research and write about a favorite subject: the history of your area, places to visit for free, a movie star, the high school basketball team . . .
- Design your own recipe book, featuring family favorites and/or holiday treats.

"It Was a Very Good Year"

Make a photo collage, fill a scrapbook, or make a shadow box to remember this year's good times.

Sawdust Cupcake Firestarters

1. Place cupcake papers in muffin tins.

2. Fill each paper ⅔ full with sawdust.

3. Melt paraffin or candle stubs *slowly over* hot water. (It ignites easily—be careful!)

4. Carefully pour melted paraffin over the sawdust. Let the cups cool and harden.

5. Create a card explaining how to use the firestarters: "Place beneath the kindling wood when building your fire."

Plant a Gift—Give a Plant

- Force-start a pot of hyacinth, narcissus, daffodils, and tulips. Check a garden book or nursery for instructions.
- Take a cutting of your favorite plant. Begonias, philodendron, ivies, and many others are easy to propagate. Be sure to start several months before Christmas and check a basic

gardening book for details. Put your healthy growing gift in a pretty and/or unusual pot.

Fancy Notepaper

1. Collect clean and perfect flowers. Small, delicate flowers such as pansies, primroses, and delphinium are ideal.
2. Put the flowers between layers of blotting paper, then under a stack of books. Leave them undisturbed for two weeks.
3. Carefully glue the flattened flowers to some nice stationery or parchment paper.

Homemade Decorations

Check Chapter 3, "Tinsel and Treasures," for some great ideas and "how-to's," including

- pomander balls
- Advent calendars
- candles and candle holders
- tree ornaments of straw, needlework, dough, fabric . . .
- holiday noisemakers
- a shadow box crèche

GIFTS FROM YOUR KITCHEN

Mary Lou's Carrot Cake is a priority item in our family's Christmas kitchen. We make several batches: a ring pan to serve with hard sauce on Christmas Eve, a loaf to slice for the open house, and several small fluted cakes (each adorned with a cherry) to give to friends and neighbors.

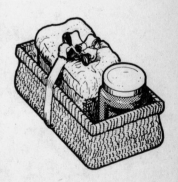

A baker's repertoire of holiday goodies is as personal as a signature. Many people are at their creative best in the kitchen—not in the workshop, at the sewing machine, or behind the camera. For them, edible creations make fulfilling projects and resourceful gifts.

If you choose to offer gifts from your kitchen, use the same consideration for the needs and preferences of the recipient as you would in selecting any other gift. Trying to lose weight, coping with allergies, following doctor's orders, or adhering to preferred diets, some people take extra care in selecting what they eat. Don't tempt dieters with something they shouldn't have. (A friend with diabetes can't eat sugary candies but would probably enjoy a loaf of homemade bread.) Keep the quantity appropriate: a little tin of fudge might be appreciated by someone living alone, but wouldn't last long in a large family. (How about a "variety pack" of assorted treats for that household?) Let your gift display your talents and your creative genius. A gift of food should be attractive and generous—not excessive.

How about:

• A foursome of jams, jellies, preserves, and/or relishes (prepared months ahead at the peak of harvest).

• Tins of home-roasted or home-glazed nuts.

• A basket of homemade "brown-and-serve" rolls. (Bake rolls half the normal time; enclose directions for storing and heating.)

• A cheese ball made from softened cheeses flavored with herbs, salsa, minced onion . . . Press nuts, olives, chives, or bacon bits onto the outside for a delicious finishing touch.

• Blackberry brandy, Irish cream liqueur, or some other "spirited" beverage. Find recipes in holiday publications and cookbooks. Be sure to seal and store appropriately, and label your gift.

• A dessert tray of elegant cookies, candies, and other nibbles—all made fresh from your family's favorite recipes.

• A selection of homemade ice cream toppings—perhaps with a jar of maraschino cherries and chopped nuts for do-it-yourself sundaes!

MARY LOU'S CARROT CAKE

3 eggs	2 c. shredded carrot
2 c. sugar	1 13-oz. can crushed
½ c. oil	pineapple (juice pack),
2 c. flour	not drained

1 tsp. cinnamon	1 c. chopped nuts
1 tsp. salt	1½ c. shredded coconut
2 tsp. baking soda	2 tsp. vanilla extract

1. Beat eggs, add sugar and oil, and beat well. Combine flour with cinnamon, salt, and soda; blend into egg mixture.

2. Add other ingredients and mix well.

3. Grease pan (one 9″ × 13″ angel food or bundt cake pan). Fill ⅔ full of batter. Use any remaining batter to make cupcakes.

4. Bake in preheated 350° over 50 minutes or until a toothpick inserted in the center comes out clean. (Cupcakes take about 30 minutes). Watch carefully; don't overbake! Let cakes cool 45 minutes in pans, then remove and cool on racks.

5. Dust with powered sugar; serve with hard sauce or whipped cream if desired.

Gift Wrappings

Under wraps, our gifts become secret treasures. Colorful papers and ribbons do more than decorate. They bundle items together, protect our breakables, and tease the recipient by hiding the identity of those mysterious packages.

The Swedish *Julklapp* is a gift hiding beneath many layers of tissue and a red wax seal. The giver delivers the gift secretly, tossing it through an open door or window and quickly disappearing.

Sixteenth-century gifts were often collections of several items—something useful, something pleasant, and something with which to discipline. German gifts were called "Christ Bundles"—parcels full of Christmas treasures.

On the following pages are some instructions for creating wrapping papers, package decorations, and disguises for your gifts. As with any do-it-yourself project, you'll get best results if you first read all directions and exeriment with a few samples.

Many of these projects are great for kids. Even preschool-

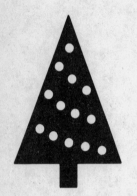

ers can try block prints and rubbings; older children will enjoy designing a unique wrapping paper for a special gift. Of course, preparation, adequate supervision, and cleanup are keys to success!

Remember that not all gifts need elaborate wrappings. An attractive item may be given "as is"; contrasting trim or a small Christmas memento may add the right finishing touch to such a gift.

DECORATING THE PAPER

Block Print Variations

Remember doing this in grade school? Tempera paints, a potato, and a simple design transform a piece of newsprint into customized wrappings.

For pattern printers:

• Carve a simple pattern (star, letter, tree, bell) onto a smooth, semihard surface—a potato, cork, slab of rubber, dense sponge, eraser. (Use a sharp knife with a good point.)

• Use cookie cutters, spools, jar lids, kitchen utensils, sponges.

• Cut a design from a piece of an inner tube and glue it to a wooden block.

For papers: Try coated stock paper, tissue paper, butcher paper, brown wrapping paper, or newsprint.

Block print paints: Tempera or poster paints, or ink. (An inked stamp pad works well, too.)

Choose bright colors that complement the paper you have chosen. Keep it simple—one or two colors—until you feel confident and creative.

Or use bleach: Dip your pattern maker (not rubber) into a dish of diluted bleach. Print on colored tissue paper or other colored paper; the bleach removes the color from the printed areas.

Spills, Spatters, and Sprays

• Use straws to blow paint across papers.

• Paint with cotton swabs, toothbrushes, cotton balls, or toothpicks.

• Put a large blob of runny paint in spots one or two inches apart across the top of your paper. Hang the paper from a wall in your garage, letting the paint drip to make parallel lines. This may be repeated, turning the paper ninety degrees before making the next set of lines.

• Dip a string into a dish of paint. Drop it onto your wrapping paper—or pull it across the paper to make any sort of "wormy" design. Tweezers make this process less messy.

• Fold the paper in quarters or diagonally into triangles. Paint a design into one of the inside sections with a liberal amount of paint. Being careful not to smear the paint, refold the paper. Open to dry.

• Try stencils, silk-screening, watercolors, and stamp pads.

Colorful Variations

• Color the paper with chalk. Spray with hair spray to "fix" your design.

• Make rubbings of interesting flat things: embossed Christmas cards or ornaments, feathers, pennies, leaves, and dried flowers are good choices. Place the item under your paper, then lightly rub a crayon over the top until the design comes through.

• Doodles are fun! Practice some Christmas doodles (trees, wreaths, crosses, "JOY") and fill a space with your creations. Or trace your children's handprints again and again across the paper.

(Look at the Christmas card suggestions beginning on page 74 for more ways to decorate wrapping papers.)

CLEVER CONTAINERS

Cover cardboard tubes with paper, foil, or fabric. The ends of the wrapping may be gathered, folded, taped, or tied.

Cover a box: glue fabric or paper directly onto a shoe box, cigar box, wooden band box . . . If there is a lid, that can be covered as well.

Get a softer look by first wrapping the box with a layer of

batting material. Glue the batting in place, then sew or glue fabric over the top. Satin ribbons and lace might add a nice finishing touch—or dress up your "pillow box" as a gingerbread house with gingham windows, a felt roof, and button flowers.

Other Wraps and Containers

canisters   a lunch box   a bucket   a pan
a basket   an empty coffee can   luggage   a funnel
a recipe box   freezer cartons   a backpack
a cookie tin   a handbag   glassware
a toolbox   a pillow case   shelf paper   lace
fabric   hair ribbons   table linens   measuring tape
washcloths and towels   a laundry bag   a poster
comic pages from Sunday's newspaper

Make a different wrapping paper or container every week during Advent. Or spend an entire day experimenting with Christmas crafts. You may want to invite some friends over to share the fun. Collect all possible materials in advance—including lots of newspapers *and* your sense of humor!

PACKAGE DECORATIONS

Ribbons and bows, papers and containers aren't the only items with which to decorate your holiday gifts. Here are some ways to give extra flair to your presents and packages.

• Add a Swedish touch with a chain of hearts cut from glossy red paper; string them across brown wrapping paper.
• Use scalloped or pinking shears to cut the paper. Or tear the edges, brown them with a candle, cut them into fringes.
• Trim an old Christmas card to make a gift tag or package decoration.
• Cut small stars, diamonds, hearts, or chevrons from a wide ribbon.

• Cut pieces of ribbon to form a star or tree across the top of a package. Try with one or several colors of ribbon.

• Cut a manger scene out of brown paper. Glue it onto the flat side of your package. Add a star, some straw, maybe a halo.

• Broadly trace the recipient's name onto pattern paper. Cut it from paper that contrasts with the wrapping. Attach it invisibly, using two-sided tape, glue, or adhesive spray.

Organize a wrapping center in your home during the busy before-Christmas days. Keep scissors, tape, wrappings, ribbons, pens, and pencils there—plus a sign that reads "Do Not Disturb—Creative Person Working!"

ATTACHMENTS

Tantalize the senses with what you affix to your package.

• Make a joyful noise with jingle bells, maracas, or a rattle.

• Add a pleasant fragrance. Bundle some potpourri or your own selection of whole herbs or spices, dried flowers, or dried citrus rind. Sew them into a sachet, or use nylon net or a tea ball to hold your selections. Try lemon and mint, rose petals, pine, and sage.

• Attach a small bottle of perfume or herbal oil, some peppermint candies, or a small fan of evergreens.

• Tie on some Christmas cheer: a tree ornament, some tinsel, or a Christmas candle. Cotton ball snowmen, mistletoe corsages, and pinecone bells are fun to make for package trims.

• Attach a little gift to the ribbons and bows: cookie cutters, fish lures, postage stamps, a silver spoon, flower seeds or bulbs, a kitchen gadget—it could be a clue to what's inside!

• Add a bit of whimsy: a silly snapshot, a small toy, a party favor.

GIVE A SURPRISE—

• Plan a scavenger hunt to find a gift. Hide clues around the house. (The first clue could be wrapped as a gift.)

• Put your gift in an unexpected place: in the refrigerator, on the seat of the car, in a file cabinet, in the bathtub . . .

• Find someone to deliver your gift to the recipient's door. Maybe you could offer to deliver for someone else in return.

—OR A DISGUISE!

• Change the shape of a gift by padding it with crushed tissue paper.

• Enclose a small loose object (such as a marble) that will rattle when the gift is shaken.

• Disassemble a gift and wrap the parts separately.

• Fill an egg carton with a dozen small gifts.

• Pack a small gift in a large box.

PUT IT IN THE MAIL!

1. Package it carefully. Wrap individual items separately. Select a sturdy box and fill with packages and packing material. Crumpled papers and styrofoam chips work well to fill the spaces and prevent breakage.

2. Wrap your parcel correctly: use plain paper and reinforced tape (not string and masking tape). If staples are used, remember to cover them with tape.

3. Address it clearly and accurately. Use dark, permanent ink, zip codes, and proper names. Mark special handling instructions in bold letters. Be sure to include a return address and add a simple Christmas decoration. (Christmas seals add a decorative touch *and* support a charitable cause.)

4. Mail it on time. (Check with the post office for this year's mailing schedule.) Usually, overseas packages should be mailed by mid-October, domestic packages by December 10.

Tips for Mailing Food

Only some foods ship well. Choose goodies that won't crumble easily or get stale quickly. Most bar and drop cookies, nuts, and some breads are good choices. Fruitcake holds to-gether well and keeps forever. Beverages, fresh fruits, and glass containers are risky to send. If you must send these fragile gifts, use sufficient packing material around and be-tween each item. *Fill* the parcel but don't *pack* it down. Mark the outside of the package "PERISHABLE. HANDLE WITH CARE."

THE STOCKINGS WERE HUNG . . .

Long before Christmas trees were readily available, stockings were hung on the fireplace in anticipation of Santa's arrival and the gifts he would bring. Like the wooden shoes set out by Dutch children, those stockings were well-worn, everyday apparel—far different from the oversize and personalized Christmas stockings hung by children today.

A century ago, a great debate pitted evergreen trees against the then traditional Christmas stockings. In time, most families adopted both customs; today Christmas stockings and Christmas trees are happily featured—and amply decorated—in many American homes.

St. Nicholas threw gold into the stockings of three poor maidens. (Page 57 has the story.) Although few of us can afford to fill stockings with gold, we enjoy Christmas stockings as festive decorations and receptacles for gifts.

Stockings can be any size, shape, or construction—from Cinderella's glass slipper to a logger's cleat-studded boot. And any stocking can be personalized with appliqués, ribbons, bells, sequins, and charms.

Also—

• Let the stockings collect hopes, dreams, and secret messages by allowing only written or symbolic gifts.

• Hang stockings early so all family members can drop gifts in.

• See the list of stocking stuffers on page 78.

• Encourage inexpensive, recycled, or simple handmade gifts.

• Hang only one stocking for the entire family.

• Hang a stocking for Baby Jesus: ask each member of the family to put something in it—a promise written on a piece of paper, a check for world hunger, a symbol of an intention to change a bad habit.

SET A GIVING MOOD

Before opening gifts, take a few moments to focus on the spirit of Christmas.

• Say a prayer as you gather around the tree.

• Sing a carol on your front porch. Pause to be thankful for Christ's birth, then reenter your home to open the presents.

• Fill a box with peace and love, with an "Open me first" tag attached. Place a few sheets of tissue and a note inside the box: "This box is filled with enough peace and love to last all year! Share it generously and you will find a renewed Christmas spirit this day!"

German children awaken early on Christmas Day. They dress in their Christmas finery and eagerly await the sounds of the bells of the gift-bearing Christ Child or the Weihnachtsmann (Christmas Man). The family joins in singing carols and reading from the Bible in the candlelit living room— and then begins the exuberant search for the hidden gifts.

Letters we have written you
    All our wishes stating,
Do not pass our chimney-flue,
    Where we children watch for you,
Father, mother, grandpa too—
    Der Weihnachtsmann we're waiting!
              —German folk song
              translated by Alice Mattalath

Becoming a Gift

Rings and jewels are not gifts, but apologies for gifts.
The only gift is a portion of thyself.
—Ralph Waldo Emerson

There are hundreds of ways to become a gift. Enjoying a concert with a friend, teaching a neighbor to fish, baby-sitting for a relative . . . Sharing yourself with those on your gift list is a wonderful celebration of the spirit of Christmas. Here are a few ideas.

• Attend the practice session of a favorite team. College and professional teams will occasionally open the stands to the fans. Call the team office to inquire.
• Trade homes with a young family—but have their children stay with you. Mom and Dad will enjoy all the comforts of *your* home—away from the kids! Leave the makings for a candlelight supper, put soft music on the stereo, and unplug the telephone. Plan to do something special with the children in the meantime.
• Do some daily gift giving—but keep your plans a secret. Put a nickel in a stranger's expired parking meter, offer daily compliments, buy a "just because" gift, or try harder to appreciate someone who "bugs" you!
• Help someone be a Santa. Check community organizations for Christmas sharing programs that help parents prepare for Christmas. You may be able to provide money, transportation, or child care to make shopping feasible—or give gifts of toys, food, wrappings, decorations, or a tree.

David Dunn is a man obsessed with giving. *Try Giving Yourself Away* is the title of his book—a small volume filled with true accounts of his gift-giving experiences. Expecting nothing in return, he shares "unbuyable gifts" every day: notes of appreciation, a listening ear, thoughtfulness, kind words, tolerance, and forgiveness.

Our Christmas lists record our intentions of giving happiness to many people. In preparing for giving, we would do well to heed Dunn's words:

> You are trying to give pleasure to someone, and you know from experience what trifling things give you pleasure. Such simple gifts as a compliment on your home or your children or your new hat, a note, a telephone call, or a simple act that reflects thoughtfulness or friendly interest, will set you up for an hour, perhaps a whole day. They are the truest form of giving, because they come from the heart—they are literally a portion of the giver.[2]

Yuletide gift-giving traditions have evolved from the precious gifts of the Magi to twentieth-century buying sprees. Christmas cards, packages, and stockings are fun-filled traditions that express our caring for others and deepen our understanding of that first Christmas. Giving inspires us to look beyond advertised expectations of the season, reclaim the generosity of the Magi, and share in their joy of our Savior's birth.

[2] David Dunn, *Try Giving Yourself Away* (New York: Coward-McCann, 1929.)

CHAPTER 3
Tinsel and Treasures

The holly's up, the house is all bright,
The tree is ready, The candles alight;
Rejoice and be glad, all children tonight!

—Carl August Peter Cornelius
"Der Christbaum"

F irst greenery and candles . . . then bonfires, Yule logs, Advent wreaths, crèches, Christmas trees, elves, and Santa became traditions. Decorative possibilities are now endless. But that has not always been true. The early Church rejected evergreens and candles. These decorations adorned the homes of Romans celebrating the Saturnalia and the Birthday of the Unconquered Sun. Regarded as tokens of pagans, and therefore inappropriate Christian symbols, the Church prohibited their use.

Some Christians agreed and spent the "Festum Nativitatis Domini Nostri Jesu Christi" (The Feast of the Nativity of Our Lord Jesus Christ) contemplating the Incarnation. Others, unwilling to forsake familiar and attractive decorations, displayed evergreens and candles. Adopted by a new faith, these pagan props in time became Christian symbols: greenery represented God's eternal qualities, and candles symbolized Christ as "The Light of the World."

Because of the limitless decorating possibilities, planning is essential. Questionnaire B (begins page 23) includes decorating traditions and ideas. As you share, consider these suggestions for holiday decorations:

BLUEPRINT FOR PLANNING HOLIDAY DECORATIONS

• Be creative. Is there a theme you want to feature—perhaps a line from a Christmas carol, poem, story, or Scripture? Encourage all family members to share their ideas.

• Discuss what images you would like to project: joy, reverence, mirth, "cuteness," beauty. Use colors to convey these images more effectively. Reds and yellows are stimulating colors which attract attention and make decorations seem larger. Blues, blue-greens, and violets are quiet and inspiring. Greens are warmer but tranquil. Contrast warm and cool colors, create new color combinations . . . enjoy experimenting!

• Consider all areas of your home, indoors and out. Are there rooms that should be reserved for privacy and reflection during the holidays?

• Determine your decorating priorities: indoor, outdoor, trees, lights, hearth, crèche, heirloom ornaments . . .

• Be realistic. Magazine photographs of rooms glittering with holiday decor are the work of professionals. Regard periodicals only as resources that help you create decorations reflecting your family's values and abilities.

• Use what is available. Nineteenth-century settlers in Nebraska created Christmas trees by attaching cotton to oak branches. You may not be this desperate, but let availability inspire you. Experiment with regional plants; check the fabric scraps on hand; find out what colors are lurking in those paint cans in the basement.

• Plan your decorations around a focal point—such as a crèche, sleigh, or the indoor Christmas tree seen from the outside. Aim for simplicity and avoid gaudiness.

• Seek a visual balance by keeping the size and scope of your decorations appropriate to the size of your home and yard.

• Make a long-range decorating plan. Some ideas may take years to complete, but each step can be attractive and meaningful.

• Consider if your decorating ideas would be appreciated by your neighborhood. Would lights or music disturb neighbors?

• Determine supplies, skills, time, and money needed to complete your proposed project(s).

• When decisions are made, discuss how to approach the project(s) and schedule family work parties.

Above all else—HAVE FUN TOGETHER! Enjoy planning and creating your decorations, and take pride in their uniqueness.

INDOOR DECORATIONS

Prepare the way of the Lord,
make his paths straight.

—Mark 1:3

Indoor decorations are shared with family and friends. These decorations are usually visual reminders of the season, but the spirit of Christmas can be discovered through sound (page 151), fragrance (page 166), and taste (page 169). There are even tactile reminders (page 180) of Christmas—the softness of a velvet dress, or a fire's warmth on a cold December evening. When we use all of our senses to celebrate Christmas, the spirit of the birth at Bethlehem descends upon us through many and more varied experiences.

Visions

When what to my wondrous eyes should appear . . .
—Clement C. Moore
"A Visit from St. Nicholas"

Christmas is visually stimulating: greenery is woven into wreaths and garlands that adorn houses, light posts, fences, and windows; Christmas trees exchange a simple verdant attire for lights, tinsel, and homemade treasures; candles, Advent calendars, mangers, and greeting cards decorate our homes.

How did this array of decorations become intertwined with our celebration of a birth marked by simplicity? From this panorama, how can we select or create the most appropriate decorations to express our faith and feelings?

O, may our faith be as ever green
And ever kind our deeds to all.

—"'Tis the Eve of Christmas"
German carol

Decorating homes with evergreens is not a unique practice, but a four-thousand-year-old tradition. To Yule celebrants who faced harsh winters and entertained doubts about spring's return, evergreens symbolized immortality and fertility. These plants lived when all others had died. Their existence was the only sign that the life force had not abandoned the earth. Their powers were impressive: a fir branch placed across the foot of the bed prevented nightmares; a partially burned fir stick put under the bed protected the house from lightning; fir sticks bound together and hung over the barn door dispelled evil spirits who wanted to steal the grain.

Germanic tribes feared the spirits who menaced the earth during the winter months. These evil spirits left the earth void of vegetation. Only the evergreens survived. Their survival was proof that this greenery possessed the power to repel demonic forces. So, to safeguard their homes and families, tribes carried evergreen sprigs indoors.

To the Romans, evergreens held magical qualities. They were harbingers of luck and protectors against evil. During the Middle Ages, celebrants could not bring evergreens into their homes before Christmas Eve nor take them down before January 6. (Pity the poor soul with allergies!) The deadline for discarding greens was February 2 (Candlemas), and then, only dry sprigs could be burned.

Fortunately, science and faith have freed us from these superstitions and schedules. Evergreens are no longer safeguards against disaster, but attractive and symbolic decorations.

LOCATING AND GATHERING GREENS may be a greater challenge than deciding when to decorate. For some, gathering involves simply a walk into the backyard or a drive to a friend's acreage or farm. Others may have to check with produce markets, the local Park Bureau, the Forest Service, or classified ads. When you find greens—

• Make sure they are fresh.
• Store cut ends in sugar water (1 cup sugar to 1 quart water).
• Store in a cool place.
• Locate displays away from heat sources.
• Discard dried greens and replace with fresh sprigs.

Discover new greenery possibilities in your yard, your neighborhood, and nearby markets. Consider ferns, camellia, strawberry or palm leaves, succulents, or herbs.

Eache roome with yvie leaves is drest,
And every post with holly.

—"Juvenilia"

Holly

According to legend, the Crown of Thorns was wound with holly whose white berries turned red after the Crucifixion. To early Christians in Northern Europe, holly signified Mary's love for God. In France and England, this prickly plant was hung over doors to show that Christ resided therein. In medieval England, unmarried women fastened a holly sprig to their beds to avoid being turned into witches, and Germans took home the holly branches from their church decorations to use as amulets against lightning.

Juniper

Believed to have concealed Mary and Joseph in their flight into Egypt, the juniper is considered a tree of refuge. Juniper sap smeared over houses and stables repelled evil spirits. In Italy, juniper sprigs were hung on doors to discourage witches, who always stopped to count the leaves. When this proved hopeless, the witches left.

Laurel or Bay Leaves

Romans celebrating the Saturnalia decorated their homes with laurel to signify victory. Early Christians adopted this practice, but for them, laurel symbolized Christ's victory over sin and death.

USING THE GREENS offers a creative and resourceful opportunity. Even though your decorations may assume traditional forms, such as wreaths (page 107) and garlands (page 111), they can reflect your own personal flair.

! ! ! ! ! ! !

WARNING!!! Plants can be harmful to your child's health. Learn if a plant is toxic before determining its use and location. Check with libraries, nurseries, or state/county extension offices. Know the names of your plants so that in an emergency, you could inform a physician or poison control center what plant(s) had been ingested or touched. Since your friends and relatives may not have poison-proofed their homes, watch the children carefully when you visit during the holidays.

! ! ! ! ! ! !

WREATHS

Originally a pagan decoration, Christians used the wreath to express their love and faith. Its circular shape symbolized God's eternal love, and its greenery signified Christ's immortality—his victory over death.

Before you begin, consider:

- What do you want to express?
- Who will see the wreath?
- Where and how will it be displayed—indoors? outdoors? over the mantle? over the dining table? hanging in the hall? resting on a table?
- Does the location require a certain shape?
- Is any shape possible? Heart, triangle, oval, pretzel . . . ?
- What ornaments will you use? How will they be attached?

Supplies needed to make a wreath—

• The BASE can be a wire frame or straw base. These are available at craft and floral shops. If you want to create a special shape, take wire coat hangers, remove the hooks, bend into the desired shape, and secure with wire.

• HEAVY TWINE looped through the base will provide the hanging loop for the finished wreath.

• STURDY WIRE is needed to attach the greens to the frame and the ornaments to the greenery. Green floral tape can also be used, and florists' pins work well with a straw base.

• WIRE CUTTERS.

• GREENS can include plants and foliage that are holiday favorites or nontraditional selections from your yard, neighborhood, or community. Turn to page 104 for suggestions on locating and gathering greens.

• PRUNING SHEARS are needed to cut the greens into pieces 3″ to 6″ long.

• SNUG GARDEN GLOVES will protect your hands.

• ORNAMENTS. (See page 112 for suggestions.)

To make the wreath—

• Cut a length of twine long enough to tie around the frame and to provide a hanging loop when the wreath is complete.

• Add greenery. You may work in one direction, filling in the entire wreath as you go, or attach sprigs to the frame's perimeter first, the inside second (if it's circular), and its front surface last.

• When the greenery is in place, add the ornaments, and display your work of art!

Ornaments can express family interests, talents, or hobbies.

• Etchings, cornhusk figures, quilted or knitted ornaments, embroidered designs, dough art, family photographs, a child's drawing, miniatures, decorative spoons, origami, cookie cutters, seashells and sand dollars, home-decorated cookies, baby toys and blocks . . .

Some ornaments hold special significance.

• STRAW DESIGNS were ancient tributes to the agrarian spirits and, later, reminders of the Bethlehem stable. In Norway, straw crosses were hung over doors to ward off evil spirits.

• SHIPS are uncommon holiday decorations in the States but popular symbols abroad. Saint Nicholas sails from Spain to Holland in a ship bearing gifts, as does the gift-laden Saint Basil, who arrives in Greece by sea. "I Saw Three Ships" is an English carol which describes Mary, Joseph, and Jesus arriving on Christmas morning.

• PRETZELS were rewards. For learning their catechism, seventh-century students of an Italian monk received *pretiola* or "little rewards." Made from leftover bread dough, pretiola were shaped to resemble arms crossed in prayer.

• HERBS and Christian legends are intertwined.

So on the trembling rosemary
    She laid them one by one,
And strong the rosemary held them
    All morning to the sun.
          —Phyllis McGinley
          "Ballad of the Rosemary"

Rosemary

According to two Christian legends, rosemary aided the Holy Family in its flight into Egypt. Once, the herb opened its branches to conceal Mary and Jesus from Herod's soldiers. In another instance, Mary hung some of the Christ Child's garments to dry on a rosemary bush. After the clothes dried, the once white flowers of the rosemary turned fragrant and blue. For centuries rosemary was significant during the holidays: it was hung in doorways to welcome elves and placed in churches to protect congregations from evil spirits.

Sage

Its fragrance was a blessing bestowed by Mary after it concealed her from Herod's forces. During the Middle Ages, sage was thought to prolong life, prevent chills, console the grieving, and avert toads!

• An herb kitchen wreath would be attractive, fragrant, and useful. Grab a pinch of oregano for the sauce, sprinkle tarragon on the beans, rosemary on lamb.

Other ideas:

• A Thanksgiving wreath of straw, decorative corn, gourds, and dried flowers. By adding candles and Christmas ornaments, this Thanksgiving decoration becomes an Advent wreath.

• Search those kitchen shelves for wreath-making materials awaiting your creative genius. Dried pasta, nuts, peach stones, seeds, popcorn kernels, and dried beans can be glued onto a cardboard or wood frame.

Although used in the Kings' Cake on Epiphany because it was considered a sacred vegetable, the bean has not always enjoyed such a virtuous status. In ancient times it supposedly caused nightmares and insanity; the aroma of beans even repelled ghosts.

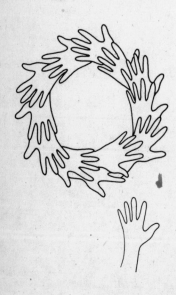

• The Green Hands Wreath: Trace the outline of your children's hands on green construction paper, or green and white wallpaper. (Let the children do this if they can). Cut out at least twelve prints; using glue, join hands together to form a wreath, and add red circle stickers for the berries. A large bow would be a colorful finishing touch.

• A Wreath of Branches: Take slender tree branches (birch works well) or grapevines, soak in water until branches become malleable, and then shape into a wreath. Hold together with wire or twine. Let dry before adding ornaments, ribbons, fruits, holly leaves, and berries.

• Consider using fabric, crumpled green tissue paper,

yarn, wood shavings, acrylic or oil paints, nuts and pinecones, clay, or candy.

Create a wreath reflecting your family's values, talents, and/or concerns. Who knows, you may even opt to make more than one!

GARLANDS

Deck out the walls with garlands gay . . .

—Anonymous

Garlands are ropes covered with evergreen sprigs. They are quite versatile and can adorn stairways, porches, door and window frames, and other spaces that often remain bare.

Look around your home. Where might garlands be attractive? In the entryway to contrast with poinsettia? Above the mantel with large bows accenting the garland scallops? Over the doorway to the dining room or around the sideboard? Down the basement stairs? Crisscrossing the ceiling over the Ping-Pong table?

Or you might frame a banner, painting, or statue. Use garlands to outline a manger or Santa's workshop and decorate with wood, fabric, or paper ornaments/figures.

Supplies needed to make a garland include:

• A BASE—This should be a ⅜″–⅝″ rope. Measure the area to be covered. Decide how you plan to hang the finished garland. These can be fairly heavy, so large hooks may be necessary. If your garland requires a loop to be hung, allow 5″–10″ for each loop at one or both ends.

• WIRE or STURDY THREAD to attach the greenery to the rope.

• WIRE CUTTERS.

• GREENS—Just as with wreaths, these greens can be traditional favorites or new discoveries. (See page 104 for suggestions.)

• PRUNING SHEARS to cut the greens into 6″–10″ lengths.

    • SNUG GARDEN GLOVES.

    • ORNAMENTS—These can range from ribbons winding around the garland and a large bow at a garland's peak to fragile bouquets of dried flowers. Or attach Christmas cards, red apples, cinnamon clusters with plaid ribbons, gingerbread cookies, and so on. As with wreaths, the possibilities are endless—have fun deciding and selecting.

To make the garland:

    • Cut the greens into the desired lengths.

    • Cut the rope. Beginning at one end, loop the wire a few times around the rope and then add the greens, several sprigs at a time. Point the ends of the sprigs in the same direction. Continue to bind the wire around the rope, adding sprigs until the rope is completely covered.

    • Some ornaments can be added before hanging the garland, such as a ribbon wound around the garland. However, it is easier to hang the garland first and then add the ornaments.

    • Lift the garland into place and secure.

    • Fill in any gaps by attaching more sprigs, and decorate.

SPARE SPRIGS

Evergreen balls are made with the leftover sprigs from the wreath and garland creations. To make these decorations, you need:

    • One whole white potato (its moisture will keep the greens fresh).

    • Evergreen sprigs measuring 4″ or less.

    • A 15″–20″ wire for hanging.

    • An ordinary nail for piercing the potato.

    • Ornaments.

    • Wire or thread for attaching the ornaments.

To make, push the hanging wire through the potato until

2″ appear on the opposite side. Hook the 2″ length back into the potato for support. Pierce the potato many times so inserting the sprigs will be easier. Insert greens, attach ornaments, and hang from light fixtures, ceilings, or in doorways.

Omit the hanging wire and create a table centerpiece. For individual place settings, use a portion of a potato. Cover with greens and attach an ornament the guest can take home.

FLOWERS

> Come with us, sweet flow'rs,
> and worship Christ the Lord.
> —"Carol of the Flowers"

As much as we enjoy the British heritage of decorating with greenery, blooming plants introduce focal points and create moods. Consult local nurseries or mail-order catalogs to learn what is available for the holidays.

Poinsettia plants are popular. Called the "Flame Leaf" because its leaves turn brilliant red around Christmastime, or "The Flower of the Holy Night" in Mexico, the plant became "poinsettia" in the States when Dr. Joel Roberts Poinsett, a botanist, introduced it to Americans around 1830. A Mexican legend tells of a small boy who was to visit the Christ Child on Christmas Eve. Sad because he had no gift, the boy knelt to pray. As he rose, a beautiful red-leafed plant grew before him. Joyously, he entered the church to present his scarlet gift to the Babe.

Legend has it that the chrysanthemum bloomed to direct the Wise Men to the stable. When King Malchior saw the flower and recognized how its petals resembled the rays of the star, he knelt to pick it. At that moment, the door of a nearby stable opened to reveal the Holy Family.

When Advent begins, it has been a custom in parts of Europe to break off a branch from a cherry, pear, or hawthorn tree, bring it indoors, and place it in a container of water. If the branch blossoms by Christmas, good luck will follow.

Other plants can be nurtured to bloom in December.

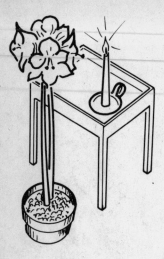

• Amaryllis—specifically the deep red hybrid called "Christmas Joy."

• Begonias, crocus, kalanchoe, veltheimia, Crown of Thorns, Dutch hyacinth, and Mediterranean narcissus.

• Lilies—Amazon lily has white flowers, and the Aztec lily is red.

• Star of Bethlehem—The Star, having guided the shepherds and kings to the Christ Child, burst, carpeting the fields with these yellow starlike flowers.

Darkness, moisture, and cool (not cold) temperatures are necessary to force bulbs to bloom. Consult nurseries and gardening books for specific directions.

> 'Twixt lilies white and roses gay,
> Sleep sleep,
> On thy bed of hay;
> —" 'Twixt Gentle Ox and Ass So Gray"

Once in bloom, make flowers the focus of attention or the colorful backdrop for a crèche or other Christmas figures.

Greenery, herbs, nuts, flowers . . . what a variety of holiday accessories whose presence beautifies the home and hints of a special event.

THE CHRISTMAS TREE

> Christmas in lands of the fir tree and pine,
> Christmas in lands of the palm tree and vine.
> —Philip Brooks
>   "Everywhere, Everywhere, Christmas Tonight"

The banana tree in India and the stalk of the century cactus in Rhodes are Christmas trees. They contrast with our vision of the pine as *the* Christmas tree—a tradition inherited from Northern Europe.

Confronting the pagan belief that evergreens offered protection from evil spirits and catastrophes, Christian missionaries encouraged the Northern Europeans to accept Christ as The Protector. Old symbols were reconciled to a new faith: the fir tree became a symbol of Christianity—the tree of the Christ Child.

The fir tree of the Middle Ages was decorated with apples, to represent the Garden of Eden in the German Paradise plays. This portrayal of the creation of Adam and Eve, the Fall, and banishment from the Garden was an Advent favorite since it closed with the promise of Christ's coming. The fir tree became a symbol of the coming Christ:

> O Christmas tree, O Christmas tree
>   You come from God, eternal.
> A symbol of the Lord of Love
>   Whom God to man sent from above.
> O Christmas tree, O Christmas tree,
>   You come from God, eternal.
>
> —"O Tannenbaum"

By the late eighteenth century, evergreen Christmas trees were popular throughout Germany. Three or four decades passed before the custom was introduced to Eastern Europe, Scandinavia, France, and England. English writer Charles Dickens called it "the new German toy." German immigrants, not English, brought this "toy" to eighteenth-century colonial America. Opposition to the tree and other Christmas "trappings" came from New England Puritans. They decried the "wanton Bacchanalian Christmases" with its "revelling, dining, carding, masking, mumming, consumed in compotations, in interludes, in excess of wine, in made mirth."[1] To free themselves of such vices, the Puritans simply outlawed Christmas! Celebrants were punished and publicly shamed.

Despite these protestations, the Christmas tree was an American institution by the 1840s.

[1] Irene Corbally Kuhn, "Christmas in Lexington & Concord," *Gourmet*, December 1976, pp. 17–18.

> Once the pride of the mountainside,
> Now cut down to grace our Christmastide . . .
> —John H. Hopkins
> "Gather Around the Christmas Tree"

The evergreen tree seems necessary to our celebration of Christmas. If we have one, where we get it, and how we decorate it are influenced by tradition and convention. But the true meaning of the tree must come from the celebrants.

As a family, discuss the role the Christmas tree plays in your holiday season. Be honest. Ask yourselves:

• Do we want an indoor tree? Why? Real or artificial?

• If real, do we want it cut or potted? Professionally shaped or naturally asymmetrical?

• If artificial, will we make it or buy it? (See page 126 for tree-making ideas.)

• How large a tree do we want? How many and for what locations?

• What is the best way for us to obtain our tree(s)?

OR

• Do we want to forego a tree and channel the time and money into another family project or community service?

In 1900, a tree in Nome, Alaska, cost from five to twenty-five dollars. Some households would avoid this expense and make the seventy-five mile dogsled trip into the woods to cut their own trees.[2]

If you choose to cut your own:

• Contact state or federal agencies about obtaining permits to cut trees on government property.

• Consult newspapers for U-Cut tree farms. Follow up with telephone calls for cost comparisons and directions.

[2] John E. Baur, *Christmas on the American Frontier 1800–1900* (Caldwell, Idaho: The Caxton Printers, 1961), p. 287.

• Check with friends, forest product companies, and even rural churches to learn where "tree seekers" can roam, looking for a tree to "grace their Christmastide."

• If you like spontaneous outings, go for a family drive in search of a tree farm.

If going to a tree lot or a produce wholesaler's is the most appropriate choice for your family, transform the experience into an adventure.

• Go as a family and take your time.

• Hike to the lot and carry the tree home.

• Enjoy a special treat at one of your favorite eating-out places before or after you get the tree.

• Sing Christmas carols in the car both going and coming.

Caution!

If you purchase your tree at a lot, buy it early in the season. It is better to buy early, take it home, and place it in water. Trees that stand for days in the lots lose freshness that could be preserved if they were stored properly.

If your family prefers a living tree:

• Check with nurseries, produce wholesalers, tree farms, and state or federal agencies.

• Decide if you will reuse the tree each Christmas or transplant it outdoors. If you plan to pot the tree for next Christmas, inquire from a nursery where to store the tree and how and when to fertilize and shape it. If you want to transplant the tree, research how and when: technique and timing vary according to climate.

If it is impossible for the entire family to get the tree, make plans to enjoy it when it is brought home.

• Young children might enjoy carrying the tree around the block before bringing it indoors to decorate.

• Have a tree-decorating party complete with cocoa, simple treats, and holiday music.

• Share the decorating with another family.

Mail-order trees are also available from reputable growers who ship fresh trees nationwide. If interested, phone or write:

The National Christmas Tree Association (NCTA)
611 E. Wells Street
Milwaukee, WI 53202
Phone: (414) 276-6410

✓ Make plans for a special celebration when the tree arrives!

LIGHTS

> The Christmas-tree with lights is gleaming,
> And stands in bright and festive glow.
> As if to say—Mark well my meaning,
> Hope's image green and bright I show.
> —"Christmas Message,"
> a German carol

Medieval Christians constructed pyramids of flaming candles to symbolize Christ, The Light of the World. Centuries later, Christmas trees replaced the wooden tiers, but candles, now attached to evergreen boughs, remained popular throughout England and Europe. Today strands of Christmas lights provide that radiant nimbus.

Tree lights are optional. You might place lights around the window to frame the tree, or use a spotlight.

If you opt for lights, consider:

• What is the best bulb size for your tree? Large bulbs? Small ones? Varied sizes?

• All one color? Twinkling? With reflectors?

• What is the condition of the lights you own? Are cords frayed? Any burned-out bulbs?

• How expensive are new lights?

Before you put the lights on the tree:

• Secure the tree firmly in place.
• Plan how to proceed so the light plug is near the outlet when you finish.
• If you have different sizes of bulbs, place the bigger ones on the heavier branches, and near the trunk.

BE SAFE:

• Purchase only U.L.-approved bulbs.
• Turn off the lights when you are away from home.
• With young children around, plug outlets with safety covers so lights cannot be turned on when adults are out of the room. Consider putting lights only on the top branches to avoid breakage, cuts, and, yes, even ingestion.
• With older children, establish rules for plugging in the lights.

TREE ORNAMENTS— FROM HEX SIGNS TO GOD'S EYE

> Every tree throughout the world bloomed and bore fruit on Christmas Eve; nature silently, but brilliantly, celebrated the Birth of Christ.
> —legend told by Georg Jacob, tenth-century geographer

Tree ornaments continue this celebration by heralding our joy at Christ's birth and reflecting the season's merriment.

Ornaments vary. They may be symbols: the apples and white wafers hung by Germans on their Paradise trees represented the Fall of Adam and Redemption through Christ. Or amulets: the Pennsylvania Dutch added a geometrical star-shaped ornament called a hex sign, possibly to bring blessings

upon the household and discourage evil spirits. They may also be decorative designs and trinkets that simply look nice.

Whatever the category, ornaments may be elaborate or simple—from fragile *pysanky* eggs with intricate designs to bulky paper chains assembled by inexperienced hands and rivers of glue.

Families moving west across the Plains created simple, yet symbolic, decorations reflective of their isolation and austerity. There were stars whittled from yellow soap, ribbons, colored beads, Montgomery Ward catalog pictures, and flowers cut from bright flannel.[3]

Our joy and merriment can find expression through purchased ornaments as well. A commercial ornament or an artist's creation may capture our sentiments and become a holiday favorite. Acquiring these ornaments can be a year-round pastime.

- Explore estate and garage sales.
- Attend arts and crafts fairs.
- Collect ornaments on your vacation.
- Host an ornament exchange party.
- Be alert to creations that do not have a Christmas theme but could become holiday ornaments—stained glass, origami, cornhusk figures . . .

Over the years, your collection of these ornaments may become so large that you will want to decorate two trees—one with purchased ornaments and the second with homemade creations.

When thinking about how you want to decorate the tree, return to the ornament suggestions for wreaths (page 107) and review the following pages of ornament ideas and directions. When these instructions call for "decorating" the ornament, select the medium (or media) you prefer—felt pens, paints, stickers, glitter, fabric scraps, felt, rickrack, trim, sequins, cotton. Loops for hanging can be made from yarns, gold or

[3] Ibid. pp. 119–120, 133–134, 215–216.

silver thread, fabric, rickrack. Feel free to experiment and enjoy the process. You are not creating a tree for a magazine cover, but one that reflects your family's personalities, interests, and talents, however humble or inexperienced.

With Paper and Paints and String . . .

The Ol' Paper Chain: Traditionally, this is cut from red and green construction paper. Use other types of paper, magazine pages, or foil. Try cutting the strips (you determine length and width) with pinking shears. Decorate with glitter and join circles with tape, glue, or staples.

Paper "Cookies": Bring out the cookie cutters. Trace their shapes onto colorful paper. Cut, decorate, and hang.

Stained Glass Windows: Cut two identical shapes and sizes (2"–6") from black construction paper (these are the frames) and another from tissue paper or cellophane (the window). Place the frames on top of each other and fold twice. Cut as for a snowflake but with fewer and larger designs. Unfold. Sandwich the tissue or cellophane window between the frames, glue in place, and trim edges. Attach hanging thread.

Cornucopias: hang cone-shaped paper or fabric ornaments filled with holiday goodies. Create a pattern by using a compass (or a large round plate) to make a circle whose diameter is 12"–14". Cut the pattern into equal quarters. Each quarter makes one cornucopia. Cut out the paper or fabric (consider felt or calico prints) cornucopias. Form a cone by overlapping the straight sides, and secure with glue or thread. Attach paper or fabric handles. Decorate with paints, stickers, felt pens, fabric scraps, fancy trim, or lace. Hang and fill with nuts, popcorn, dried fruit, colorful candies, dried flowers, small toys.

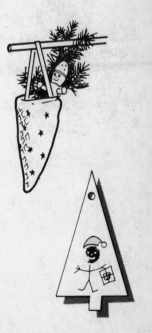

Thumb paints: Supplies needed for these decorations include thumbs or fingers (toes?), paper, colored stamp pads or paints, and felt pens. Transfer thumb and/or fingerprints onto paper. Draw faces, animals, trees, suns, moons, flowers. Use embroidery cloth (Aida cloth)* instead of paper. With fabric

* Made specifically for cross-stitch and available at fabric stores.

paints, make the thumb print and embellish with cross-stitch designs. Cut, frame, and hang.

God's Eyes: The Huichol Indians of Mexico feature God's Eyes, or Ojos de Dios, in their religious festivals. Made from dowels and colorful yarn remnants, these symbols of God's presence are an ancient folk art. To make them, take two sticks of equal length (twigs, Popsicle sticks, wooden skewers, even toothpicks) and place them at right angles to each other. Glue and let dry. Tie a piece of yarn around the center of the cross. Carry the yarn over and around one stick and then move on to the next stick. Always go over the stick, never under. Do not overlap yarn, but wrap lengths right next to each other. New yarn can be added with a double knot. When finished, tie the end of the yarn to a stick. Add thread to hang.

From Popcorn, Pasta, and "Hidden Treats"

Popcorn Balls and Wreaths: Make your favorite popcorn ball recipe. Place on waxed paper to dry. Wrap each in plastic wrap or colored cellophane and gather ends with a 9″ piece of ribbon. Tie ribbon ends into a bow, leaving a loop for hanging.

For Popcorn Wreaths: Before mixing the syrup, make wreaths by stringing popcorn and tying string ends together to form a circle. One cup of popped corn makes three 4″-wide wreaths. Prepare syrup. Dip the wreaths into the syrup and set on waxed paper. To decorate, press candies, décors, ribbons . . . and hanging hooks into the wreaths before they dry.

SYRUP RECIPE

⅔ c. sugar
½ c. water
2 ½ tbsp. white corn syrup

Combine ingredients in saucepan over medium heat and stir until sugar is dissolved. Bring to a boil. Cover and continue boiling for three minutes. Remove from heat and start dipping! Makes ⅔ c. syrup—enough to dip three or four popcorn wreaths.

Macaroni Bands or Pasta Paste-ups: To dye pasta, in a jar add several drops of food coloring to 1 cup uncooked pasta. Seal container and gently shake until pasta is evenly tinted. Let pasta dry on waxed paper.

- To make bands: String macaroni on colored yarn. Tie yarn ends and hang.
- For paste-ups: Glue pasta onto shapes cut from posterboard or heavy paper.

PCC's (Pretzels, Cereal, and Crackers): For these ornaments you will need:

- Pretzels of assorted shapes and sizes.
- Dry cereals.
- Small crackers.
- Waxed paper.
- Glue.
- Ribbons or yarn for hanging.

These fragile ornaments have no foundation: the pretzels, cereal, and crackers are glued together to form any design you choose. Work on waxed paper and let the ornaments dry for several hours.

Hidden Treats or *Julgranskaramell*: Swedish children enjoy these bright surprises that rest on the branches of their Christmas trees. Wrapped in brightly colored tissue paper, the treat inside remains a mystery until the tree is taken down and the *Julgranskaramell* distributed to the eager children. To make these treats, take cardboard tubes from toilet paper rolls and fill with nuts, dried fruits, candies, and small toys. Cut tissue or wrapping paper 4″ wider than the length of a cardboard tube. Wrap tubes, gather ends with yarn, and fringe the paper. Decorate, label, and place on the tree branches since these decorations are too heavy to hang.

And There's More

Balsa Ornaments: Balsa is a light wood that can be fashioned into decorative tree ornaments: flat shapes, geometric designs, weavings, miniature boxes. Necessary supplies include:

• Balsa—the wood comes in sheets and blocks. Select the thickness most suitable for your project(s).
• Modeling knives with interchangeable blades.
• Grade 0 sandpaper.
• Grain filler or sanding sealer.
• Soft brush.
• Gloss enamel paints. (These come in ¼-oz. bottles, and the color choices are endless.)
• Brush cleanser solution.

To make:

• Determine a design and make a pattern from paper.
• Cut the balsa and make a hole for hanging the ornament.
• Seal ornament with grain filler or sanding sealer.
• Sand.
• Reapply filler or sealer, and sand several times until balsa surface is perfectly smooth.
• Paint.

Spare Spools: Transform spools of thread into Christmas fare with paints, paper, and fabric scraps. A spool with purple thread could be the attire for a Wise Man, red for a Santa's suit, and blue for an angel's gown. Use another spool (with thread, or without) for the heads. With felt pens add faces, yarn for hair, rickrack for crowns or halos. Attach hanging thread under hair, hat, or crown.

"A Stitch in Time": Have available 4″ or 5″ squares of muslin and different colors of embroidery thread. Embroider a design or scene on the fabric. Supervise younger children and help them thread the needle, tie knots, untangle threads. When finished, take the stitchery and, with another fabric square, batting, and ribbon, make a "pillow" ornament to hang on the tree.

Variations of this idea:

- Brush on the design with fabric paints.
- To create a sachet, fill with potpourri instead of batting.
- Create simple cross-stitch designs on Aida cloth.

Metal art, stained glass, needlepoint, batik, tole painting, mosaic work, ceramics, etchings, wax sculpture, woodworking, macramé . . . the list is endless.

Tree decorations reveal our faith and joy. Whether we purchase or create them, they are extensions of ourselves. As we grow and change with the years, we may wish to decorate our tree in ways that are more accurate and up-to-date reflections of ourselves.

"Make it Memorable"

Your family's choice might be a tree that displays memorabilia.

- graduation tassels
- awards, certificates, medallions (no large trophies, please!)
- photographs of family, relatives, friends; or old photos featuring ancestors from long ago (truly a family tree)
- "treasures" found while beachcombing, spelunking, camping, or walking home from school

The resources for tree decorating are limitless. Discuss and explore these possibilities as a family. By planning and working together, the results can be fun, creative, inexpensive, and expressive. Your tree is a unique creation.

Gather around the Christmas Tree!
Gather around the Christmas Tree!
Ev'ry bough bears a burden now,
They are gifts of love for us, we trow;
For Christ is born, His love to show,
And give good gifts to men below.
—John Henry Hopkins
"Gather Around the Christmas Tree"

CREATING A TREE

If bringing a tree into your home is impossible or undesirable, create one. The result will contrast with traditional images but can capture the spirit of the holidays.

TABLE TREES are usually small creations intended for rooms with limited space. Centuries ago, Italians constructed the *ceppo*, or "tree trunk," a pyramid of shelves whose shape resembled a Christmas tree. The bottom shelf was the largest and held the manger scene, with higher shelves displaying presents, candles, and special figurines. Later, the *ceppo* became a popular Christmas decoration in Germany and England, where celebrants added nuts, apples, and other fanciful decorations to this Italian creation.

Create a ceppo using wood strips and plywood. Place nativity figures on the bottom shelf, add small presents to the second shelf, and decorate with candles, greenery, and special ornaments. If you have the know-how (or want to learn a new skill), motorize your ceppo so it revolves.

In addition to wood frames, table trees can be made using paper, Styrofoam, or mesh wire for the conical frame. Glue shelled nuts, beans, lentils, or pasta to a paper cone. Lollipops and gumdrops skewered with toothpicks can be inserted into a styrofoam base. Evergreen sprigs thrust into the cone would cover the bare places. Mesh wire frames covered with soaked sphagnum moss provide enough moisture to keep sprigs of evergreen, holly, herbs, and flowers fresh for days. Wire or thread tied around candy canes, animal cookies, ribbons, miniatures, and so forth, can be attached to the wire cone.

Some table trees require no base. Dried thistles, teasels, and pinecones are prickly enough to retain their form without a base. Arrange in concentric circles beginning with a 12"–15" diameter. Bright ribbons and small ornaments can be added.

DOWEL TREES can range in height from six inches to six feet. They consist of a ¾"–1" dowel that serves as the tree trunk, and smaller dowels as branches. If purchased in craft stores, the dowels will usually be birch wood. To make a dowel tree:

• Decide the height of the tree and its shape. For a pyramid, smaller branches are on the top, with branches proportionally larger closer to the base. For an oval, the smaller branches are at the top and bottom of the tree, with the longer branches in the center.

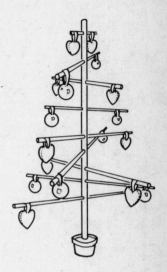

• Determine the number of branches and their length.

• Purchase dowels.

• On the trunk, mark where you will drill holes for the branches.

• Drill holes the diameter of the dowel branches through the dowel (trunk) shaft.

• Paint or varnish.

• Attach a base or set in a container filled with patching plaster. When the plaster hardens, the tree is definitely secure.

• Decorate.

Icelanders decorate their dowel Christmas trees with candles and homemade paper ornaments. Foliage may be tied to the "branches" if the snow thaws enough to make some greenery accessible.

ESPALIER TREES require a wall for support. Here are some ideas.

• Cut mesh wire into a tree shape, spray-paint, hang, and decorate.

• Cover strands of heavy wire with evergreen sprigs, attach to a wall to form a tree pattern, and decorate.

• Crochet, knit, or macramé a tree.

• Cut a triangular tree out of cardboard, paper, wood, or foil.

• Omit the tree background altogether and let the ornaments define the tree shape.

You may want to decorate an evergreen tree in one room and create one or two of these styles for other locations. Feel free to experiment and discover the tree(s) most suited to your needs, resources, and taste.

The Christmas tree, with its candles gleaming,
A glow is kindling in all our hearts.
It speaks of God's pure love-light streaming;
It brings us hope, and joy imparts.
— "The Christmas Tree with Its Candles Gleaming"
traditional German carol

The unavoidable task of putting away the ornaments may be depressing, as it signals the close of the holiday season. Transform this humdrum task into an occasion. Consider hosting an Epiphany party (page 37), where everyone helps and merriment reigns.

Discarding the tree may also be a dismal task. Prolong the joy by taking the bare tree outdoors and redecorating it with food for the birds. (See page 150 for food ideas.)

Discarding the Tree Responsibly

RECYCLE: Contact a recycling switchboard in your area or phone City Hall for information about recycling.

PICKUP: Check newspapers or radio stations to learn what service organizations, school clubs, businesses . . . are collecting trees.

COMPOST: Enrich your soil by composting the branches and mulch the trunk.

CANDLES

And this is the judgment, that the light has come into the world . . .

—John 3:19

Early Christians in Rome chose candles to represent Christ and Mary's purity. To the clergy this symbolism was disturbing. After all, candles were pagan ornaments and viewed as inappropriate Christian symbols. In time the Church revoked the sanctions forbidding candles. During the Middle Ages the Church even elected to celebrate Candlemas on February 2 (also The Feast of the Purification of Our Lady and the Presentation of Child Jesus in the Temple). On this day priests blessed candles and distributed them to church members. Through Candlemas, the Church officially acknowledged that candles were appropriate and powerful Christian symbols.

Even now, when electricity has replaced candles as the source of light, we return to that simple wax taper and wick as our symbol of "The Light of the World."

• As a family, purchase or make a Yule candle that is to be lit daily from Christmas through Epiphany, January 6.

• Discuss who will light the candle (take turns); when (select a time when everyone is usually together . . . breakfast, dinner, early or late evening); and the format for doing so (music, singing, Scripture, prayer, personal sharing . . .).

• St. Jans Cathedral in Gouda, Holland, is emblazoned with one thousand candles each December. Envision a cluster of candles on your dining or coffee table, mantel, entryway.

• Use varnish, paint, fabric, or wrapping paper to transform scraps of lumber into candle bases. A nail (use wire cutters to remove the head), driven into the wood base, will hold the candle in place.

• Place a candle securely in a wide glass bowl or aquarium. Decorate with evergreens and ornaments.

• For a centerpiece, turn clay flowerpots upside down and insert candles into or atop the drainage hole. Wrap ribbons around the pots and add greenery, gingerbread cookies, ornaments.

• Cut bamboo stalks into different heights; use clay to hold candles upright.

• Borrow from America's past and hold a Moravian Candlelight Christmas Eve service, affectionately known as a *love-feast*. The choir sings while the congregation enjoys coffee and soft Moravian buns. Toward the end, lighted beeswax candles, symbolic of the Coming of Light into the world, are carried into the service and distributed by women dressed in white to every member of the congregation—a sign that God's love is shared with all through Christ.

MORAVIAN LOVEFEAST BUNS

1 package active dry yeast
¼ c. warm water (105°–115°)
1 c. sugar
1 egg, beaten
¼ c. margarine or shortening, softened
1 tsp. salt
¼ c. warm mashed potatoes
7 to 8 c. flour
2 c. warm water (105°–115°)
Melted butter or cream for glazing

1. Dissolve yeast in ¼ c. warm water. Mix sugar with beaten egg, then add softened margarine or shortening, salt, warmed mashed potatoes, and yeast mixture.

2. Stir in 3 c. flour and warm water alternately; mix until smooth. Add enough flour to make a soft, firm dough. Knead until smooth. Place in a warm bowl and cover with a clean cloth; let rise until double in bulk.

3. Punch dough down and form balls three or four inches in diameter. Arrange an inch apart on greased cookie sheets.

4. Cover with cloth and let rise again until double. Bake at 400° about 20 minutes or until golden brown. Brush with cream or melted butter.
Makes 18 to 20.

Remember the fire hazard candles present. Be watchful and establish rules for lighting and extinguishing candles.

Versatile and easy to obtain, candles transform a room in a way electric lights can never hope to duplicate. The commonplace becomes extraordinary in the presence of faith.

Custom Inspection

Ireland

"May the Virgin and her Child lift up your latch on Christmas night"—This Irish toast referred to the custom of leaving the door unlocked in the hope that these visitors would arrive. Window sills held candles as a sign to the Holy Family that the hosts would welcome and feed them.

Germany

Believing that the Virgin Mary and Child were traveling through the countryside on Christmas Eve, Germans left candles burning in the window as invitations to Mary and Jesus to enter for food and rest.

Syria

Candles were placed in windows to direct Jesus as he traveled again to the manger in Bethlehem.

Siberia

Portions of the Christmas feast were left on candlelit windowsills to aid any escaped prisoner.

Scandinavia

A candle burning in the window welcomed any traveler to drop in for food and shelter. A member of the household was assigned the task of keeping the candle lit. If extinguished, misfortune would befall the household during the year. Some homes featured two candles—one representing the wife, and the other, the husband. The order the candles burned down indicated which spouse would die first.

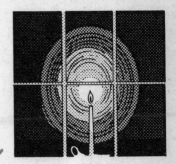

Denmark

Even the candle stubs were of great value. The Danes burned them during storms to protect their homes from lightning. While the stubs were fed to the poultry to increase productivity, candle wax was smeared on the plows to ensure a good harvest.

ADVENT WREATH

An Advent wreath intertwines symbols of God's eternal love (the evergreens and the circular shape) and Christ, the Light of the World (the candles). This "circle of life" not only beautifies but offers new meaning to the weeks preceding Christmas. These days become a season of preparation and repentance based on our year-round belief that Christ fulfills God's promise:

> In many and various ways God spoke of old to our fathers by the prophets; but in these last days he has spoken to us by a son, whom he appointed the heir of all things, through whom also he created the world. He reflects the glory of God and bears the very stamp of his nature . . .
>
> —Hebrews 1:1–3

The traditional Advent wreath has five candles, with one of these being the Christ candle. The first candle is lit four Sundays before Christmas and rekindled daily through Advent. Celebrants light another candle each Sunday—the radiance intensifies as Christmas draws near. The Advent wreath pulls us toward December 24, when the lighting of the Christ candle celebrates the birth of Jesus. We acknowledge God's gift and mark the King's humble entry in our world.

> I am the light of the world; he who follows me will not walk in darkness, but will have the light of life.
>
> —John 8:12

To make a simple wreath, you will need:

• evergreen sprigs (these depict immortality)
• four purple candles (purple denotes royalty and is the liturgical color for Advent and Lent—ecclesiastical seasons of preparation and repentance)
• one white candle—the Christ candle (white signifies purity)

Place the five candles equidistant in a circle or place the Christ candle in the center. Arrange the sprigs around the candles. (You may choose to add a decoration each day, making the wreath an Advent calendar as well.)

On each of the four Sundays of Advent, light a new candle and enjoy a special celebration: read, sing, and do some sharing together. Review the suggested celebrations on the following pages—use, revise, or create your own. Poems, thoughts, song, and prayers appropriate to Advent may be discovered or composed by members of the family throughout the year. Weave these personal offerings into your Advent celebrations.

THE FIRST WEEK OF ADVENT

Hope
See the loveliest blooming rose,
   Hal-le-lu-jah!
From the branch of Jesse grows,
   Hal-le-lu-jah!
     —"Let Our Gladness Know No End"

Read Isaiah 11:1–2 and Matthew 1:17.
Light one purple candle.

The Scripture selections refer to Christ's genealogy, or his family tree. Isaiah suggests that the line of Jesse, a descendant of Abraham and the father of King David, would yield up greatness—"a shoot from the stump of Jesse."

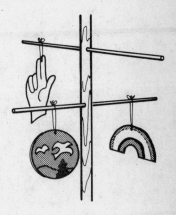

Sing or read aloud "O Come, O Come, Emmanuel," an Advent carol originating with anthem verses sung in medieval churches on the seven days before Christmas. Each verse celebrates Christ's coming.

O come, O come, Emmanuel,
And ransom captive Israel,
That mourns in lonely exile here
Until the Son of God appear.

REFRAIN: Rejoice! Rejoice! Emmanuel
Shall come to thee, O Israel!

O come, Thou Rod of Jesse's stem,
From every foe deliver them
That trust Thy mighty power to save,
And give them victory o'er the grave.

REFRAIN

O come, Thou Dayspring from on high,
And cheer us by Thy drawing nigh;
Disperse the gloomy clouds of night,
And death's dark shadows put to flight.

REFRAIN

O come, Thou Key of David, come,
And open wide our heavenly home;
Make safe the way that leads on high,
And close the path to misery.

REFRAIN

O come, O come, Thou Lord of might,
Who to Thy tribes on Sinai's height
In ancient times didst give the law,
In cloud, and majesty, and awe.

REFRAIN

O come, Desire of nations, bind
All peoples in one heart and mind;
Bid envy, strife, and discord cease;
Fill the whole world with heaven's peace.

REFRAIN

Possible mealtime or pastime questions—

• In the Old Testament, what is Israel hoping for?
• How is Advent similar to Israel's waiting? How is it different?
• Is it hard for you to wait for Christmas?
• When have you experienced "waiting" this week?
• What can be learned from waiting?
• What can be done while waiting?
• Does hope make waiting easier?

Activities—

• Assemble the crèche and place photos or personal mementos around it. Leave the crib empty until Christmas Eve.
• Combine your talents and ideas to make an Advent calendar (see page 140).
• Or make a Jesse tree.

A JESSE TREE is a potted tree branch decorated with ornaments depicting Christ's spiritual heritage and ancestors . . . the apple, Abraham's pillar of sacrifice, Noah's Ark, the Ten Commandments. A dove, star, or the sun represents Christ. On Christmas Eve, the decorations can be transferred to the evergreen tree to symbolize the fulfillment of the messianic promise. In preparing a Jesse Tree—

• Review the key people and events in the Old Testament.
• Create twenty-four symbols (use paper, fabric, balsa . . .) to be hung December 1 through December 24. As you place the ornament on the tree, explain its significance.
• If you seek resources to guide you, consult your church curriculum, religious bookstores, or libraries. An excellent book is *The Jesse Tree—The Heritage of Jesus in Stories and Symbols of Advent for the Family*, by Raymond and Georgene Anderson.

Close with a prayer that expresses your reasons for enjoying Advent and seeks God's help in preparing for Christ's coming.

THE SECOND WEEK OF ADVENT

Faith

. . . looking to Jesus the pioneer and perfecter of our
faith . . .

—Hebrews 12:2

Read Psalm 31:21–24 and Hebrews 11:1–3.
Light two purple candles.
Sing "O Come, All Ye Faithful."
Mealtime or pastime questions—

• Is faith different from belief? How?
• What does it mean to "grow in faith," "to be faithful,"
"to have faith in others"?
• Share how you have faith in the different members of
your family.
• How does faith in others differ from faith in Christ?

Encourage a family prayer, where willing participants
share a sentence or two.

THE THIRD WEEK OF ADVENT

Joy
Here is joy for ev'ry age,
Ev'ry generation;
Prince and peasant, chief and sage,
Ev'ry tongue and nation:
Ev'ry tongue and nation,
Ev'ry rank and station,
Hath today salvation: Alleluia.

—"Ecce Novum Gaudium"
Thirteenth-century carol

Read Psalm 98, Isaiah 35:10, and John 15:11.
Light three purple candles.
Sing "Joy to the World."
Based on Psalm 98, Isaac Watts composed this carol in

1692, when he was eighteen years old. As a teenager in South-ampton, England, he noticed the congregation's lack of enthusiasm for the songs and composed his first hymn at the age of fifteen. Often called "The Father of English Hymnody," he is thought to have written six hundred hymns and songs.

Talk about some of the joyous times you have had as a family and as individuals.

- What were you doing?
- Whom were you with?
- What made these times so joyous?
- Does joy differ from happiness?
- When you sing "Joy to the World," what does that mean to you?

Distribute paper and pencil to everyone and ask each person to write a prayer. Take turns reading them or give the written prayers to one person who will read them aloud.

Share some joy with your neighborhood.

- Distribute homemade goodies.
- Invite some neighbors over for a meal.
- Drive another family around town to see the lights and decorations.
- Go caroling.

THE FOURTH WEEK OF ADVENT

Love
Thou camest, O Lord,
With the living word
That should set
Thy people free . . .

   —Timothy R. Matthews
    "Thou Didst Leave Thy Throne"

Read Leviticus 19:17–18 and Matthew 22:36–40.
Light four purple candles.

Read the words to "Love Came Down at Christmas":

Love came down at Christmas,
    Love all lovely, Love divine;
Love was born at Christmas;
    Star and angels gave the sign.

Worship we the Godhead,
    Love incarnate, Love divine;
Worship we our Jesus,
    But wherewith for sacred sign?

Love shall be our token;
    Love be yours and love be mine,
Love to God and all men,
    Love for plea and gift and sign.
                        —Christina G. Rossetti

Mealtime or pastime questions—

• What does it mean to "love God with our heart, our soul, and our mind?" How can we do this?
• What does it mean to love your neighbor as yourself? Who is your neighbor?
• Do you feel closer to other people at Christmas? Why?

Activities—

• Have everybody write a love letter to him or herself. Seal in stamped, self-addressed envelopes, and as a family, walk down to the mailbox to send the letters.
• This week, do one loving deed for each member of the family—unasked!

CHRISTMAS EVE

How silently, how silently
    The wondrous gift is given!
                        —Phillips Brooks
                        "O Little Town of Bethlehem"

Read Luke 2:1–20 and John 3:16.

Light the four purple candles. Before lighting the Christ Candle, encourage the family to recall times during the year when Jesus was very real to them.

Sing "Hark! The Herald Angels Sing."

The church bells on an eighteenth-century Christmas morning inspired Charles Wesley to write this carol. The composer of almost sixty-five hundred hymns, Wesley is often called "The Prince of Hymn Writers" and "The Poet Laureate of Methodism." Charles was a brother of John Wesley, founder of Methodism.

Activities—

• Place the Christ Child in the crèche.
• Give Baby Jesus a gift of yourself—write it on a slip of paper and place it in the crèche.
• If you stay home tonight:

—Search the Bible for the different names given to Christ.
—Draw your impressions of an angel.
—Play twenty questions about the characters in the Christmas Story.

Prayer—

Be near me, Lord Jesus:
I ask Thee to stay
Close by me forever
and love me I pray.

Bless all the dear children
in Thy tender care,
And fit us for heaven
to live with Thee there.

—Anonymous
"Away In a Manger"

Continue to light all the candles daily until Epiphany, January 6. After removing the candles, redecorate the wreath with food for the birds (see page 150) and place outdoors.

ADVENT CALENDAR

Advent calendars are visual reminders that Christmas is approaching. The calendar may be a picture of a Christmas scene with numbered windows, one of which is opened daily, revealing another, but much smaller, Christmas scene or Scripture. Or a paper chain of twenty-four links with celebrants removing a link each day beginning December 1. Perhaps the family wants to use a small tree as an Advent calendar and add an ornament each day. Whether we remove a link in the holiday chain or eat a wrapped treat, we are reminded each day that Christmas approaches.

There are many ways to use an Advent calendar. It might be featured at mealtimes along with songs, readings, and devotions. Individuals may want their own Advent calendars to accompany personal devotions or to decorate their bedrooms and bulletin boards.

Technically, Advent begins the fourth Sunday prior to Christmas, so the number of days in Advent varies. Most Advent calendars begin December 1 and end December 24 with a nativity scene.

How you use the calendar may determine if it is purchased or homemade. Scandinavian import shops and stationery stores often carry a delightful assortment. If you choose to make one, the homemade calendar can be simple or intricate.

• Cut up old Christmas cards, and each day paste a picture on your family calendar.

• Use paper, poster board, or felt as the backdrop. Cut into a Christmas shape: tree, wreath, bell. Add a sticker, drawing, felt ornament, or design daily.

• Create twenty-four paper windows, using small rectangles. On one side, draw holiday symbols, quote Scripture, or suggest activities—take a short walk, feed the birds, and so forth. (See the Family Christmas Calendar on page 31 for suggestions.) Fold cards, seal, and number 1 through 24. Attach cards to backdrop.

• Appliqué a Christmas symbol onto cloth. Purchase or create twenty-four ornaments. Wrap each individually. Each day, select one ornament to unwrap and attach to the Christmas symbol. Attach with thread or a small pin.

• Make a paper chain with twenty-four rings. Remove one ring each day.

• Decorate a plant or small tree with pretzels and red ribbons. Pick a pretzel daily and enjoy it!

• Create a Jesse tree to use as an Advent calendar (page 135).

• Let your Advent wreath also serve as an Advent calendar (page 133).

Custom Inspection—The Mysteries of Christmas Eve

Norway

After the Christmas housecleaning, the brooms were hidden so witches would not ride them on Christmas Eve. Outside, the family inspected the pole sheaf set out for the birds. If birds were resting on the sheaf, the corn harvest would be good. If the family had not placed the sheaf of grain on the pole but birds were already resting on the sheaf, someone in the family would die in the near future.

Normandy

At midnight, the bees hummed the Hundredth Psalm: "Make a joyful noise to the Lord, all the lands! Serve the Lord with gladness! Come into his presence with singing! . . ." If Christmas was on a Monday, a long, cold winter would follow. However, if New Year's fell on Wednesday or Saturday, a warm summer with plentiful harvests was assured.

Germany

Celebrants could learn their fate by looking at their shadows cast by the lighted Christmas tree. If the shadow had no head, death within the year was certain.

Poland

Only the saints could see Jacob's ladder returning to earth each Christmas Eve. Descending the rungs were angels bringing peace to all people.

Switzerland

With eyes closed, a courageous soul opened a Bible to Psalms and blindly pointed to a chapter. The number of verses in the chapter revealed how many more years that person would live.

Ireland

The Gates of Heaven opened at midnight, and any soul dying then entered Paradise straightaway.

Greece

Homes were marked with a black cross in hopes of discouraging the *Kallikantzaroi*, half-human monsters with large heads, red eyes, tusks, monkeys' arms, curved nails, and hairy bodies. They ran rampant from Advent until Epiphany. Their mischief making included entering homes (usually when the occupants were sleeping), breaking furniture, consuming the Christmas meal, and fouling the water and wine. Peace offerings of sweets and sausage might be hung in the chimney. Occupants also tried to discourage the monsters' entry by burning a Yule log or old shoes—these odors being offensive to the hairy beasts. Despite these safeguards, the most successful course was to wait until Epiphany, when the home was blessed by a priest and the spirits fled.

THE STAR OF BETHLEHEM

"At this time of the rolling year," the spectre said, "I suffer most. Why did I walk through crowds of fellow-

beings with my eyes turned down, and never raise
them to that blessed Star which led the Wise Men to
a poor abode! Were there no poor homes to which its
light would have conducted me!"
> —(Jacob Marley's ghost)
> Charles Dickens
> A *Christmas Carol*

The appearance of the first star on Christmas Eve signals
many Eastern European families to begin their celebrations.
For their "Festival of the Star," Polish families break wafers
blessed by a priest and exchange good wishes; Lithuanians
offer prayers of thanksgiving before enjoying a vegetarian meal
of twelve courses commemorating the Twelve Apostles; and
Ukrainians end their forty-day meatless fast. Christmas begins
for them, as it did for the Wise Men, with the sighting of a
special star.

This star was a beacon, guiding the curious to a rustic
stable. As a signpost, its importance derived from the message
it told—"Christ is here."

> Star of the East, the horizon adorning,
>> Guide where our Infant
>>> Redeemer is laid!
>> —Reginald Heber
>>> "Brightest and Best of the Sons of the Morning"

By placing stars on our doors and windows during the
Christmas season, we communicate that same message.

A five-pointed crepe paper star hanging in the front
window is the most important Christmas decoration in the
Philippines. A twenty-six-pointed star is a Moravian tradition
originating in Germany around 1850. Made of translucent
paper, the star honors God the Creator, the Old Testament
promise of the star that "shall come forth out of Jacob"
(Numbers 24:17), and the Wise Men.

143

Celestial Creations for the Home

• Mark your front door with a star: consider a foil star with crepe paper streamers, a patchwork star trimmed with lace or rickrack, or a balsa star decorated with intricate designs.

• Create a star mobile to hang from a ceiling or light fixture.

• Adorn your windows with a galaxy of stars. Cut yellow tissue paper into 4″ squares. Crumple each one separately and dip the center into liquid starch. Place on a window. Cut an 8″ square. Crumble, starch, and place amidst the others. With tempera paints, add rays of light emanating from the largest star.

• Attach a string of outdoor Christmas lights to a star-shaped frame. Hang on a door, the roof, the outside the chimney, or in a window.

THE CRÈCHE

The heavenly babe you there shall find
To human view displayed
All meanly wrapped in swaddling bands,
And in a manger laid.
  —Nahum Tate
    "While Shepherds Watched Their Flocks by Night"

Until the thirteenth century, Christians generally overlooked the humble conditions in which Jesus was born. St. Francis of Assisi reminded them. He had visited the East, including Bethlehem, in 1219–1220, where he was spiritually moved by the simplicity of Christ's birthplace. Carrying this image of the manger home with him, he was dismayed by the contrast between Christ's birthplace and the Church's lavish celebrations. St. Francis returned Jesus to the manger by re-creating the rustic stable for a Midnight Mass on Christmas Eve in 1223. Village residents and live animals were included

. . . to enact the memory of the Infant who was born

Low lies His head with the beasts of the stall;
Angels adore Him in slumber reclining,
    Maker and Monarch and Saviour of all.
        —Reginald Heber
          "Brightest and Best of the Sons of the Morning"

In re-creating the humble setting of Jesus' birth, St. Francis paid special attention to the stable animals. His Nativity stable inspired farmers not to work the animals, and to provide extra hay for them during the twelve days of Christmas. Sometime during the Middle Ages, the animals' presence in the manger was given new interpretation. No longer mere observers, they became understanding servants: the cow breathed on Jesus to keep him warm; the robin, fanning an ember to rekindle a dying fire, remained too close to the flame and seared its breast; the stork plucked its own feathers to make a warm bed for the Christ Child; and the firefly, hiding in the manger straw, searched and presented to Jesus the most fragrant strand of hay. To reward their efforts, Jesus made the stork the patron of all babies everywhere and gave the firefly its small twinkling light.

To honor the rooster who was thought to have announced Christ's birth, Welsh congregations in the nineteenth century gathered at 4 A.M. on Christmas morning to celebrate the Crowing of the Cock, or the *Plygain*, with a sermon and "hymnfest" until dawn. Likewise, in Brazil and the Dominican Republic, the Midnight Mass on Christmas Eve is called the *Missa do Galo*, or the Mass of the Rooster.

And birds sit brooding in the snow.
                        —William Shakespeare
                        Love's Labour's Lost

Danes sheltered these fragile creatures by hanging a sheaf of corn in a tree, and Norwegians scattered oats. In the American Midwest, Scandinavian settlers not only attached the fullest grain sheaves to a pole so the birds could feed and rest, but cleared a circle of lawn at the pole's base so the birds could exercise.

exchanges share a message of good cheer and hope. Happiness is reflected in the Finnish *"Hauskaa Joulua!"* (Merry Yule) and the Portuguese *"Boas Festas!"* (Good Holidays). In Rumania the message is longer but very direct: "May the birth of Christ bring you happiness!" Even our "Merry Christmas" is really more than a wish for a fun-filled holiday, since "merry" originally meant "blessed, peaceful, and pleasant."

When December arrives and holiday greetings are shared at work, in stores, and among friends, listen and respond sincerely and appropriately. Be creative: come up with some new greetings (foreign greetings and their translations may provide ideas); telephone a relative or friend just to say, "We're thinking about you!"; tape your greetings; or send a singing telegram.

There's the danger that frequent holiday greetings can become automatic, like the phrase "Have a nice day." Be alert. List the different greetings you hear and receive during the day; and initiate greetings with business associates, clients, store clerks, and commuters. Let your greeting be one way you share your enthusiasm.

CHRISTMAS CAROLS

What sweeter music can we bring
Than a carol for to sing
The birth of this our heavenly King.

—Robert Herrick

The word *carol* originates from the Greek *choraulein—choros* is "dance," and *aulein* means "to play the flute." Greek "carols" were circle dances performed in the Greek theater. During the third and second centuries B.C., these dances appealed to the Romans and were woven into the Saturnalia, town festivals, weddings, and special celebrations.

The Romans took the carol to France and Britain, where for centuries it had no connection with religion. To the medieval French, "carol" was an amorous song-dance honoring spring's arrival, and the English referred to a ring dance with singing as a "carol." Not until the fourteenth or fifteenth centuries did carols evolve to mean songs, not dances.

Lighthearted folk carols contrasted sharply with the solemn hymns by the monks. Ignoring the poetry of the Bethlehem event, the monks' sacred songs dwelled on the theological implications of the Incarnation. This chasm between the masses and the monasteries was bridged in St. Francis of Assisi's Midnight Mass. His re-creation of the Bethlehem manger included new songs extolling the birth of Jesus.

> The child Jesus had been forgotten
> and St. Francis resurrected him.
>
> —Francis X. Weiser
> *The Christmas Book*

His followers, the Franciscans, composed Nativity songs of joy, which extolled the divinity of Christ's birth while celebrating its humanity. One of these Franciscans, Jacopone da Todi (1228–1306), created poem/songs, earning him the title "The Father of Christmas Carols." Unlike other Church Fathers, he wrote many songs in Italian, not Latin. Just as St. Francis re-created the realism of Jesus' birthplace, Jacopone captured its simplicity and beauty in verse. His relationship to the Christ Child was not distant, but personal. Affectionately, he referred to Jesus as *Bambolino* (Little Baby) and *Jesulino* (Little Jesus).

> She with left hand cradling
> Rocked and hushed her boy,
> And with holy lullabies
> Quieted her toy. . . .
> Little angels all around
> Danced, and carols flung;
> Making verselets sweet and true,
> Still of love they sung.
>
> —Jacopone da Todi

The spirit of these carols was contagious; soon, Europeans

153

were singing songs of joy and building mangers in honor of the Infant "resurrected" by the saint from Assisi.

In 1224, the Franciscans visited England. The "carol spirit" and popular carols intertwined to pave the way for pure English carols. The earliest of these were really lullabies:

> I saw a sweet, a seemly sight,
> A blissful bird, a blossom bright,
> That mourning made and mirth among:
> A maiden mother meek and mild
> In cradle keep a knave (boy) child
> That softly slept; she sang and sung:
>   Lullay, lulla, balow
>   My bairn, sleep softly now.

Some carols of the fifteenth and sixteenth centuries were poems describing the Crucifixion and Redemption:

> It was dark, it was dim
> For men that leved in gret sin;
> Lucifer was all within,
>   Till on the Cristmes day.

These serious carols were an exception. Some believers, dismayed by this lighthearted trend, wrote solemn carols and tried to revive religious customs so "bright shoots of ever-lastingness" could shine through "all the fleshly and material dress of the Festival."[4]

Their intentions were pure but their scheme too grandiose. Neither the carols nor customs changed. In the seventeenth century, Robert Herrick, "the last of the old English carol writers," described the festive mood prevailing at Christmas:

> "To do him honour who's our King

---

[4] William Muir Auld, *Christmas Traditions* (New York: The Macmillan Co., 1933), p. 70.

And Lord of all this revelling"

English Puritans reacted to the holiday revelry by outlaw-ing Christmas in 1645. This solution seemed extreme to other European Protestants. They encouraged believers to celebrate Christmas more reverently, but composed lively new carols. Religious lyrics were set to folk melodies. Congregations received these carols enthusiastically.

In 1660, the Restoration occurred in England, and carols (and Christmas!) won public favor once again. New carols, however, did not address the Nativity or Redemption, but described secular customs—figgy pudding, boughs of holly, and the Christmas goose. Again, mirth had replaced religious concerns.

A century later, composers and lyricists created many of the carols that remain our favorites.

"ANGELS FROM THE REALMS OF GLORY" first appeared in a Sheffield, England, newspaper on December 24, 1816. The words were the creation of the paper's editor, Scotsman John Montgomery (1771–1854), who wrote over four hundred songs. Incarcerated twice for his fervent efforts to reform social injustices, his imprisonment gave him time to write hymns. Henry Smart (1813–1869), a notable London organist, composed the music several decades later.

"ANGELS WE HAVE HEARD ON HIGH" is often called the "Westminster Carol" since it was sung in London's Westminster Chapel at Christmas. While the verses are of French-English origin, the "Gloria in Excelsis Deo" chorus was a Latin chorale during the Middle Ages.

"AWAY IN THE MANGER"—Although this song is called "Luther's Cradle Hymn," it was not written by the Reformation leader. German Lutherans in Pennsylvania were the likely creators of this poem, which first appeared in Phil-adelphia in 1885.

"GOOD KING WENCESLAS" recounts the Bohemian legend of Wenceslas the Holy, Duke of Bohemia. This be-nevolent tenth-century ruler was renowned for his kindness to the poor. The "Feast of Stephen" is December 26.

"IT CAME UPON A MIDNIGHT CLEAR"—A Unitarian minister from Massachusetts, Edmund H. Sears, was moved to write these words on a wintry December day, as he sat at his study window and marveled at the snow-covered landscape. His verses were published in 1850, and Richard S. Willis, former student of Mendelssohn's and a music journalist, rearranged one of his earlier hymns to accompany Sears's poem.

"O HOLY NIGHT" is a poem set to music by the nineteenth-century French composer Adolphe Charles Adam. Adam's father had wanted his son to enter law, but Adolphe preferred to teach himself music. He went on to become a professor at the Paris Conservatory of Music, and a distinguished composer.

"O LITTLE TOWN OF BETHLEHEM"—Bishop Phillips Brooks visited Bethlehem in 1865 and wrote these lyrics three years later for his Sunday school at Philadelphia's Holy Trinity Church. Lewis H. Redner, the organist at Holy Trinity, composed the melody.

"O TANNENBAUM (O Christmas Tree!)" is a medieval drinking melody with nineteenth-century German lyrics.

"SILENT NIGHT"—On Christmas Eve, 1818, the parish priest at Oberndorf, Germany, learned that the organ could not be used at the Midnight Mass. To compensate for this loss, Father Joseph Mohr wrote the words and asked the organist, Franz Gruber, to compose a melody. Within hours, Gruber fulfilled Father Mohr's request, and "Silent Night" was sung a cappella at the Midnight Mass.

> Yea, the heavenly child is born!
> Let us sing of the sacred morn!
>
> —Olga Paul

• Annually tape your child(ren) singing Christmas carols. Play them to create a Christmas mood at the "On Your Mark" family meeting in September (page 13). Make copies of the tape to share with relatives.

• Learn a new carol each year.

• Starting in the fall, check out Christmas records and tapes from your local library. Play as background music or at

a time when you are able to listen more attentively. Ask yourselves: How do you feel when you listen to the carol? What
images do the words and music create? What do you think
the lyricist and composer intended?

• Concentrate on the lyrics of Christmas carols by reading
them for graces or family devotions.

• As a family, select a carol and individually paraphrase
it. Take twenty to thirty minutes to write and share your in-
terpretations. Have paper and pencils available for this
project.

• With family and/or friends, take turns sharing the title
of a favorite carol and the reasons for your choice. Try to
remember when you first (or most memorably) sang it. Who
was with you? Where were you? What images do the lyrics or
melody create?

• Play "Name That Carol." This game can be played with
two or more people. One person hums the first three notes
of a carol and the others try to guess which carol it is. Hum
another note if the audience is stymied. This is a good game
to play while traveling or waiting in line.

• Explore the lyrics of carols to get ideas or themes for
indoor/outdoor decorations, Christmas cards, holiday wrappings, and entertaining.

• Gather family and friends together to go caroling. (Consider a sleigh ride or an old-fashioned hayride, where everybody can ride together!) Welsh singers caroled at dawn on
Christmas morning to arouse celebrants. Grateful for being
awakened, families served refreshments to the holiday
minstrels.

• Transform caroling into star-singing. In Eastern Europe, Scandinavia, Mexico, and Alaska, carolers bear a large
star representing the Star of Bethlehem. Fashioned out of
paper or wood, the star is usually decorated with lace frills,
bells, a candle, and a picture of the Holy Family. Star-singers
often reenact Nativity scenes, including the visit of the Wise
Men. Stalking the singers in hopes of destroying the Star were
costumed evildoers who represented Herod's soldiers dis-
patched to kill all the male children in and around Bethlehem.

• Begin your caroling or star-singing with a snack, and

enjoy a full meal together afterward. Il Cenone and the Brazilian Ceia (pages 300 and 251) are two-part meals that might be perfect for your celebration. A progressive dinner is also a pleasant accompaniment to caroling. This way you can sing, enjoy a course, travel to another hospital, care center, or senior citizens center, sing, enjoy another course, etc. See the Posada Procession on page 284.

• Today, citizens around Lexington and Concord, Massachusetts, gather annually to sing carols. Public singing of Christmas carols in the colonies, and later the States, was discouraged for years due to the Puritan influence. Boston held its first organized caroling on Christmas Eve in 1908, and St. Louis followed suit in 1909. Consider organizing a caroling party in your community. Take into account location (indoors or outdoors), necessary equipment, musicians, emcee, choice of carols, publicity, funding, and permits.

• Host an annual Christmas carol contest. Entrants submit original carols or new lyrics set to familiar carol melodies.

• Strike up a holiday band. Begin in late summer to round up fellow musicians. Practice carols for your own pleasure or arrange December performances in churches, care centers, hospitals, senior citizen centers. You might want to be minstrels-on-the-move strolling through the community like the Italian shepherds who for centuries entered Rome during Advent to play their bagpipes before the "sidewalk" shrines of the Madonna in order to charm away her labor pains.

• Approach local radio stations requesting that they record school choirs for holiday broadcasting.

• Attend musical performances—Singing Christmas Tree, choir and "pops" concerts, Handel's *Messiah*, and special musical programs at local churches.

Handel's Messiah

The Messiah took twenty-four summer days for the fifty-six-year-old George Frederic Handel to compose in 1741. Isolating himself in a small room, he often ignored the food brought to him. Handel confessed that during these three weeks, "I did think I did see all Heaven before me and the Great God Himself."[5]

Not all of the composition was new. Handel borrowed portions from his previous works, and scriptural passages were chosen and organized by Charles Jenner.

The Irish were the first to hear *The Messiah* at a benefit performance in Dublin in 1742. They received it enthusiastically. One year later, publicity for *The Messiah*'s opening performance in London became a controversial issue. Clergy were appalled that a religious work would be advertised on a playbill and presented in the Covent Garden Theatre—"a place of worldly amusement."[6]

Despite the opposition, Handel performed this oratorio in London in March 1743. It was a failure. Nobility called it dull, and clergy condemned it as irreligious. Two years passed before *The Messiah* was performed again in London. By 1750, it was overwhelmingly popular. Two decades later, *The Messiah* was heard in the colonies—in the George Burns' Music Room of the New York City Tavern!

Carols introduce us to lyrics that express our feelings and thoughts better than we can ourselves; they offer meditative, reassuring, and enthusing melodies and can transport us to a manger thousands of miles and years away.

> With joy I gaze upon Thy face,
>   Thy glory and Thy splendor
> Are greater than my heart can praise,
>   And songs can fitly render.
>
> —Martin Luther
> "Beside Thy Manger"

---

[5] Robert Manson Myers, *Handel's Messiah—A Touchstone of Taste* (New York: The Macmillan Co., 1948), p. 63.
[6] Ibid. p. 116.

PLAYS, PAGEANTS, AND DANCING

To inform their congregations about the birth and life of Christ, churches in the Middle Ages used mystery plays as educational tools. These "sight and sound" presentations were extensions of the liturgy, performed in Latin. The Nativity Story portrayed the mystery of the birth of Christ, and the "Office of the Star" honored the Magi's visit.

In the decades to come, the plays left the sanctuary and were performed in the streets and town squares. Irreverence reigned. The "Office of the Star" was abolished as a liturgical service and became known as the "Feast of the Star." The most logical choices to portray the Magi were honest-to-goodness Christian kings. These regal actors offered gifts of gold, frankincense, and myrrh to the Christ Child. This typecasting might have been a symbolic gesture: the state (represented by the kings) was submitting to a higher authority, the Church (i.e., the Babe).

Some of these productions were quite elaborate. The "Feast of the Star" in Florence, Italy, in 1466 was so magnificent, according to Machiavelli, "it kept the whole city busy for several months in arranging and preparing it."[7]

These Nativity celebrations made their transatlantic crossing with German immigrants. The first Nativity pageant on the eastern seaboard of the United States was at Boston's Holy Trinity Church in 1851, when children carried gifts to the altar and then paraded through the streets.

In Mexico and Southern California, an annual pageant, the Pastorela, featured the shepherds who visited Christ's manger. In some of the California missions the Pastorela was a musical presented on Christmas Eve, but in other locales it was a theatrical event demanding months of rehearsals. Elaborate scenery and decorative costumes were needed to depict "a multitude of heavenly host" appearing before the shepherds, battles between angels and devils, and fearsome glimpses of hell.

[7] Clement A. Miles, *Christmas in Ritual and Tradition, Christian and Pagan* (London: T. Fisher Unwin, 1912), p. 147.

Often, plays and pageants were followed by dances of thanksgiving. Eighteenth-century Pueblo Indians enjoyed the buffalo dance—"a rhythmic ritual of prayer and thanksgiving for the year just past."[8] On the other side of the globe, a Ceylonese devil dance performed amidst fireworks and bonfires celebrated Christ's victory over evil.

Custom Inspection

Germany

The *Herbergsüchen* is a pageant dramatizing Mary and Joseph's search for lodging.

> Who's knocking at my door?
>   Two people, poor and low.
> What are you asking for?
>   That you may mercy show;
>   We are, oh sir, in sorry plight,
>   O grant us shelter here tonight.
> You ask in vain
>   We beg a place to rest—
> It's "no" again!
>   You will be greatly blessed.
> I told you, no! You cannot stay,
> Get out of here, and go your way!

> —Francis X. Weiser
> *The Christmas Book*

This musical drama usually ends happily as the Nativity takes place in a peaceful but humble cave.

France

In Les Baux, France, during the Midnight Mass, newborn lambs are brought to the altar in carts.

---

[8] Baur, op cit. p. 47.

Peru

On January 6, the Day of the Kings, statues of the Christ Child and Madonna are carried through the streets to a platform in the town square. When the statues are in place, the Magi appear to pay tribute. One king is a Spanish conquistador, another an Inca, and the third an Ethiopian. Each honors Jesus with a speech.

During the holidays, "either actor or audience be."

• Find a play to perform: check libraries, church school curriculum, or write the play yourself. Staging does not need to be elaborate.

• Begin rehearsals in the fall and during December, perform it before friends, churches, community groups, or care centers.

• Organize a church or community pageant, and invite participants to come in costume. There may be short plays during a pageant, plus songs, games, dances, and refreshments.

• Stage an Impromptu Play (no practice necessary!) with families, friends, youth groups. Choose a familiar Christmas story or setting. Select a narrator, who will set the scene. Then have characters make up their own lines and engage each other in conversation. The narrator should move the story along by filling in details and asking the characters to share their feelings and thoughts with the audience or each other.

• Enjoy the variety of a cosmopolitan community. Attending a St. Lucia Festival (Swedish) or Los Pastores (Spanish) introduces one to new customs and celebrations. Search local newspapers for announcements about these events.

Take delight in home "productions" as well.

• "Listen" to your Christmas cards. Have each person choose and read a card the family has received. (This could be a grace at a meal.) Then share silence, a prayer, and/or a discussion about the sender.

• Obtain serious or lighthearted Christmas literature to

read with your family. Consider recordings of Christmas stories, legends, and poetry.

• Centralize your Christmas library during the holidays or place the books and tapes in several favorite at-home reading places—in the den, on the coffee table, next to the bed.

THE SOUND OF BELLS

Ding dong! merrily on high
    in heav'n the bells are ringing:
Ding dong! verily the sky
    is riv'n with angel singing.

E'en so here below
    let steeple bells be swungen,
and i-o, i-o, i-o
    by priest and people sungen.
              —G. R. Woodward
            "Ding Dong! Merrily on High"

The Chinese called bells "singing stones," and Egyptians, Jews, and Greeks rang them for their feasts and ceremonies. To Christians, bells became heralds calling believers to worship.

In the Middle Ages, bells were sources of inspiration announcing Christ's Redemption of the world. Upon hearing the chimes, believers were to respond with devotion and proper reverence.

Bells were also protectors. They dispersed storms and terrified evil spirits. By A.D. 400, their importance to the safety and spiritual well-being of a community was so great that priests blessed the bells before hoisting them into position.

On Christmas Eve, bells continued their heraldic role. They called Scandinavians to church and signaled Italian and Peruvian families to begin their Christmas Eve festivities. To inspire devotion, they tolled solemnly an hour before midnight, warning Satan of the coming birth of Jesus. At the stroke of midnight, a triumphant pealing replaced the tolling as an announcement of Satan's death and the Savior's birth.

Bells buried for safekeeping during wars were thought to chime on Christmas Eve but were supposedly heard only by those who listened with a proper attitude.

London church bells on Christmas morning inspired Charles Wesley to write "Hark! The Herald Angels Sing." Over a century later, in 1863, and three thousand miles west of London, Henry W. Longfellow penned "I Heard the Bells on Christmas Day." Having just learned that his son had been seriously wounded in a Civil War skirmish, Longfellow was pondering the horrors of war and the prospects of peace:

And in despair I bow'd my head:
  "There is no peace on earth," I said,
"For hate is strong and mocks the song
  Of peace on earth, good will to men."

Then pealed the bells more loud and deep:
  "God is not dead, nor doth He sleep;
The wrong shall fail, the right prevail,
  With peace on earth, good will to men."

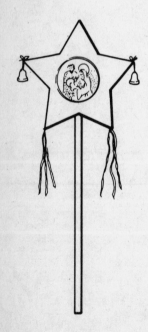

Steeple chimes were not the only bells used during the holiday season. At one time, almost every parish in England had hand bell ringers who accompanied carolers. Star-singers in Mexico, Eastern Europe, and Scandinavia carried staffs or wooden stars with bells attached.

For over fifteen centuries, bells have reminded believers of a special birth in Bethlehem. Their contemporary significance derives from our use and enjoyment of them. At home and in the community, the sound of chimes can signal an opportunity or reflection.

• Place bells on or over a door to announce the comings and goings of friends and family.
  • Hang a wind chime.
  • Ring a bell to call the family to meals and devotions.
  • Make a necklace, bracelet, or corsage using bells.
  • Attach bells to children's shoelaces.
  • Affix bells to Christmas presents.

• Use bells in outdoor or indoor decorations.

• Obtain handbell recordings from the library.

• Discover if there are any hand bell performances in your community.

• Take a tape recorder and, as a family, go search for chimes.

• Check out a book on the history of bells and adapt the information and designs to homemade Christmas cards, wrapping paper, and home decorations.

• Arrange a collection of bells as a centerpiece or room decoration.

MAKE A JOYFUL NOISE TO THE LORD

It is unlikely that you will imitate the old German custom of firing guns on Christmas Eve to drive away the evil spirits and announce the birth of Christ. Nor are you likely to stage a Midwinter Horn Blowing, as did nineteenth-century Dutch farmers. On the first Sunday of Advent, they used hollowed elder branches and trumpeted the message from farm to farm that Christ was coming.

Don't save the noisemakers for New Year's Eve!

• Create a homemade band to accompany your caroling. Try oatmeal boxes, spoons, pans, or a few dried beans in a can. This celebration is akin to the Carnival of Horns. Begun in Germany, the carnival included drumming iron kettles and tin pans and ringing sleigh bells through the town. When immigrants brought this custom to America, it was not enthusiastically received by neighbors! By 1868, the din and revelry had become so irksome that the carnival was outlawed.

Participate in the stillness of a night.

The time draws near the birth of Christ:
The moon is hid; the night is still.

—Alfred, Lord Tennyson
"Voices in the Mist"

• Take a silent walk at night with friends or family. Tune in to the sounds around you. When you return home, share what you heard. What were your expectations? Did you hear any "Christmas sounds"?

• Make time for yourself and enjoy the absence of others. Your calendar may fill up rather quickly during the holidays, leaving little time for you to be alone. Find a quiet place and relax. Enjoy a cup of tea, a book of poetry, a letter from a friend. . . . Be nurtured in silence.

• Discuss what holiday sounds are present in your home. How do these compare with the rest of the year? What sounds and noise levels are reassuring? Irritating? When is silence enjoyed in your home?

• Imagine the sounds in the stable in Bethlehem.

Listen with the "Ear of your Heart."

• Learn from listening. Seek out older people and ask them to describe how they celebrated Christmas as children.

• Become sensitive to what people don't say. Words are symbols, and sometimes they express our feelings and thoughts inadequately. Watch facial expressions and body language: learn to read between the lines.

During an average day, your sense of hearing is bombarded at every turn. Some sounds may be unavoidable: the weather, traffic, appliances, office machinery, neighbors, the dripping faucet. Other sounds, like music and TV, are optional. Exercise control wherever you can by selecting what you hear. Concentrate on listening so it resumes its place as a "learning sense," and weave into your holiday those sounds that enhance the celebration of Christ's birth.

Fragrances

Fresh hay, O fresh hay,
Fragrant as the lily!

You are the cradle
For the Son of Mary.

—"Cradle of the Hay"
traditional Polish carol

The visions and sounds of the stable may be easier to imagine than the fragrance. What is the scent of hay or a feed box? How does "a newborn babe wrapped in swaddling clothes" smell? Shepherds? Farm animals? Are we able to complement our visual and auditory images with olfactory ones?

Advent is a delightful season to sharpen the olfactory sense. Evergreens, scented candles, peppermint candy canes . . . a cornucopia of holiday fragrances exists. They can provoke a twinge of nostalgia, help create a festive atmosphere, or complement a quiet, reflective mood.

With family and friends—

• Share the holiday fragrances you remember as a child.

Then I would be slap-dashing home,
the gravy smell of the dinners of others,
the bird smell, the brandy, the pudding
and mince, coiling up to my nostrils . . .
—Dylan Thomas
"A Child's Christmas in Wales"

• Enjoy a game played in Japanese parlors. While sitting together in one room, individually jot down as many scents as you can discern. Share your findings—high score wins.

• Over dinner, discuss what smells you find pleasant and unpleasant. What holiday fragrances do you enjoy the most? The least?

When decorating the home for the holidays—

• Take time to inhale the scent of the evergreens. If you want this fragrance to waft through the house, place evergreen sprigs in a saucepan, add water, and simmer. Herbs and spices, including citrus peel, vanilla bean, and cinnamon stick, can be added.

• Use scented candles and incense; vary the scents throughout the house.

• Select fragrant flowers for your holiday decorations.

• Use a large rosemary plant as a table tree, and decorate.

• Place sprigs of fragrant herbs in the crèche or around holiday decorations.

• Hang a pomander ball in a room or closet. To make—

1. Use an orange, kumquat, lemon, lime, or apple for the base.

2. Insert cloves as close to each other as possible until the fruit is covered.

3. Dust thoroughly with cinnamon and allspice.

4. Let the fruit dry in a warm place for a week before adding a ribbon, since the fruit will shrink.

5. Tie a bright ribbon around the pomander and hang.

• Hang sprays of pomanders and fragrant herbs. (Keep pomanders from year to year, but be sure they have dried completely before storing them. To restore their fragrance, wash them in warm water, adding a drop or two of clove or cinnamon oil. Redust with spices, wait for a few days, add a ribbon, and enjoy the familiar fragrance once again.)

As you shop—

• Use your nose while shopping—in choosing a pineapple, entering the bakery, or selecting a blend of coffee or tea.

. . . the blended scents of tea and coffee were so grateful to the nose. . . .

—Charles Dickens
A Christmas Carol

• Compare the aroma of a bakery to a deli; a print shop to a bookstore; a toy store to a kitchenwares shop. . . . As you travel from store to store, try to detect differences between sachets, scented candles, perfumes, floral arrangements, sealing wax, incense.

• When you are preparing food, try to distinguish the varied aromas.

Sharing scents from home to home—

When sending holiday cards or thank you notes, include a sprig from a fragrant herb. Comment on the herb's history and religious significance. Refer to pages 106, 109, and 110 to learn the historical and religious significance of juniper, bay leaves, rosemary, and sage. Lavender relieved fatigue, and thyme cured depression. Brides put dill in their shoes to bring luck. Wishful thinkers wore balm to make their wishes come true. One of the bitter herbs consumed at Passover was coriander.

Over the centuries herbs and symbolism have intertwined. Basil represents love; a clove is dignity; juniper berries, protection; tarragon, generosity; mint, virtue; and thyme, courage. Perhaps the recipient of your holiday greetings would enjoy a sprig of costmary, which Pilgrims placed in their Bibles "to sweeten the times while sermons lasted three hours long. . . ."[9]

• Make sachets: Create calico drawstring bags, trim with lace, and share with relatives and friends during the holidays.

As our education in fragrances advances, we realize that smells, in addition to visions and sounds, can play a memorable role in our holiday celebrations. And this new awareness may help us imagine the manger more clearly than ever before.

Tastes

. . . the raisins were so plentiful and rare, the almonds
so extremely white, the sticks of cinnamon so long

[9] Violet Schafer, *Herbcraft* (San Francisco: Yerba Buena Press, 1971), p. 49.

and straight, the other spices so delicious, the candied fruits so caked and spotted with molten sugar as to make the coldest lookers-on feel faint and subsequently bilious. Nor was it that the figs were moist and pulpy, or that the French plums blushed in modest tartness from their highly-decorated boxes, or that everything was good to eat and in its Christmas dress. . . .

—Charles Dickens
A Christmas Carol

The Early Church designated Christmas as a day of fasting and meditation. But this official position quickly met with opposition. After all, food and special occasions were fused in many traditions; why should Christmas be an exception? Most celebrants disregarded Church sanctions, although some honored meatless "fasts" during Advent.

There are menus reserved for Christmas Eve alone:

Denmark
Dinner begins with rice pudding, then goose with prune-apple stuffing, potatoes browned in sugar, and sweet red cabbage.

Austria
Fish soup, carp, potato salad, and Sacher torte are served.

Sicily
A twenty-four-hour fast precedes Il Cenone, an elaborate meal which may include as many as twenty fish dishes! Eel is a popular entree. Seasonal vegetables, plaited breads, fresh fruit, spumoni, cookies, roasted chestnuts, hazelnuts, almonds, and walnuts are holiday favorites. Strong coffee and liqueurs are the finishing touch to this festive occasion. (See page 300 for our version of Il Cenone.)

Perhaps one or two seasonally unique dishes will grace the Christmas table.

Bolivia

Picana—a stew consisting of three to four types of meat and several vegetables is traditionally served after the Midnight Mass on Christmas Eve.

Peru

Pachamancha—pork, lamb, chicken, and potatoes are wrapped in banana leaves and cooked over heated stones.

New Zealand

Hanga—lamb is stuffed with sweet potato and pumpkin, then barbecued.

Norway

A home-brewed special Christmas beer is served with pork as the main Yule dish.

Czechoslovakia

Masika, a fruit stew, accompanies plaited white Christmas bread.

The Ukraine

A twelve-course Christmas dinner commemorates the Twelve Apostles. The meal begins with *kutya*, boiled wheat with honey and poppy seed. After blessing this special dish, the head of the family takes a spoonful and throws it against the ceiling for luck.

England

Plum pudding began as a frumenty (wheat boiled in milk and seasoned with spices and sugar). It was a fasting dish, but over the years, meat, eggs, dried fruits, and liqueurs were added. (See page 236 for a plum pudding recipe.) The burning brandy on the plum pudding symbolizes the sun's rebirth.

> The boar's head in hand bear I,
> Bedecked with bays and rosemary . . .
> Our steward hath provided this,
> In honor of the King of bliss,

Which on this day to be served is,
In Reginensi atrio (In the Queen's hall)
—''The Boar's Head Carol''

For five hundred years, a boars' head has been served during Christmas dinner at Queen's College, Oxford. Legend has it that a medieval student was strolling through the woods on Christmas Day when a wild boar charged him. Using the only weapon at hand, a book by Aristotle, the student crammed the treatise down the boar's throat, decapitated the beast, carried the head to the college, and presented it to the students at dinner.

Sometimes, just an ingredient added to an everyday dish creates a Christmas treat.

• Citron is mixed into Christmas stollen and used quite liberally in fruitcakes. In the Middle Ages, it was regarded as a powerful antidote for poisons.

• Nuts and honey flavor the Christmas baking. Rumanians take delight in the *türte*, a cake with melted sugar (or honey) and walnuts sandwiched between the thin layers. *Beigli*, a pastry with grated nuts and poppy seed filling, is a holiday favorite in Hungary. Nuts and honey were used for more than flavor enhancers. People believed nuts encouraged the fertility of the earth and honey extended wishes for a New Year overflowing with sweetness.

• Germans used to add seven spices to honey cakes to commemorate God's creation of the world in seven days.

• Christmas pastries and breads are often tinted and flavored with saffron, a very expensive seasoning. And with good reason: it takes eight thousand flowers to make 3½ ounces of saffron! Ages old, saffron was used to dye Persian robes. Water colored with saffron was sprinkled on public buildings and streets during Greek and Roman festivals. On these special occasions, cities were literally "golden" in hue.

• In times of scarcity, people used whatever was available in their celebrations: A frontier South Dakota family in the nineteenth century was pleased with seed popcorn. And Alaskan Indians savored strawberries preserved in seal oil. One Christmas feast on the American frontier featured:

> Roast wild goose
> Potatoes, turnips and bread
> Boiled buffalo rump
> Boiled buffalo calf
> A dish of dried moose nose
> White fish fried in buffalo marrow
> Buffalo tongue
> Beaver tail[10]

• With our many-course ham and turkey dinners, it is hard to imagine that a tablespoon or two of sugar added to breads,

[10] Baur, op cit. p. 118.

coffees, or puddings could transform a dish into a holiday treat. This was certainly the case with Captain John C. Fremont's men on Christmas Day 1843:

> Coffee was poured, and there was some sugar. The lake they had camped beside on Christmas Eve at least had drinkable water. Fremont named it Christmas Lake in honor of the day, and there was something right about this name applied to a lake in this remote, desolate land so much like the wilderness beyond the walls of Bethlehem.
>
> —Ferol Egan
> *Fremont, Explorer for a Restless Nation*

Custom Inspection— *Foods & Superstitions*

Denmark

A portion of the Christmas bread crumbled and added to the seed ensured a bountiful harvest.

Germany

Breads baked on Christmas and moistened with Christmas dew were magical. If thrown into a raging fire, the holiday bread calmed the menacing flames.

England

No mold would grow on breads baked on Christmas Day.

Pennsylvania Dutch

Families placed three different kinds of food on the windowsill. A portion of each dish was to be eaten by everyone on Christmas Day to prevent fevers.

Switzerland

An elaborate Christmas ritual was performed by the grandmother of the household. Taking the best onion from the cellar, she halved it and peeled off twelve layers, with each representing a month. She filled each layer with salt. The next morning, the family learned the weather forecast for the year to come: peelings containing damp salt would be months of precipitation, and those holding dry salt would be fair.

Christmas celebrations may be marked not so much by special foods, but by ordinary foods elaborately prepared: Germans bake a bread called stollen, shaped to resemble the Babe in swaddling clothes. Simple foods may also hold a special treat: Scandinavians hide an almond in rice pudding, and the finder is rewarded with good fortune. (See the Scandinavian Julbörd beginning on page 275.)

With your family—

• Make a practice of discussing the food you share as a family. What are your favorite at-home foods? When did you last enjoy them?

• Together brainstorm what you think are the perfect menus for Christmas Eve and Christmas Day (assuming you have unlimited time, money, equipment, and ingredients). How do these menus compare with your traditional holiday meals? Evaluate which suggestions could be prepared and enjoyed during the holidays.

• Imagine what foods the Holy Family may have eaten as they were housed in the manger. What might Mary and Joseph have considered a treat in those days?

Cheese from the dairy, bring they for Mary
And, not for money, butter and honey.
—G. R. Woodward
"Past Three a Clock"

During the holidays, as well as throughout the year, make an effort to try new foods:

• With family/friends, organize a Palate's Delight. Prepare new recipes plus several family favorites. Take time to savor each bite. Describe the flavor and decide if it "delights your palate."

• Host "tasting parties" featuring a foreign cuisine, old family recipes, childhood favorites.

• Prepare holiday favorites from other countries: cardamom bread, Christmas stollen, Bûche de Nöel (page 305), Ensalada de Noche Buena (page 288).

• Enjoy a culinary adventure by working your way through a cookbook or digging out those recipes snipped from magazines or newspapers.

• Acquaint yourself with foods you unintentionally ignore: litchi nuts, kiwi, leeks, patés.

• Add new ingredients to a familiar dish.

• Experiment with different herbs or spices.

God could have created all food as a bland mixture of proper nutrients: something like wheat-germ, yoghurt and honey in a cake form, or some sort of fruit which would have contained everything necessary to good health. However pleasant the mild flavor might be, we cannot imagine eating just one single flavor all the time, the reason being that we have been created with taste buds, a delicate sense of smell, and a sensitive appreciation of and response to texture and colour.

—Edith Schaeffer
Hidden Art

Through this variety of foods we can creatively express and savor the "specialness" of the event. Enjoying taste is not a license for gluttony; it is an opportunity to include another sense in our celebration of Christmas.

Touch

Through the sense of touch, we receive information and sensations that reassure, educate, and provide a feeling of belonging.

FIRE, WARMTH, AND FELLOWSHIP

To combat the chill of an arctic winter, Northern Europeans stayed close to the hearth. Fire and sunlight were their only sources of heat and light. When the sun's intensity waned during the winter solstice, they kindled large bonfires whose warmth and light would restore the dying sun.

With Christianity, bonfires acquired new religious significance. Epiphany bonfires burned in England to celebrate Christ's ministry and encourage a good harvest. Farmhands set thirteen fires on Epiphany morning—the largest fire represented Jesus, and the twelve smaller ones, the Apostles. All bonfires burned down except the Judas fire, which farmhands stomped out.

In Syrian churches, bonfires were set to warm the Magi en route to Bethlehem. At home, Syrian families used a fire as a special accompaniment to holiday celebrations. The wood was set as the youngest son read the gospel account of Christ's birth. Then the father lit the fire. Singing followed, while the family enjoyed the warmth and fellowship. Later, celebrants jumped over the glowing embers and made wishes for the year to come.

> The fire, with well-dried logs supplied,
> Went roaring up the chimney wide;
> > —Sir Walter Scott
> > "Christmas in the Olden Time"

In England, the Yule log became a Christmas custom. An enormous tree, large enough to burn for twelve days, was chopped down. Decorated with ivy streamers and saddled with children, the log was dragged into the house. Once in place, corn, wine, or ale might be sprinkled on it to ensure a good harvest.

French families sang carols as they carried the log indoors. Before lighting it, the youngest child poured wine over the log in the name of the Father, Son, and Holy Ghost. Similarly, in Yugoslavia, the burning *Badnjak* log (Christmas log) received offerings of grain and wine to ensure bountiful harvests of both.

The *ceppo*, or "tree trunk," in Northern Italy was significant to believers. Imagining the birth of Jesus in a manger exposed to the ravages of winter, Christians in northern Italy were moved to provide a warm haven for their beloved *Jesulino*. Before attending Midnight Mass on Christmas Eve, a household lit its ceppo for Mary and Jesus, who might enter and warm themselves while the family was away.

> In Bethlehem is born, is born the Holy Child,
>   born the Holy Child,
> On hay and straw in winter wild,
>   On hay and straw in winter wild;
>
>   "In Bethlehem"
>   an Italian carol

At the close of the twelve days, when the Yule log had burned down or was extinguished, the charred remnant (or brand) and ashes were not discarded. The brand was saved to ignite next year's Yule Log:

> Kindle the Christmas brand, and then
> Till sunset let it burn;
> While quenched, then lay it up again
> Till Christmas next return.
>
>   —Robert Herrick
>   "Epiphany"

Thinking the ashes possessed curative powers, German farmers mixed them into cattle feed to exterminate vermin. Ashes used as mulch protected household crops from insects. Some English celebrants might discard ashes, but never on Christmas Day. In tossing them out, "they might be thrown in Christ's face."[11]

If a family had no Yule Log, they fastened ash sticks together with wood bands and burned them. As each band

---

[11] *A Celebration of Christmas*, ed. Gillian Cooke (New York: G. P. Putnam's Sons, 1980), p. 64.

snapped, a bowl of cider was drunk; or, at an inn, the breaking of the first band signaled a round of free drinks. Sometimes the bands were named for girls in the family, or pairs of lovers. The order of the breaking bands indicated in what order those family members would marry.

The hearth was a haven on chilly December evenings. Basking in front of the holiday fire, a community of well-wishers enjoyed conversations, games, and refreshments. This fellowship was a fusion of warmth and the Christmas spirit.

> Heap on more wood!—the wind is chill;
> But let it whistle as it will,
> We'll keep our Christmas merry still.
>
> —Sir Walter Scott
> "Marmion"

Fires continue to create an atmosphere that invites sharing. Amidst this warmth and security, we feel free to express ourselves. How appropriate, then, to include fires in Advent and Christmas celebrations!

• Invite friends over to enjoy a fire and conversation. Gather around the hearth and make merry with good talk and fine food.

• Schedule an evening for the family to gather around a blazing fire. Ask each person to bring a project to work on (knitting, reading, letter writing, "busywork" . . .). Play Christmas music softly and serve a light snack.

• Light a fire during one or several of the Five Family Celebrations (see Chapter 1).

• If you have no fireplace, use candles instead. Place several around the room or on a table and turn the lights down.

• Prepare a meal over a fire.

• Create a decorative Yule log for Advent. Add evergreen sprigs, bow, candles, figurines, small presents. Display in the fireplace, on the mantel, coffee table, or as a table centerpiece for a holiday dinner. Burn the log sometime during the holidays or save from year to year.

TEXTURES, TEXTURES EVERYWHERE

Through the sense of touch, we become aware of the textural variety of our world—satiny, prickly, moist, gritty, sticky, furry, soft, mushy, hard. Tactile experiences occur every waking minute.

During the holidays, enjoy and compare the tactile experiences that may be seasonally unique.

• When decorating, consider the variety of textures you are using—prickly spruce, satiny ribbons, mushy papiermâché.

• As you purchase or make Christmas presents, feel the textures of the materials (fabric, wood, glass, food, paper . . .). If you are creating the gift, how does the project change in texture as you work with it? How does the sweater compare to the yarn? Rough wood to sanded? Freshly baked bread to the flour, salt, yeast, and other ingredients?

• Create a "touch book" and introduce a young person to the variety of textures. Include bits of fabric, lace, yarn, sponges, wood, dried flowers, shoelaces, foil, cellophane.

• While outdoors, stop and feel the trees, rocks, frozen grass, handrails. Which textures are unique to winter?

• While indoors, place some Christmas objects in a paper sack and see how many a blindfolded friend or family member can identify.

A SENSE OF BELONGING

Touch Hands
Ah friends, dear friends, as years go on and heads
    get gray, how fast the guests do go!
Touch hands, touch hands, with those that stay.
Strong hands to weak, old hands to young,
    around the Christmas board, touch hands.
               —William H. H. Murray
               "John Norton's Vagabond"

Just as temperature and texture are perceived through the

skin, so is a sense of belonging. By touching and being touched, there is a feeling of acceptance that may not come with words. This holiday season, communicate affection and belonging through the sense of touch.

- Hold hands during grace.
- Take time to hold your children close to you— on your lap, in an embrace.
- Share hugs more frequently.
- Give back rubs to each other.
- Enjoy mistletoe in your home.

Sacred to the Druids, mistletoe was cut from oak trees with a golden sickle and, along with two white bulls, offered to the gods for peace and good fortune. Thinking mistletoe possessed powers to heal diseases and counteract poisons, the Druids named it "all-heal." Sprigs of mistletoe adorned door-ways and rooms to protect the inhabitants from witchcraft and express goodwill to all visitors. Enemies meeting under the mistletoe cast their weapons aside, greeted each other amiably, and honored a one-day truce. A kiss under the mistletoe meant love and the promise of marriage.

Considered a pagan symbol by Christians in medieval England, mistletoe was allowed only in one church, the Cathedral of York, and then only on Christmas Eve. Placed on the high altar, the "all-heal" of the Druids symbolized the healing powers of Christ.

> Forth to the wood did merry men go,
> To gather in the mistletoe.
> —Sir Walter Scott
> "Christmas in the Olden Time"

More decorative than a sprig of mistletoe is a kissing bough—a decoration that friends and lovers have enjoyed for centuries. There are several variations.

- Use an evergreen branch as the base. Attach mistletoe,

181

ribbons, and ornaments to the branch and display over the doorways or from ceilings or light fixtures.

• Select an orange, apple, or potato. Pierce this base with a nail or darning needle before inserting the mistletoe and other greens. Add ribbons or other decorations.

• To make a "kissing ball," take an embroidery hoop and make a cage by placing the smaller hoop inside the larger one. Fasten securely with wire or ribbon so the hoops are at right angles to each other. Hang the mistletoe from the top of the hoop cage. Decorate with other greens, candy canes, cinnamon sticks.

"Greet one another with a holy kiss," Paul admonished the Christians in Rome and Corinth. The church community is called to share each other's joy and sorrows. A tear, wink, handclasp, a kind deed, an embrace . . . these gestures show others that we care about them.

In your worshipping communities—

• Greet friends with a handshake, a hug, or a gentle touch on the arm.

• As a congregation, hold hands during songs, prayers, or graces prior to a church dinner.

While visiting—

• Hospital patients and people confined to homes or care centers may need to be reassured that the church community includes them. A gentle touch can renew their sense of belonging.

> And with true love and brotherhood
>   Each other now embrace;
> This holy tide of Christmas
>   All other doth deface.
>   —"God Rest You Merry, Gentlemen"
>   eighteenth-century English carol

Indoor decorations include a tapestry of creations and experiences. They may be visual or tactile, fragrant or auditory, and are appreciated by a diverse group of people—our family, friends, neighbors, and a host of guests. In the midst of this diversity, there is a unifying purpose: indoor decorations "prepare the way" by turning our attention to the Bethlehem event and reminding us of the intent and spirit of the holiday season.

OUTDOOR DECORATIONS

Let your light so shine . . .

—Matthew 5:16

To "Let our light so shine," we create outdoor decorations that reflect our faith, thoughts, feelings, and priorities. This is a way we can share ourselves with friends, neighbors, and even strangers.

As with indoor decorations, don't try to do everything in one year. Design a plan that may take several years to complete, but is attractive and meaningful at each step. Begin by carefully looking at the outside of your home and yard. Come up with some decorating possibilities.

Return to the questions and suggestions regarding indoor/outdoor decorating beginning on page 101. Share answers as they relate to outdoor decorating. Turn to Questionnaire B in Chapter 1 (page 23) to review your original ideas and jot down new ones.

YOUR HOME

From the Street to Your Door
• Welcome your guests with lights around the door or along the walkway. (Use only weatherproofed outdoor lights.) An inviting custom in New Mexico is to line the entryway with luminaries—paper bags partially filled with sand and holding lighted candles.

• Decorate a gatepost with paper lanterns, as Christians do in Korea.

• Place a three-dimensional crepe paper star over a light post—a favorite Christmas decoration in the Philippines and Hawaii.

• Set potted poinsettia or small holly trees bedecked with red ribbons on the porch.

At the Door

Christ was born on Christmas Day;
Wreathe the holly, twine the bay.
> —"Christ was Born on Christmas Day"
> fourteenth-century German carol

• Create wreaths, symbols of God's eternal love. Their versatility allows a wide range of personal expression. Ideas for creating and displaying wreaths are featured beginning on page 107.

• Drape garlands over the crosspiece, around the door, along a banister. Attach a garland to the door so it hangs vertically, or create a holiday shape (see page 111).

• Hang baskets filled with evergreen sprigs, flowers, angels, Santa and elves, and small gifts to be shared with holiday guests.

• Transform a door into a package: use foil and a large plastic ribbon; (or with sunshine guaranteed) tape brown parcel paper onto the door, paint on a ribbon, and mount designs cut from colorful self-adhesive paper.

• Cheer up your mail carrier with a holiday decoration or message. Use evergreens, ornaments, and decorative tape to highlight the mailbox.

The Windows

• Using tempera paints, create Christmas scenes on the "inside" of windows.

• Let your windows frame an indoor decoration: Christmas tree, crèche, wreath, and so on. Accentuate the display by outlining the window with lights or garlands.

• Attach paper or star lanterns at window corners, to the crosspiece, or along the windowsill.

Chimney and Roof

• Place Santa, elves, St. Nicholas, or La Befana hovering around your chimney, or use the chimney as a backdrop for a star, stockings, decorated garland, wooden gingerbread figures, or Christmas message. Try to camouflage or hide spotlights and extension cords.

• Place a lighted display on the roof.

Decorating the Entire House

• Outline your house with lights along the eaves, around the windows, doors, hedges, and trees. Too many lights look gaudy and may be expensive. You can ask your power company for a cost estimate of your plans.

• Feature a Christmas scene in your front windows. Spotlight these creations and consider "broadcasting" appropriate music.

YOUR YARD

Determine where your yard has the greatest visibility. In discussing outdoor decorations, what are your family favorites?

• Old-fashioned Christmas images with sleigh rides, caroling, expeditions to get the tree?
• Pictures of Santa's workshop?
• Scenes from Bethlehem?
• Images from your ethnic background?

What size decorations are most appropriate for your yard? Could hedges or shrubbery be used as background, or complement a window display? How about your trees? Can they be decorated with lights, lanterns, or food for the birds? If you feature a crèche, tree branches can hold the angels and stars, with the manger set at the base of the tree.

YOUR NEIGHBORHOOD

• Enjoy decorating a neighbor's home in lieu of or in addition to your own.

• Work with several families to decorate the most visible home.

• Every house in the neighborhood can be decorated. Hold a block party in the fall and discuss the idea. A single theme could tie the individual displays together.

—"Twelve Days of Christmas"

—"Journeys to Bethlehem," featuring Mary and Joseph, the shepherds, the Wise Men

—"Christmas Comes But Once a Year," showing ways we prepare for the holidays—getting the tree, decorating the home, wrapping presents, baking goodies, worshipping together

• Create a neighborhood Christmas fair on your street or in a park. Set up booths for gifts, refreshments, and games. Consult local authorities about obtaining permits for the event.

The annual *Christkindlmarkt* has been a tradition in Vienna since 1842. From November 18 through December 24, the square in front of Vienna's city hall is bedecked with lights. Booths selling gifts and sweet treats fill the square.

As you develop a particular idea, consult hardware and variety stores to learn what supplies you will need. Do this early so you will have time to pursue another idea if you run up against unavailable or unaffordable supplies.

YOUR COMMUNITY

Your home and yard are not your only opportunities for outdoor decorating; the family car can be adorned with a wreath or garlands. Paint a Christmas message and secure it to the top or sides of the vehicle. Imitate nineteenth-century rancheros in California, who decorated carts and horses for their Christmas Eve procession to Midnight Mass.

- Decorate your motorcycle, bike, or moped.
- Become a holiday message! Obtain a Santa's outfit and walk through town. (Practice your "Ho ho ho" and North Pole chatter before you go!)
- Rent a billboard to express your holiday greetings.

Let your holiday decorations reflect your ideas and concerns. Create displays that are appropriate to your home, apartment, or neighborhood. Enjoy your neighbors' decorations. Take time to drive or stroll past to appreciate their efforts and creations. For family fun, drive up to your home as if you were guests or passersby.

These tangible expressions are "tinsel and treasures." They attract our attention and evoke feelings and impressions of Christmas Past and Christmas Present. Visual, fragrant, tactile . . . Christmas can come to us through a variety of senses.

Christmas decorations are indoors, outdoors, all around the town. They hint of a special occasion—an event in history that touches our lives today. Our faith grows as we imagine the stable more clearly—see the shepherds, hear the lowing of the cattle, inhale the fragrance of hay, taste the simple foods, and touch the soft skin of the newborn Babe. Having returned to the manger, we can create decorations that more accurately reflect the spirit of Christmas.

CHAPTER 4
Where Two
or More Are
Gathered

O welcome all! Our honored Squire;
Begs ye fulfill his high desire,
That Lord and Lady, youth and maid;
Give reign to mirth and let not fade;
The tumult of unceasing joy!

S uch a welcome greeted many a guest at Christmas meals in seventeenth-century England. Menus included ample portions of peacock pie, baron of beef, Yorkshire pudding; and wassail—with jesters, a choir, and trumpets adding to the merriment.[1]

These elaborate Christmas feasts are no longer standard fare in England, but they have become a holiday tradition at the Ahwahnee Hotel of Yosemite National Park. The annual feast is patterned after a meal described in Washington Irving's *Country Sketches*.

> The table was literally loaded with good cheer, and presented an epitome of country abundance, in the season of overflowing larders.
> —Washington Irving
> "At Bracebridge Hall"
> *Country Sketches*

Medieval England's Christmas feasts were incredible. The menu of a dinner served in 1560 included seventeen main dishes and sixteen salads—plus an uncounted number of stews, vegetables, breads, pastries, and sweets. In 1770, a four-wheel cart was used to carry a Christmas pie measuring nine feet around. The pie contained two bushels of flour, twenty pounds of butter, four geese, two turkeys, two rabbits, four wild ducks, two woodcocks, six snipes, four partridges, two beef tongues, seven blackbirds, and six pigeons![2]

[1] A. Seiden, "Yosemite Christmas," *Travel*, December 1976, pp. 52–53.
[2] Francis X. Weiser, *The Christmas Book* (New York: Harcourt, Brace and Co., 1952), p. 144.

Such abundance was expected at great celebrations. Feasts often lasted nine hours, from afternoon until midnight. The poor often received generous portions of the feast, which they, in turn, shared at their own celebrations.

In contrast, the Puritans decried such gluttony, calling the feasts pagan and inappropriate for the Holy Nativity. Coming to power in England in 1645, Puritans declared December 25 a day of fasting and penance—an "Anti-Christ Mass," it was called. For twelve years, these restrictions were enforced in England, and were carried across the Atlantic to the struggling New England colonies.

The Puritans were not alone in spurning the Yuletide frivolity. Amish and Mennonites, Presbyterians, Baptists, Methodists, and Congregationalists all looked askance at the "wasteful" festivities and honored a more traditional Holy Sabbath on Christmas. The Quakers also bypassed the celebrations, considering each day equally holy.

Envy may have stirred the hearts of some of those protesters, but mostly, their objections grew out of a desire to preserve the sanctity of the season. For them, frivolity obscured the significance of that long-ago birth.

Looking at modern expectations for Christmas entertaining, one may be equally troubled. The holiday parties depicted in magazines, newspapers, and on television feature the finest tableware and cuisine, as well as an atmosphere of elegant calm that is foreign to many of us. The decor seems more important than the guests, and the food more significant than the cause for celebrating.

Such rigid formality is quite a contrast to the stable birth of the "first Christmas." Only a few unassuming guests were at the manger, the site of one of the greatest celebrations of all time.

And in that region there were shepherds out in the field, keeping watch over their flocks by night. And an angel of the Lord appeared to them, and the glory of the Lord shone around them. . . . And the angel said to them, ". . . I bring good news of a great joy which will come to all the people; for to you is born

this day in the city of David a Savior, who is Christ the Lord. And this will be a sign for you; you will find a babe wrapped in swaddling cloths and lying in a manger." . . . The shepherds said to one another, "Let us go over to Bethlehem and see this thing that has happened, which the Lord has made known to us." And they went with haste, and found Mary and Joseph, and the babe lying in a manger. . . . And the shepherds returned, glorifying and praising God for all they had heard and seen."

—Luke 2:8–20

Jesus' birth was but the first of many celebrations in his presence. His ministry offers some wonderful models for entertaining.

• He made the most out of ordinary well water for a wedding at Cana.
• He fed thousands of people—without any preplanning—on a beautiful hillside overlooking the sea of Galilee.
• He chose mealtime to talk with Zacchaeus, the distrusted tax collector who sought another chance.
• He shared the honored Passover meal with his disciples, an odd group that included three fishermen, a tax collector, Simon the Zealot, Thomas the skeptic, and Judas Iscariot, who betrayed him. Gathered at one table in the Upper Room, Jesus led them in a new understanding of their faith: "This bread is my body . . . this cup is the New Covenant. . . . Do this in memory of me." (Mark 14:22–25)

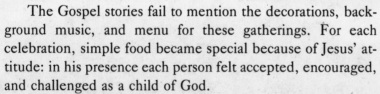

The Gospel stories fail to mention the decorations, background music, and menu for these gatherings. For each celebration, simple food became special because of Jesus' attitude: in his presence each person felt accepted, encouraged, and challenged as a child of God.

The example he set is still before us, and his attitude can be ours as well. "Wherever two or three are gathered in my name, there am I in the midst of them," he said (Matthew 18:20). As we gather to share in the spirit of love that *is* Christmas, we can be assured that Jesus is with us and that his caring is ours to share.

If only our Christmas parties would always express that spirit! If only we—like Jesus—would take the time to listen to, share with, and enjoy those around us! If only we would stop waiting for the "right time" and celebrate the "right-now time!"

> The happy Christmas comes once more,
>   The heavenly Guest is at the door,
> The blessed words, the shepherds thrill,
>   The joyous tidings, peace, goodwill.
>   —Gruntvig, Krauth, Balle
>   "The Happy Christmas"

A *true* celebration fills the premises with joy. The spirit of festivity is made evident by

—enthusiastic conversation
—hugs and handclasps
—comfortable surroundings
—delicious food and drink
—time to relax, relate, reflect, and refresh!

Festivity then is a time set aside for the full expression of feeling. It says yes to experience; it entails joy, which explains why we wish people happiness on holidays and consider a party successful if "a good time was had by all."

>   —Harvey Cox
>   *Feast of Fools*

FOCUSING ON YOU AS A HOST

If you can get past the advertised images of holiday parties—the myths of caviar and crystal, elegant attire, and a different wine with each course—you may be able to see entertaining as a viable option for you. Your hospitality is a unique gift awaiting expression, and the opportunities are endless. Think of a holiday celebration as a festive, affordable, and enjoyable occasion for all participants, *including* the hosts. Let go of any rigid expectations. Reach for new ideas and formats that will be fun and meaningful for hosts and guests.

Be sure to include family members in your plans for entertaining. Share the excitement of formulating a party idea, the responsibilities of planning and preparing, and the satisfaction of welcoming guests. If a family member is truly indifferent to all aspects of entertaining, respect his or her wishes and arrange to entertain without imposing.

> You'll never get a good party going without giving things a bit of a push. It boils down to the same formula most times: good setting, good food, good drink and plenty of goodwill, as is right at this time of the year.
>
> *—The Duchess of Duke Street Entertains*
> Michael Smith, editor

Before going any further, take a good look at your preferences and assets as a host. Spend a few minutes answering these questions:

What do you and your friends most enjoy doing together? (Talking and relaxing, working on a project, experiencing something new . . .)

What hobbies and interests do you enjoy that might work into your entertaining plans? (Cuisine and traditions from other countries, craft projects, music, dancing, and games . . .)

What foods do you most enjoy preparing for your family? For your guests?

What entertaining space does your home have? (Living room, family room, recreation room, dining room, patio, kitchen—large or small) What are the personalities of these rooms? (rustic, formal, cozy, playful . . .)

What are some special features of your home that might be enjoyed by guests? (Fireplace, beautiful view, piano, pool table, swimming pool, barbecue . . .)

If you think your home is inadequate for entertaining, do you have access to other entertaining space? (A church, recreation hall, community center, country club . . .)

How much support and assistance can you expect from the other members of your household? Ask them—don't just guess!

—Total cooperation?
—Help with specific jobs? (List who, describe what jobs.)
—General support (greeting, conversation, etc.)?
—Little or no support? (Will you entertain elsewhere, by yourself, or not at all?)

Each family member involved in the entertaining should answer the following questions:

As a host, which of these entertaining goals is most important to you? Rate their importance from 1 (most important) to 5 (least important).

_____ The comfort of your guests?
_____ Introducing a new experience?
_____ Meeting "society page" standards?
_____ Ease of preparation and cleanup?
_____ Your own enjoyment of the celebration?

What entertaining jobs do you enjoy most? Least? Rate the following jobs from 1 (most enjoyable) to 6 (least enjoyable).

_____ Decorating?
_____ Preparing refreshments/meals?
_____ Serving refreshments/meals?
_____ Greeting guests and conversing?
_____ Planning and leading activities?
_____ Cleaning up and postparty relaxing?

Is there anything about entertaining that you dread, dislike, or are especially fearful of, such as social faux pas, culinary disasters, cost overruns, or general confusion?

Look over your answers. As a host, what can you offer your friends this Christmas?

CHRISTMAS: A SEASON TO CELEBRATE!

Traditionally and historically, the weeks between Thanksgiving and Epiphany are marked with dozens of celebrations that honor saints, offer social occasions, and provide opportunities for holiday baking. The calendar on the next few pages describes some of these celebrations. Their variety sparks ideas for new ways you can enjoy the season.

Christmas celebrations puzzled Malcolm Boyd.

> The big mistake we have made is to place it *back there*. We have made it ancient history instead of modern life. It concerns angels, shepherds, Mary, Joseph and an inn keeper, but not us.
>
> We have decided, too, to confine Christmas to Christmas. On December twenty-fourth, it has not arrived ("Santa Claus does not come, Johnny, until tomorrow.") On December twenty-sixth, it is over ("We've got to get the tree outside, sweep the room and clean up. It's all over, dear.")
>
> So we don't really let Christmas come at all. By its very nature, it cannot be contained any more than God can be bottled up inside a church building to be visited once a week for an hour, or Jesus can be invoked in prayer to act as a convenient magician on call.

> Fortunately, despite the fact that we don't let Christmas come at all, it is here all the time.
>
> —*Malcolm Boyd's Book of Days*

November 1—All Saints' Day: Recognizing "all, known to man or known only to God, who, in whatever circumstances and whatever states of life, have contended manfully in this life and now enjoy the blissful vision of God for ever in Heaven."[3] This may be a good time to work on your Christmas planning—the "Go" celebration that begins on page 27.

November 25—St. Catherine's Day: In honor of the patron saint of unmarried women, this can be a day for a mother-and-daughter luncheon, women's day out, or a time to address an issue of particular importance to women.

November 30—St. Andrew's Day: German Christmas preparations begin today—no dancing or weddings till after Christmas!

December 1—The first day on many Advent calendars. (See the Advent calendar on page 140.)

December 4—St. Barbara's Day: Celebrants honor a third-century woman imprisoned by her father to protect her from the evils of the world. She converted to Christianity during her imprisonment and later was put to death for refusing to honor pagan ceremonies. Syrian children go from house to house seeking blessings and gifts. Wheat is symbolic of St. Barbara: baklava and other wheat pastries and candies are prepared in her honor. How about baking a favorite Christmas goodie to share with a friend?

December 6—St. Nicholas' Day: Truly a children's holiday! Loads of gift-giving celebrations and ceremonies occur worldwide. See page 52 for some fun-filled traditions.

December 12—Fiesta of Our Lady of Guadalupe. This important Mexican festival commemorates an Indian boy's vision of the Virgin Mary in 1531. Read about Mary in Luke 1:26–56. Imagine what Mary was thinking and doing in the days before Jesus was born.

---

[3] *Butler's Lives of the Saints*, Vol. IV, (New York: Harper and Row, 1956).

December 13—St. Lucia's Day: A Scandinavian celebration honors the Queen of Light with candle-studded crowns of evergreens and the commencement of Yuletide festivities. See the Scandinavian *Julbörd* celebration beginning on page 275.

December 16—Posadas Day: In Latin America, celebrants play the parts of innkeepers and pilgrims to reenact the drama of the Holy Family's journey. The *posada* occurs each night between now and Christmas Eve. See the Posada Procession, page 284.

December 21 or 22—Winter Solstice: The sun is at the lowest point of the year—a cause for pagan fears, rituals, and celebrations that were once thought to compete with sacred Christmas activities. Read about the symbolism of evergreens (page 104) and decorate your dinner table with a simple centerpiece of evergreen branches.

December 23—Night of the Radishes: Citizens of Oaxaca, Mexico, carve huge squash-sized radishes into elaborate scenes of Christ's birth, the Crucifixion, or contemporary life. *Bañuelos*, puffy fried breads, are the traditional treat. Make *bañuelos*; the recipe is on page 290.

December 24—Christmas Eve: ". . . and while they were in Bethlehem, the time came for her to have a baby." (Luke 2:6) Christians around the world welcome Christmas with midnight worship and family festivities. *Il Cenone* (page 300), Le *Réveillon* (page 304), and the Brazilian *Ceia* (page 251) are party plans based on these traditions.

December 25—"The Birthday of the Son of the Stranger on High" in Arapahoe terms and *"Joy Day"* for the San Jacinto Indians. Just as the sun provides longer days, the Son of God brings us Light: "Glory to God in the Highest, and on earth, peace among all!" (Luke 2:14)

December 26—St. Stephen's Day commemorates two saints with the same name: the first Christian martyr (Acts 7:59–60) and a ninth-century missionary venerated as the patron saint of horses. It is an Irish tradition to carry a caged wren through town while singing a ballad that tells of the wren that betrayed St. Stephen to the Roman soldiers. In England, this was Boxing Day, when gifts were shared with tenants, employees,

᛫ S᛫ Stephen ᛫

mail carriers, and anyone who renders a service, and when the coins in the church alms box were counted. This might be a good day to decide on some special year-end gift you can give to a mission, charity, or other project.

December 27—Feast of St. John the Evangelist: A day devoted to visiting friends. Let's go!

December 28—Holy Innocents' Day or Childremas: An unlucky day remembering Herod's massacre of infants. Say a special prayer today for the world's children.

December 31—St. Sylvester's Day, honoring a fourth-century pope. Usually festivities are part of the New Year's celebrations, as in Germany, where carp and St. Sylvester's punch are enjoyed. As *you* greet the New Year, remember other holiday seasons and give thanks for the year ahead.

January 1—The first day of the year is known by many names: the Octave of Christmas, the Commemoration of the Circumcision, the Feast of Fools, and St. Basil's Day. In England and colonial America, this wasn't referred to as New Year's Day until 1752, two hundred years after the shift to the Gregorian calendar. On page 310, you will find descriptions of January first customs from around the world. Enjoy the New Year's In or Out celebration (page 311), a festive but flexible way to welcome the year.

January 5—Twelfth Night: The eve of Epiphany and the end of the Christmas season in many countries. The Twelve Days of Christmas (December 25—January 6) were marked with gift-giving, visiting friends and family, and relaxing, to enjoy the season. Some believe the powers of darkness run rampant during this time—a good reason to stay in at night and to be suspicious of strange goings-on!

January 6—Epiphany: Celebrations honor the Magi's visit to Bethlehem and the official end of the Christmas season. A world of customs has evolved around the "Three Kings," the guiding star, and dismantling the decorations. (See the Epiphany Experience, page 35.) The Irish celebrate "Women's Christmas" on this date, honoring the miracle of the wedding at Cana of Galilee. It is said that all water becomes wine between sunset, January 5, and sunrise on the sixth.

> There was a quaintness, too, mingled with all this revelry that gave it a peculiar zest; it was suited to the time and place, and as the old Manor House almost reeled with mirth and wassail, it seemed echoing back the joviality of long-departed years.
>
> —Washington Irving
> "At Bracebridge Hall"
> *Country Sketches*

Of course our celebrations aren't always based on historical or ethnic experience. A look back at your questionnaires beginning on page 22 should bring to mind some of the Christmas celebrations you and your family have enjoyed most—inviting Aunt Martha to dinner, baking cookies with the children, trimming the neighborhood tree, attending a Christmas concert.

Some of these are time-honored occasions linking Christmas past and present as the event is repeated yearly. Other events are spontaneous and may only happen once, or be the start of a new tradition.

North America's first Christmas party was on Christmas Eve of 1492, when a flagship belonging to Columbus's expedition shipwrecked off the island of Santo Domingo. The hearty explorer and his crew were rescued by islanders and enjoyed a Christmas feast with the native chief. To honor that shared meal and their timely rescue, Columbus later built a small fortress nearby and named it *La Navidad*, meaning The Nativity.

Both traditional and spontaneous gatherings begin by focusing on a special event, experience, or person. The party may be thrown to celebrate St. Lucia's Day, to share a favorite recipe, or to introduce an out-of-town guest. These "beginnings" can be developed in the invitations, decorations, activities, and menu for the event. For example, set the scene for a tropical Christmas celebration (and honor Christopher Columbus!) with colorful paper lanterns, island music, and a flavorful dinner cooked on the barbecue or over an open fire.

Or allow the holiday spirit to be your reason for hosting an informal evening with friends.

How easy it is for one benevolent being to diffuse pleasure around him; and how truly is a kind heart a fountain of gladness, making everything in its vicinity to freshen into smiles!

—Washington Irving
"At Bracebridge Hall"
Country Sketches

Christmas is a season for all kinds of get-togethers. Advent through Epiphany, morning, afternoon or evening, at home or on the road, meal or snack . . . the options are endless!

Your Holiday Calendar

The wonderful world of Christmas
is a joy from the moment it starts.
The wonderful world of Christmas
should remain ev'ry day in our hearts.
　　　　　　　—Charles Tobias and Al Frisch

The December page of a home calendar is likely to fill quickly. Appointments and meetings are sandwiched between dates for school productions and office parties . . . and that "wonderful world of Christmas" may be left behind as the month speeds along. It's not at all hard to find activities that will bring home the spirit of Christmas; it *is* hard to find the time to do them all, even to balance what we *must* do with what we would *like* to do.

In working on the "Go" celebration (page 27), your family may have shared some important dates for Christmas programs, parties, shopping excursions, and so forth, and some ideas for new experiences. Refresh your memory about these dates and ideas.

List some "little celebrations" that might be fun during the holidays. Almost anything can become a celebration.

—Playing carols while unpacking the Christmas decorations.

—Reading Christmas Scripture or a poem for grace at the dinner table.

—Making a "Merry Christmas" phone call to Grandpa.

—Inviting a neighbor over to help make (and eat!) Christmas cookies.

A holiday calendar may help you pace the commitments and celebrations of this busy season. You could use your family calendar, marking Christmas activities with a red pen. Or make a date line for the Christmas season, posting the page near other calendars.

Either way, begin with a date that signifies for you the start of the Christmas season—perhaps the first Sunday of Advent, December 1, or Thanksgiving Day. On your holiday calendar:

• Note church activities, parties at work and school, and social "obligations" that are important to family members. Don't forget birthdays, anniversaries, and homecomings.
• Schedule the "little celebrations" and times for shopping, baking, visiting, and other holiday activities.
• If you have space, include the Family Christmas Calendar, page 31.

Throughout the season, keep your holiday calendar handy for planning, and use it as a daily reminder of the events and ideas that can make the spirit of Christmas come alive for you.

Are you willing to believe that love is the strongest thing in the world—stronger than hate, stronger than evil, stronger than death—and that the blessed life which began in Bethlehem nineteen hundred years ago is the image and brightness of the Eternal Love? Then you can keep Christmas, and if you keep it for a day, why not always?

—Henry van Dyke
"Keeping Christmas"

Greetings, good master, mistress, children
   Greetings, good health to one and all!
Once more we come to you with singing;
   Open your door, we've come to call!
Let us now to your heart draw near
   and with warmth and with food be welcomed!
—"Carol of the Mistletoe Singers"

GUEST LISTS

Inviting people into your home will give you a chance to get to know them a little better, catch up on what's happening in their lives, and create some memories together.

Questionnaire A on page 22 asks you, "Whom would you like to spend time with during this year's holiday season?" Alter that list to include those persons you and your family would like to invite over during the Yuletide. Include new friends, friends without families nearby, friends you only see once a year, business associates, neighbors, members of your extended family, and people who have especially enriched your life during the past year.

Your list undoubtedly includes some natural groupings: friends from school days, coworkers, members of your church, and so on. But unless you plan to entertain a well-defined group (such as a sorority or the church trustees), let your guest list cross the lines of neighborhood, church, work, and club involvements. One of the joys of hosting is introducing your friends to each other.

Whether your guests are close friends, casual acquaintances, or complete strangers to one another, you'll be wise to follow these tips in putting your guest list together:

Invite a *very* diverse group only if you will be available to guide the conversation—at a catered dinner, a fireside gathering for a few friends, *or* a large gathering where all guests know some others but nobody knows everyone. In any case, guests are likely to be more at ease if they know at least one person there besides the hosts.

Look for interests that your friends have in common. Hobbies, travel, age of children, regional background, or profession may provide a lead-in for conversation.

Don't be restricted by age. Young and old have much to share: enthusiasm, experience, sometimes even similar interests.

There are no strangers—only friends we haven't met.
—folk saying

Special Guests

Some people are easier to entertain than others. Adept at conversation, courteous but not rigid, helpful but not domineering, these friends are a pleasure anytime. But most of us are harder to please. Some special needs and idiosyncracies can be subtly dealt with by a considerate and well-prepared host.

Learn what you can about a shy guest before the party. Plan to involve this person with the others by using such conversation starters as job, hobbies, family, and birthplace.

Involve "picky" guests in some of the planning. Ask them to bring a "salad that will go well with roast duck" or "a dozen of your wonderful rolls." Let them know that you respect their opinion, and give them a specific opportunity to use their expertise.

Lonely guests may particularly enjoy the festivities. Those who are unable to spend the holidays with their families will cherish an invitation to decorate the tree, bake Christmas cookies, or sing carols. Send some Christmas cheer home with them—perhaps a homemade decoration, a loaf of holiday bread, or a recording of the evening's caroling.

Enjoy the company of foreign guests and the opportunity to appreciate another culture, as you share your own traditions. Be sensitive to language difficulties and questions about unfamiliar food or customs. Your welcome will seem more sincere if before the party you have learned where these guests are from and how to pronounce their names correctly.

Include non-Christian friends in the joy of your celebrations. Don't try to convert them, but don't hide the crèche either. Let the decorations and other traditions speak for themselves. Some details may need extra attention—for example, the grace before a meal or the choice of Christmas songs.

Actually, all your guests are "special guests." These people are the focus of your party plans and are worthy of your loving attention. Take care to provide for, include, and enjoy them, every one.

Invitations

Think of an invitation as introducing a party to the celebrants. It should provide just enough pleasant and intriguing details to lure the recipient toward a positive response—that of becoming a welcome guest at the upcoming celebration.

There are some dos and don'ts for a good invitation.

DO be clear about what's being planned. Be sure to include:

—The date and day of the week.
—Time (beginning and ending, if desired).
—Location (address and map if necessary).
—Names of the hosts.
—Occasion: honoring ———, dinner or dessert, etc.
—Attire.
—Phone number for R.S.V.P. or "regrets only".

DON'T send the invitations out late. (Remember the busyness of these days!) Most people appreciate at least one week's notice. If you must have an exact count of how many guests will be coming, send invitations two or three weeks in advance, and follow up with a telephone call a week later. A formal occasion requires a longer advance notice—a month is usually appropriate.

DO decide carefully on the style of your invitations. Except for a large dinner or formal reception, a telephoned invitation is perfectly proper. Extend the invitation by calling your guests seven to ten days before your party. Three or four days later, follow up with a second call or postcard as a reminder and confirmation.

A written invitation can be more vivid and appropriate to the theme of the celebration. It also serves as a visual reminder of the upcoming event. Check a stationery store for a broad selection of printed invitations. They may be sophisticated, businesslike, romantic, casual, trendy.

Here are some fun ways to personalize the message.

• Block-print, stencil, or sketch the design.

- Print your message on a chain of paper dolls.
- Use colored ink or stickers.
- Print up just one original and have your local printer reduce it on your choice of paper.
- Hand-deliver your invitation and attach

—a helium balloon;
—a small potted plant;
—a homemade ornament;
—or an early souvenir of your party.

Name Tags*Name Tags*Name Tags*

Don't be embarrassed to use name tags at your parties. Although they aren't always appropriate or necessary, name tags can be icebreakers that visually remind your guests who's who. Once the wearer gets past the awkward step of attaching it, he or she is apt to forget about it. But it is bound to be appreciated by fellow celebrants.

Use name tags:

- To encourage guests to introduce themselves to one another without your assistance.
- To call attention to some interesting fact about each person: hometown, favorite Christmas decoration, and so on.
- To jog the memories of guests who have met before—somewhere . . . sometime . . .

Use your imagination when making the name tags.

- Purchase stick-on tags. Decorate with Christmas stickers and ask guests to write their names and favorite Christmas activities.
- Cut Christmas symbols from red and green paper, aluminum foil, or wrapping paper, using small cookie cutters as patterns. Provide bold markers (white paint on dark surfaces,

permanent markers on foil) for guests to write their names on a selected design.

• Invite guests to create their own name tags. Provide colored paper, scissors, glitter, glue, stickers, and other supplies. Be sure to complete your own name tag before guests arrive; offer instructions and encouragement. You may want to give prizes for the most creative, colorful, inventive, and unusual name tags.

• For a dinner party, let place cards double as name tags. Write the guest's name on both sides of the card, and place it so it can be seen by others at the table.

Involving the Kids

Whenever your invitation includes family members of all ages, you'll be wise to plan ahead for the arrival of the youngest guests. Begin by giving these children the same consideration you give your adult guests. Take into account the children's ages; and prepare your house accordingly.

1. Place breakables out of reach or in a place that can be easily and constantly seen and monitored.
2. Store poisons in a locked cupboard or somewhere that is definitely inaccessible to toddlers.
3. Remember that mistletoe, holly berries, and many other plants are attractive but poisonous.

Plan some appropriate children's activities.

Free play area: Equip a playroom or area with such items as interlocking blocks, toy cars and trucks, beanbags, a child-proof cassette recorder.

Arts and crafts: Set out old Christmas cards, glue, and scissors, or Play-Doh, on an out-of-the-way (but nearby) table, or have your young guests make place cards for the dinner table. List diners' names clearly and correctly. Have a stack of index cards, red and green markers, stickers, felt scraps, sequins, and old Christmas cards. (You might ask an older child to supervise.) Or outline a large picture (a Christmas tree, Santa, a stable) on a piece of butcher paper. Tape it to the floor or table. Set out crayons, colored chalk, water-based markers, or colored pencils for embellishing the design.

Kitchen help: Involve the children in the preparations for the meal. Besides setting the table, they may enjoy:

—Making the salad (tossed greens, diced fruit, or cottage cheese plates).

—Filling bowls with crackers, peanuts, mashed potatoes, or jelly.

—Piping cream cheese into celery, buttering bread, mixing punch.

Supervise carefully—and constantly—whenever sharp knives and hot foods are involved!

Quiet time: Rent a movie or videotape of a Christmas special. This is not the best community builder, but may be a memorable (and peaceful) experience.

REMEMBER—The children are likely to have a short attention span and be excited and eager to eat (or at least sample the food).

• Plan both active play and quiet time activities.

• Provide an appealing appetizer about thirty minutes before the meal; it will make *everyone's* meal more relaxed! Good choices include

peanuts, nut cups, or stuffed celery
cheese and fruit on toothpicks
peanut butter sandwich "fingers"
(Avoid very salty or sugary snacks.)

Guest Lists: The Numbers Game

In drawing up a guest list, it's sometimes hard to know when to stop. Will a few more guests add confusion or charisma?

Will you have enough food, drink, and chairs for everyone? Will you be able to keep up with everyone and everything?

Your responsibilities to your guests are the key factor in deciding how many to invite to your party. As a *host* you'll want to make every guest feel welcome and comfortable; as a *friend* you'll want to have a chance to visit with each of your guests. Your ability to host and to chat will depend upon the type of party you plan; the size and arrangement of your home (or party location); the food and beverages served; the activities offered; and the attitudes and expectations of everyone present.

A look at four styles of entertaining will help you focus your plans. As you'll discover on the following pages, each style has its own personality, advantages, and requirements.

FOUR STYLES OF ENTERTAINING

A *Holiday Open House:* a time for "dropping in"
A *Comfortable Gathering:* just having some friends over
A *"Sit-Down" Meal:* gracious dining in your home
Parties Away from Home: a world of opportunities

A Holiday Open House

With this type of party, you and your home can work together to welcome many people at once. The come-and-go format encourages guests to fit the party into their busy schedules, whether for a few minutes or a few hours. The refreshments and activities are arranged in a help-yourself style so you can concentrate on welcoming and visiting with a steady stream of guests.

Keep your personal expectations in mind as you plan your open house. How busy will you be fixing food and drink, answering the door, and so forth? Think about the invited guests whom you haven't seen for a long time, and those whom you look forward to "catching up" with. Is this the best format to satisfy your expectations?

One example of a well-planned holiday open house is the Wassail Buffet, page 226. It includes many of the details that will help you make your open house a success.

As you consider how many to invite, guesstimate* how many people can comfortably move around your home. Even if your entire *home* is considered "open," you can assume that the party will happen in only a few areas. Where are your guests most likely to congregate? How many people can comfortably fit in these areas?

You'll also need to consider how many you can *serve*. Think in terms of purchasing, preparing, serving, replenishing, and cleaning up.

Most guests will *stay* one or two hours. For a three-hour party in a home that will accommodate twenty guests, you could probably entertain forty to fifty persons. Remember that some invited guests will be unable to come; others may stay for the entire time; and some may bring an out-of-town visitor or unexpected guest. (That's why it's called an *open* house!)

An open house often has thirty to sixty minutes of *lag time*: it may take a full hour to "get going"—or may start with a flourish but become quiet as bedtime approaches.

You may wish to host two consecutive "open house" parties in one day, perhaps inviting the punch-and-coffee crowd from 2:00 to 3:30 and your wine-and-cheese friends from 7:30 to 10:00. That way you'll only need to clean house once, yet can enjoy two distinct celebrations in one day. You are apt to be exhausted by the end of it all, but can avoid some unnecessary confusion if you:

• Allow at least two hours between parties—enough time for cleanup, preparations, and a "recess" between those slow to leave the first party and those early to arrive for the second.

* Guesstimate: between an estimate and a guess—the approximation of something you can't know for sure.

• Streamline plans for both parties, keeping food, drink, activities, and special effects as simple as possible.

• Are well rested and well prepared for both celebrations.

• Plan on some "just me" time later that evening or the next day.

A Comfortable Gathering

"Having some friends over" may not seem like *real* entertaining, but these informal gatherings often are the best parties. We use the word "gathering" here to describe just that type of celebration: inviting a few people over for a set period of time. An informal meal, a Christmas activity, or just conversation and refreshments may be the format. Less formal than a reception or a sit-down meal, the gathering is an opportunity for relaxed conversation and interaction between you and your guests.

If you will be serving a meal, plan to offer it as a buffet and to eat in the living room or family room. Trays or small tables will be helpful. Other refreshments might be served by you or placed on a tea cart, coffee table, or sideboard so guests can help themselves.

HOW MANY GUESTS?

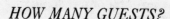

If you plan to involve guests in making gifts, caroling, or preparing a meal, the *activity* itself may dictate the number to invite. How many people will the activity involve? How much space is needed? What might the on-lookers do?

If *conversation* is to be the focus of your gathering, it may be best to invite a few more people than can be comfortably seated—and a few less than would fill the room to capacity. Having a seat for each guest lets everyone in on the conversation, but some people may feel trapped in their chairs and alienated from the mouth-watering snacks in the other room. On the other hand, a standing-room-only gathering might be inherently festive, but guests may feel unnoticed in the hubbub.

How much *food* do you envision preparing? For a meal, how many diners can arrange themselves comfortably in the room you have selected? How many settings of tableware do you have?

A "Sit-Down" Meal

A sit-down meal may be casual or formal, intimate or stately, a simple meal or a multi-course banquet. Whatever the format, this style of entertaining is likely to be quite demanding of your resources. Careful planning and orchestration, though, can make it a most satisfying way to welcome guests.

Most hosts will do best serving no more than eight to ten guests a sit-down meal. But getting outside help can expand those limitations.

• A potluck by any other name is twice as elegant! Ask guests to bring part of the meal according to a "master menu" that you have established. See the tips on page 266.

• Pool resources with a friend. You could exchange kitchen help, china, centerpieces, and chairs, or even baby-sitting and housecleaning services.

• Consider using the services of a caterer or rental outlet. These professionals can add the finishing touches to your plans. See pages 291 and 294 for more information.

• Host the meal at a favorite restaurant. Page 294 will help you plan.

HOW MANY GUESTS?

As you decide how many to invite, keep in mind these concerns:

How many *diners* can be comfortably seated around the table you plan to use? Do you have enough chairs and tableware?

What are your *menu* plans? How many servings can you realistically expect to purchase . . . prepare . . . serve . . . clean up?

What are your *budget* limitations? How many guests can you afford to entertain?

Do you have the *time* and *patience* to do all the preparations? Will you enjoy the process?

> The pleasure in giving a dinner is mostly the pleasure of giving yourself. The effort you take is your way of showing your company that you care about them enough to give them a good time.
>
> —Marguerite Kelly and Elia Parsons
> *The Mother's Almanac*

HOW TO GET THE MOST SPACE OUT OF YOUR HOME

• Use rooms that best suit the occasion. Areas in your home where you are most at ease are likely to be the most comfortable for your guests as well. Your kitchen is likely to be a gathering spot for conversation and helping hands. A garage may be the best place for a messy project. Dinner could be served in your dining room, living room, family room, patio (weather permitting), or even in a warm and cleaned-out garage.

• Make small rooms seem larger by eliminating unnecessary furniture and accessories. Don't push the furniture against the walls: passageways will be blocked and the room's boundaries will be more obvious.

• Set up seating so guests can see and hear each other. Instead of lining up the chairs in a row, make small conversation groupings away from the flow of traffic. Don't provide enough seats for everyone if you want to encourage mingling and a "help yourself" atmosphere. But remember that the danger of spills is greater whenever guests must balance food and beverages while standing.

• Arrange adequate lighting. Use direct light to call attention to a guest book, special decorations, projects, or refreshments. Keep stairs, bathrooms, and the entrance subtly lit at all times. For conversation areas, soft, indirect lighting is most relaxing—and candles are always elegant and festive. And there's nothing more cozy and comfortable than sitting around the fireplace!

Portable Feasts

Thoughts of entertaining away from home may begin and end with summer picnics. But "away from home" doesn't necessarily mean picnic, nor does "entertaining" always imply that the host is furnishing a full meal.

Here are some fun holiday celebrations that you can enjoy away from home.

• Carry a portable banquet to enjoy before a sporting event or concert. A hot and hearty meal—complete with garnishes—can be served from the kitchen of a recreation vehicle or out of your picnic basket. A Deli Dinner (page 296) and New Year's In or Out (page 311) are two celebrations that transport well.

• Go on a holiday expedition: a winter hike, a tour of Christmas displays, or a caroling hayride, followed by refreshments at a restaurant or back at home.

• Have a dollar dinner: ask each participant to spend a set amount (usually one to two dollars) on something for a potluck-style meal. This is a fun way to end a shopping trip.

• Have a box social at the ski lodge: each diner prepares a lunch, concealing it with decorative packaging. Lunches are exchanged (or bid for) at mealtime.

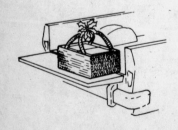

• Serve a tailgate tea: pack favorite tidbits to share before or after a favorite Christmas event.

You may choose to transport your party to a location more appropriate for your entertaining plans . . . to take in some of your community's Christmas events . . . to experience winter's beauty with other outdoors enthusiasts . . . or perhaps just to try something new. With a little imagination you'll discover a multitude of great places for special celebrations, including

—Community halls and churches (especially good places for family reunions and receptions).

—A restaurant for a meal hosted by you (see page 294 for tips).

—A college lounge or cafeteria. Comfortable seating, reasonably priced food, and interesting surroundings are part of this informal setting. (These facilities may close for winter break; call ahead to check the schedule.)

—The lobby of a museum, gallery, or convention center. Call the business office if you have any question regarding their facilities and general policies.

HOW MANY GUESTS?

Because there are so many possibilities for portable feasts, it's useless to give a formula for determining how many to invite. Ask yourself:

What are the *expenses* for your celebration? Who pays? (Be clear in the invitations if you expect guests to buy tickets, meals, or bus tokens, or contribute for gas, food, etc.) How much can *you* afford to spend?

What *arrangements* and *preparations* will you, as host, need to make? Will the number of participants affect the time needed for these responsibilities?

How many people will your plans *accommodate*? Consider the practicalities of transportation, activities, meals/refreshments.

What are your *intentions* and *hopes*? Do you envision a family outing, a special time with a few close friends, an excursion with a busload of merrymakers . . . ?

Here are some basics for any entertaining venture.

1. Make your plans well in advance.
2. Keep your expectations realistic.

Have your guests in the forefront of your plans.

Base your plans on what you know how to do and what you will enjoy doing for guests.

Don't try to do too much. Strive for simple elegance.

3. Organize your time and resources wisely.

Make lists, charts, and schedules, and refer to them often.

Have some "if that doesn't work" plans.

This kind of planning may seem to be "busywork"—but it will save you time, money, and disappointment in the long run. Think of the planning process as an investment in your confidence as a host and in the comfort and pleasure of you and your guests.

MENU PLANNING

The goal of menu planning is *satisfaction*—for the purchaser, preparer, server, and diners. It is usually best to plan the menu after you've worked out some of the other details: time of day, number of diners, preparation time, budget, and available supplies.

What style of meal do you envision? Consider theme, location, service style, tableware, pace, number and age of guests, cost, and atmosphere.

Some basics:

• Base your meal on foods that you enjoy preparing and serving, and which will be something special for your guests.

• Always include a surprise or "dining adventure": an unusual dish, a flambé, a bit of history or tradition.

• Don't serve too many courses, too many dishes, or too much food.

• Check the aesthetic appeal of the meal. Use your sensory imagination.

Contrasting colors
> earthy shades of brown, golds, and whites
> garden greens
> bright oranges and reds
> unusual blues and violets

Range of temperature

Shapes and sizes

round	chunky	diced	sliced
bite-sized	mounded	sticks	wedges

Textures

crumbly	chewy	mushy	gritty
gummy	smooth	creamy	crunchy
juicy	delicate	greasy	crispy

Aromas and flavors

sweet	tangy	sharp	light	fruity
salty	rich	bitter	complex	bland
spicy	nutty	sour	refreshing	mild
foreign	hearty	homey		

Don't overwhelm the senses. Too much is as unappealing as too little!

HOLIDAY CELEBRATIONS

The following pages contain plans for some very special holiday celebrations. Each plan includes:

• Some background or history for the idea.
• A menu with specific instructions.
• Tips on decorations, activities, and ways to adapt the celebration.

Use the following guidelines as you look through these pages:

1. Read the description of the celebration, as well as the menu and tips.
2. Then close your eyes and imagine you are a guest coming to the party. Imagine with all five senses: pay attention to your first impressions and the imagined aromas, lighting, music, centerpiece, and garnishes.
3. Jot down some notes about your imagined observations.
4. Read the party plan again. Would you enjoy doing this? Would your friends enjoy participating? Can you be relaxed carrying it off? What would you like to change—add, omit, or do differently?

As you read through the outlines and menus, you will find ⟨T⟩, our symbol for timesaving tips:

—ways to organize your time
—suggestions for utensils that will simplify your work
—tips for selecting plans that will work most efficiently for you

Also look for the ⟨*⟩, our signal that the recipe or instructions for that item are on the following pages.

For Best Results With These Recipes—
1. Read completely through the recipe before starting any preparations. Pencil in any notes about changes, timetable, and so on.
2. Prepare ingredients accurately. For example, "1 c. chopped nuts" directs you to chop the nuts *before* measuring. "1 c. nuts, chopped" denotes chopping *after* measuring.
3. Use standard measuring cups and spoons. Fill them level.
4. Follow instructions carefully.
5. Always preheat the oven.
6. Watch for these helpful symbols:
    ⟨T⟩ timesaving tips

⟨*⟩ recipe or instructions following
(P) pointers from the pros

THE WASSAIL BUFFET　　　　　Page 226
Assorted fresh breads, fruits, vegetables
⟨*⟩ Cheese & Garlic Dip
⟨*⟩ Savory Stuffed Mushrooms
Other canapés, sliced meats, cheeses
⟨*⟩ British Plum Pudding
⟨*⟩ Fanciful Date Cake
⟨*⟩ The Wassail Bowl
⟨*⟩ Wassail for All Ages

EGGNOG SOUTHERN STYLE　　　　Page 239
⟨*⟩ Holiday Eggnog
Christmas breads, cookies, and canapés
⟨*⟩ Flavored butters

THE JUBILEE BRUNCH　　　　Page 244
⟨*⟩ Jubilee Punch
Baked ham (hot or cold)
⟨*⟩ Deviled Egg Variations
Cheese cubes on pretzels
⟨*⟩ Spinach and Mushroom Salad
Fruit tray
⟨*⟩ Quick Cheddar Loaf
Warm dinner rolls or biscuits
Coffee, tea, milk
⟨*⟩ Cherries Jubilee

A BIRTHDAY PARTY　　　　Page 248
⟨*⟩ Sandwich Cut-Outs
Fruit kabobs
Hot cider or cocoa

THE BRAZILIAN *CEIA*　　　　Page 251
⟨*⟩ Brazilian Party Punch
⟨*⟩ Toast in Port
⟨*⟩ Spicy Tomato Soup

⟨*⟩ *Peru à Brasiliera* (Roast Turkey, Brazilian Style)
Green beans with lemon
Punch, juice, wine
Orange sherbet
Coffee and tea

MIDDAY DINING   Page 257
⟨*⟩ Shrimp and Avocado Salad
⟨*⟩ Spaghetti Carbonara
Bread sticks
⟨*⟩ Caramelized Pears Almondine

**A PENNSYLVANIA DUTCH
CHRISTMAS DINNER**   Page 267
⟨*⟩ Roast Goose or ⟨*⟩ Pork with Apples and Onions
⟨*⟩ Potato Filling
⟨*⟩ Purple Cabbage
Hot buttered corn
⟨*⟩ Pepper Relish
⟨*⟩ Pickled Red-Beet Eggs
Fresh bread
Butter, apple butter, jellies and jams
Cider, water
Mincemeat pie
Coffee

SCANDINAVIAN *JULBÖRD*   Page 275
⟨*⟩ Lucia Buns
⟨*⟩ Hot Cranberry Glög
Ice-cold lemonade
Crisp crackers or thin slices of bread
Pâté
Pork sausage
Lutfisk
⟨*⟩ Pickled Fresh Cucumbers
⟨*⟩ Sardines with Apples
⟨*⟩ Ham in Mustard Crust
Mashed or boiled potatoes
⟨*⟩ Vegetables au Gratin

⟨*⟩ Christmas Porridge
Spritz or cut-out cookies
Coffee, tea, milk

THE *POSADA* PROCESSION   Page 284
First Course: ⟨*⟩ *Menudo*
Soft tortillas with butter
Second Course: ⟨*⟩ *Ensalada de Noche Buena*
Third Course: ⟨*⟩ *Guajolote Relleno* (Stuffed Turkey)
   Rice
   ⟨*⟩ *Legumbres Mexicana*
   White wine, champagne, or sparkling white grape
   juice
Fourth Course: ⟨*⟩ *Bañuelos*
Coffee and hot chocolate
(whipped cream and liqueurs, optional)

THE DELI DINNER   Page 296
Fresh fruits
Salad selections
Make-your-own sandwiches
Juices, wines, teas
Chocolate truffles or other desserts

IL CENONE   Page 300
⟨*⟩ Holiday Fritters
Fresh fruits, roasted nuts
⟨*⟩ Sicilian Orange and Onion Salad
⟨*⟩ Homemade Pasta with Butter and Grated Cheese
⟨*⟩ Baked Fish in Sesame Sauce (optional)
Steamed broccoli or zucchini
Spumoni or vanilla ice cream
Hot coffee (with liqueurs if desired)

LE REVEILLON   Page 304
⟨*⟩ *Potage Noël:* a chicken bisque
French bread (preferably *baquette*)
Cheese tray: Brie, Muenster, raclette; and other favorites

Fresh fruits
⟨*⟩ *Bûche de Noël*

ELEGANCE FROM EXTRAS   Page 308
⟨*⟩ Jellied Apple & Apple Salad
⟨*⟩ Italian-Style Turkey Pie
Steamed vegetables with butter
Bread or rolls (optional)
⟨*⟩ Quick Parfaits

NEW YEAR'S IN OR OUT   Page 311
⟨*⟩ Mimosas
Hearty stew (homemade or purchased)
Hot bread or crackers
⟨*⟩ Grand Finale Cake

"Here We Go A-Wassailing . . ."

The caroling, snacking, and revelry that are known as wassailing date back to a medieval English blessing. *Wes hàl*, a
wish for wholeness or good health, was a greeting often exchanged during the Yuletide over a cup of punch. The blessing became ceremonious: the wealthy hosted fancy parties
while the poor went from house to house requesting donations
so they could buy the festive punch for their own celebrations.

A thirteenth-century carol—the earliest of vernacular
Christmas carols—includes an invitation to join in the wassail
revelry.

Lords, by Christmas and the host
of this mansion hear my toast—
　　Drink it well—
Each must drain his cup of wine,
And I the first will toss off mine:
　　Thus I advise
Here then I bid you all *Wassail*,

Cursed be he who will not say,
    Drinkhail!
        —Anglo-Norman carol, thirteenth century
        Clement Miles
        Christmas

On occasion even trees were "wassailed" when a half-finished cup of brew was thrown at a tree.

Wassail the trees, that they may bear
You many a plum and many a pear;
For more or less fruits they will bring,
As you do give them wassailing.
        —Clement Miles
        Christmas

The central attraction of wassailing has always been the wassail bowl.

It was a potation, indeed, that might well make the heart of a toper leap within him; being composed of the richest and raciest wines, highly spiced and sweetened, with roasted apples bobbing about the surface.
        —Washington Irving
        "At Bracebridge Hall"
        Country Sketches

Accompanying the wassail tradition was "toasting"—bits of toast garnishing the brew absorbed enough flavor to make them a delicacy worth a special blessing. The blessings became more clever as the party went on, and toasting became a popular ceremony of pleasantry and well-wishing.

Wassail recipes may use almost any combination of fruit juices, ale, wine, spirits, and spices. The punch is traditionally served hot, often with baked apples, nutmeats, or toast pieces floating atop. A spicy fragrance from the simmering potion will fill the room—an inviting welcome for holiday guests!

THE WASSAIL BUFFET

Here we join an old English custom with a twentieth-century American tradition, the holiday open house. Your warm welcome, comfortable home, and enticing refreshments are a delightful way to extend the Yuletide greeting for "Wes hàl"—good health—to a number of your friends. Refer to page 227 for a discussion of some of the basic considerations in planning an open house.

Completing *all* preparations before the first guest arrives is essential to this party plan. Do the paperwork—including the guest list, menu planning, timetables—two weeks before party day. Then spread the rest of the preparations out over a full week. Doing a bit at a time can help you look forward to the big event while relieving you of some of the last-minute pressures of entertaining.

HOSTING AN OPEN HOUSE

Choose an ample block of time for your open house: three or four hours is often just right. Expect guests to arrive and depart throughout the specified time period. Answering the doorbell, chatting briefly, and replenishing the serving table are likely to demand all of your time. You may wish to extend the time block if you anticipate having lengthy conversations with your guests.

As you welcome your guests, you'll want to show them where to find comfortable chairs, refreshments, and activity centers (a pool table, player piano, jigsaw puzzle, scrapbook you've set out, etc.). Except for rooms closed off for the occasion (usually a closed door implies "off limits"), your entire home should invite guests to help themselves.

- Chairs are arranged in intimate groupings.
- Refreshments are attractively displayed and easy to serve and eat.
- Activities are arranged with appropriate lighting and seating, and necessary props.
- Walkways and rooms are clean and cleared. You may wish to remove some of the nonessentials: hassocks, magazine racks, and so on.

PLANNING THE MENU

A snack buffet is an excellent menu format for an open house, and a good complement for the wassail. Use foresight in selecting the food for your snack buffet. Choose foods that will be attractive, tasty, compatible, and easy to replenish. A review of menu planning basics will be helpful (see page 218).

- Plan food for the duration of the party. Refreshments at an open house should look appealing to the last guests as well as to the first—all the while demanding minimal attention from the host. You might choose to introduce a new item midway through your party; it must be something that takes less than five minutes for you to set out during the party.

(This might be a good opportunity to bring out something with less staying power: perhaps nachos or broiler canapés.) Prepare replenishments of food and beverages, and store emergency rations in the pantry in case you run out of everything.

• Consider the "keeping" quality of your selections. Can you keep hot foods hot and cold foods cold? Is there a risk that the food might curdle or become limp—or just lose its appeal?

• Make self-service and eating easy. Remember that guests will not want to risk making a mess in order to sample an awkward morsel. Serve only finger foods, unless guests will be seated while they eat.

—Decorative toothpicks in banana chunks and a serving knife in the cheese ball invite guests to help themselves.

—Two- or three-bite portions are easy to dish up; set them slightly apart for the most accessible and elegant appearance.

—Place plates, cups, and napkins within easy reach.

• Arrange the food attractively. Place contrasting bite-sized snacks in patterns on a platter: diagonals, concentric circles, and pie-shaped wedges are appealing. Red and green foods will add a Christmas look—see page 232 for some ideas. Try to keep platters at least half-filled: as snacks are depleted, put odds and ends all on one platter or remove them from the buffet table.

The Wassail Buffet Menu is a finger-food version of a full meal. It's a light buffet that includes the salty and the sweet. Keep portions small and quantities plentiful so guests can sample several of these tidbits. Plan on five to ten items per guest.

Something Fresh (and low in calories)
    Sliced apples, pears, pineapple, oranges . . .
    Crispy vegetables with ⟨*⟩ Cheese & Garlic Dip

Breadstuff

Special breads cut in manageable slices (two- or three-inch pieces are best)

Homemade or purchased crackers, spread or topped with something simple (cheddar and salami)—or something exotic (caviar and capers)

Popcorn, pretzels, or peanuts (optional)

Substantial Fare

⟨*⟩ Savory Stuffed Mushrooms
Other canapés, sliced meats, cheeses . . .

A Sweet Treat (thinly sliced and decoratively displayed)

⟨*⟩ British Plum* Pudding
⟨*⟩ Fanciful Date Cake
or nutbreads, cookies . . .

And the Beverages

⟨*⟩ The Wassail Bowl—a traditional wine-and-ale punch
⟨*⟩ Wassail for All Ages—a hot fruit-based version (coffee, tea, and ice water should also be available)

⟨P⟩ *Serving Tips*

Fill a glass bowl—a punch bowl works well—with crushed ice. Set your fresh fruits or vegetables on top to keep them at their crispy best.

Lemon, orange, and pineapple juices will prevent other fruits from browning. Sprinkle on bananas, pears, and apples before serving.

Put the wassail in a large electric slow-cooker, or place a kettle on a hot plate or electric warming tray.

Place a dishcloth or small towel near your buffet, where it will be handy for cleaning up spills and drips.

Alabama's "fantastic" Christmas riders carried their ver-

---

* *Plum* is an early name for raisins, one of the few ingredients that has been included in the Christmas pudding throughout its history!

sion of the wassail greeting from plantation to plantation. Donning masks and costumes, they started early Christmas morning for a full day of visiting. The cups of punch or liquor that greeted them at each home refreshed the riders and encouraged them to continue the tradition.

CHEESE & GARLIC DIP

1 clove garlic	¼ c. chopped green
2 tbsp. lemon juice	onion
½ tsp. grated lemon	1 tsp. basil
rind	½ tsp. salt
2 eggs	½ tsp. pepper
½ c. Parmesan cheese	1 c. oil (may be
¼ c. fresh parsley	part olive oil)

1. Measure all ingredients except oil into a blender jar. Whirl until smooth.
2. With blender running, slowly add oil in a thin, steady stream (open the center of the blender cover to do this); stop the motor once or twice to scrape the mixture down from the sides of the blender. Cover and refrigerate. Serve as a dip for vegetables. (May also be served as a salad dressing or an unusual but delicious pasta sauce.)

Makes 2 cups.

SAVORY STUFFED MUSHROOMS

24 medium whole	¼ tsp. sage
mushrooms, cleaned	¼ tsp. thyme
1 tbsp. lemon juice	¼ tsp. salt
2 tbsp. butter or	2 strips bacon, crisply
margarine	fried and crumbled
2 tbsp. minced onions	(optional)
⅓ c. fine dry bread	¼ c. finely chopped
crumbs	almonds or filberts

2 tbsp. Parmesan cheese
⅓ c. chicken stock or
   water (may use 2 tbsp.

white wine plus ¼ c.
   water)

1. Use a melon baller or small, sharp knife to remove stems from mushrooms. Brush the caps with lemon juice and place in a baking dish in a single layer.

2. Finely chop the stems. Sauté with onion in melted butter. Stir in remaining ingredients in the order given.

3. Use a spoon and your fingers to stuff the mushroom caps with the mixture.

4. Bake uncovered at 350° for 8 to 10 minutes.

⟨T⟩ These may be prepared up to 12 hours in advance and refrigerated before baking.

Wassail, wassail, all over the town
Our bread it is white and our ale it is brown;
Our bowl it is made of the green maple tree,
In the wassail bowl we'll drink unto thee.
—"Wassail, Wassail!"
traditional English song

WASSAIL BOWL

5 small or 2 large tart
   green apples
About 20 whole cloves
2 c. Burgundy wine
2 sticks cinnamon

½ c. brown sugar
2 c. apple juice
½ tsp. nutmeg
½ tsp. ground ginger
two 12-oz. bottles or
   cans ale*

1. Core apples, but don't peel them. Large apples should be cut horizontally to make thick rings. Stud each with 3 or 4 cloves. Place the apples in a shallow baking pan. Bake at

* Buy ale from a wine shop, liquor store, or delicatessen. You may omit the ale, altering the recipe to use 1 liter Burgundy and 3 c. apple juice.

350° until they are barely tender when pierced with a fork (20 to 30 minutes).

2. Stir other ingredients together in a kettle. Heat just to boiling, stirring occasionally.

3. Float apples in wassail. Serve warm.

Makes about 9 cups.

WASSAIL FOR ALL AGES

2 qts. grape juice
1 qt. apple juice
1 pt. lemonade
¼ c. honey
2 sticks cinnamon
½ tsp. whole cloves
1 lemon cut in ¼"
    slices OR 2 baked
    apples cut in ½"
    rings

1. Core, slice, and bake apples (if used) at 350° according to instructions in recipe for Wassail Bowl.

2. Stir together first six ingredients in a kettle. Heat just to boiling, stirring occasionally.

3. Float fruit slices on top of the hot punch just before serving.

Makes about 14 cups.

SOME REDS AND GREENS: ADDING HOLIDAY COLOR TO YOUR MEAL

Reds!
    cranberries: jellied, relished, juiced
    raspberries and strawberries: in gelatin, jellies, sherbets, ice cream, punches
    cherries, crabapples, pomegranates

apples: red delicious, Rome, Jonathans
tomatoes, beets, chili beans, kidney beans
paprika, pimento, red bell peppers
peppermint and cinnamon candies
sweet-and-sour or barbecue sauce

Greens!
limes, kiwi fruit, green apples, gooseberries
watercress, spinach, parsley, mint
romaine and iceberg lettuce
green onions, pickles, celery, chives
avocado, green olives, cucumbers, asparagus
zucchini, broccoli, beans, peas
peppers: jalapeño, chile, or green bells
guacamole and green goddess dressings
lime sherbet, pistachio, and mint ice creams

English parties have always included games, drama, or other planned merriment. In the days when feasts were incredible and gluttony was in vogue, some midmeal activity was often planned as a sort of "shaking down process" to make room for the rest of the meal.

For a time in English history, Christmas was the only day of the year when games were lawful. A sixteenth-century proclamation forbade game playing by English working people, with one annual exception: Christmas. The ruling prompted rapid growth in the number and popularity of games. But when Christmas was banned by the Puritans in 1652, the English lost even that yearly opportunity to enjoy games.

Variations of many old English games are still popular today, including blindman's buff, hunt the slipper, and hoop-and-hide (similar to hide-and-seek).

One exciting game was *snapdragon:* The lights were turned low as a shallow dish of flaming brandy-soaked fruit was placed in the center of the room. Guests were challenged to snatch raisins, plums, and other morsels from the flames, blow out the flames, and eat the hot fruits.

You might enjoy playing a safer version: seat players in a circle around a shallow dish in which you have placed a button or other small object (or a collection of trinkets or candies). Call out the name of a player. He or she should try to snatch the object and sit down again before the other players can count to ten.

For *hotcockles*, one player is blindfolded and kneels, sits, or lies down. The others take turns tapping him/her on the shoulder as the blindfolded player tries to guess who is tapping.

Yawning for a Cheshire cheese was always the last game of the evening. A cheese was awarded to the guests who yawned the widest, longest, loudest.

Now try to figure out this riddle. The answer is the topic for the next few pages.

> Flour of England, fruit of Spain,
>   Met together in a shower of rain;
> Put in a bag tied round with a string;
>   If you tell me this riddle,
>   I'll give you a ring!

Large quantities of a few fine foods typify English Christmas meals. Plates are piled high with roast goose, beef, or turkey—plus stuffings, sausages, and potatoes with gravy. There's seldom a need for the appetizers or first courses popular in other Christmas cuisines.

Dessert makes a spectacular appearance. Prepared four weeks earlier, the plum pudding is greeted with the same enthusiasm shown by the Cratchits of Dickens' *A Christmas Carol*:

> . . . the pudding, like a speckled cannon-ball, so hard and firm, blazing in half of half-a-quatern of ignited brandy, and bedight with Christmas holly stuck into the top.
>
> —Charles Dickens
> *A Christmas Carol*

Legends date Christmas plum pudding back to early English history. Lost in a forest one Christmas eve, a king and his entourage had only meager provisions. Combining the odds and ends—meat, flour, apples, eggs, ale, brandy, and sugar—the clever cook designed a festive pudding large enough for the entire company.

The term *pudding* can refer to many sweet or savory dishes. Through the centuries, Christmas puddings have ranged from a stew of grains, breads, and spices to pies shaped to resemble the manger of Bethlehem. The most popular of these has been plum pudding, a steamed dessert with a rich flavor and complex texture.

The pudding was once called *hackin*, a reference to the lengthy job of "hacking" up suet, bread, candied and dried fruits, and nuts. Even today, making the pudding is no simple feat. After grinding or mincing the ingredients, egg yolks and whites must be beaten separately for fifteen minutes more. The batter is then sealed in a mold and steamed four to twelve hours, before it can be wrapped in the brandy-soaked cloth for several weeks of mellowing. Hours before the Christmas guests arrive, the spirited pudding is steamed once again and then ignited for its hot and flaming entrance.

With origins as British as the wassail cup, a plum pudding is fitting fare for your wassail open house. Festively adorned in a wreath of holly, the pudding should be carried out midway through the party, when the majority of your guests are most likely to be present. Flame the pudding for its entrance (see Flambé Fanfare, page 238), then slice it thinly and serve with hard sauce.

> Now thrice welcome Christmas
>   Which brings us good cheer,
> Minced pies and plum porridge.
> Peace and plenty for many a Christmas to come.
>
> —Irish blessing
> Paul Dickson
> *Toasts*

⟨T⟩ In the interest of your sanity, you may want to forgo the complicated preparations necessary for steamed plum pudding and prepare instead the easy ⟨*⟩ Fanciful Date Cake.

Decorate with holly, flambé, and make the festive entrance. Your version of tradition can be just as elegant—and much less work!

⟨P⟩ *NOTES OF A PUDDING STEAMER*

• Select a *steaming pot* with a tight-fitting lid, a *trivet* or *rack* that will fit inside the steaming pot, and a *pudding mold* (or other container) that will sit on the trivet inside the steaming pot with ample room for the steam to circulate (at least one inch all around).

• Grease the pudding mold well, then dust with granulated sugar. Fill no more than two-thirds full with batter. Use a tight lid, or cover tightly with foil and tie with string.

• Pour boiling water into the steamer to the depth determined on the recipe. Cover and cook over high heat until steam escapes. Reduce heat to low. Check periodically and replenish water as needed.

• At the end of the cooking time, lift the mold out of the steamer. Let it cool until it is warm to the touch. Take the cover off the pudding to let any steam evaporate before you unmold it.

• If desired, wrap the pudding in a brandy-soaked cloth. Store in a tightly closed container for a month or so. Resteam (or warm in a microwave) prior to serving.

"Stir up, we beseech thee, O Lord
the wills of thy faithful people. . . ."

So reads the Collect or prayer in the Church of England for the last Sunday before Advent. The reading has given the day the name "Stir-up Sunday," a title interpreted by many as signifying the latest date one might "stir up" the Christmas pudding.

PLUM PUDDING

¾ c. fine dry bread crumbs	¾ c. hot milk
	2 eggs

1 c. light brown sugar
¼ c. orange juice
½ c. coarsely chopped
  walnuts
1 c. raisins
1 c. chopped dates or
  candied fruit
6 oz. suet, finely
  chopped or ground
(available from
  your butcher)
1 tsp. soda
1 c. flour
½ tsp. salt
1 tsp. cinnamon
½ tsp. mace
½ tsp. cloves

1. In a small mixing bowl combine bread crumbs and hot milk. Let stand 10 minutes.

2. Beat sugar and eggs until light. Stir in orange juice, then bread crumb mixture.

3. Sift dry ingredients over suet, fruits, and nuts. Gently stir with a fork. Blend into other mixture.

4. Pour pudding into a greased and sugar-dusted pudding mold (about 1½-qt. capacity). Cover with foil. Tie with string (or close tightly with lid).

5. Place a trivet in the bottom of your slow cooker. Pour boiling water in to 1″ depth. Place pudding on the trivet. Cover cooker and cook on high setting 6 hours (or steam on the stove according to directions in Notes of a Pudding Steamer, page 236). Cool pudding 10 minutes before unmolding. If pudding is not to be eaten immediately, leave in mold or wrap in brandy-soaked cloths; resteam 30 minutes to warm before serving.

6. Top with:

HARD SAUCE

½ c. butter
2 c. sifted confectioners' sugar
1 tbsp. rum or brandy—or 1 tsp. vanilla flavoring

1. Whip butter until light. Gradually add confectioners' sugar, continuing to beat until creamy. Stir in flavoring.

2. Spoon into serving dish. Chill.

⟨T⟩ Use a grinder or food processor to make bread crumbs and grind the suet. Grind meat once, freeze 10 minutes or more, grind again, and return to the freezer while preparing the other ingredients.

FANCIFUL DATE CAKE

2 c. chopped dates (about 12 oz.)	2 eggs
	1 tsp. vanilla
2 c. boiling water	2 tsp. soda
1¼ c. sugar	1 tsp. salt
½ c. butter or margarine	2¾ c. flour
	1 c. chopped nuts

1. Pour the boiling water over dates. Set aside.
2. In a large mixing bowl, combine the sugar, butter, eggs, and vanilla. Beat with an electric mixer until creamy. Sift in dry ingredients. Stir, then blend in date mixture and nuts.
3. Grease an angel food cake pan, bundt pan, or two smaller loaf or ring pans. Pour batter into prepared pans.
4. Bake cakes at 350° for one hour or until a toothpick comes out clean when poked in the center of the cake. Cool on a wire rack for 10 minutes before turning cake out of pans.

⟨P⟩ FLAMBÉ FANFARE

• Be sure the plum puddings, fruit compote, or kabobs are hot, as flames don't do well on cold or lukewarm foods.
• Use cassis, brandy, or rum to carry the flames. Don't risk failure by using too little liquor.
• Slowly warm the liquor before igniting. Never pour liquor directly from the bottle onto flames. The fire may travel upstream and cause the bottle to explode.
• You may ignite the liquor before or after adding it to the food. Although the flames usually die as the liquor burns off, avoid disaster by having the pan lid handy to extinguish wayward flames.

- Place a protective mat over your tabletop during the "fireworks."
- For best results, practice before your flaming debut!

EGGNOG SOUTHERN STYLE

Southern hospitality thrives at Christmas. Holiday specialties like pecan cakes, bourbon balls, and eggnog are often served as dessert or sweet snacks for family and guests.

As with much of Southern cooking, the recipe for eggnog is akin to recipes for beverages from many other cultures. German settlers enjoyed an *egg punch* made with milk and wine. The English were partial to *syllabub*, originally made by milking a cow directly into the serving bowl; the still warm and frothy milk was flavored with sherry and sweetened to taste. *King William's posset* was a custardy beverage with the distinctive addition of ale. Another British specialty—*Bosom Caresser*—contained sherry and brandy, with cayenne pepper, egg, sugar, and nutmeg.

This party plan is great for the first-time host as well as for anyone who is short on time during the holidays. The menu is simple and flexible, centering on a bowl of fresh and frothy holiday eggnog.

This eggnog is the real thing: egg yolks and whites are beaten separately, combined with real whipped cream, sweetened, and then flavored with vanilla or rum. Imagine the richness of this specialty as you select your accompaniments. (Avoid sharp flavors and heavy sweets that might overwhelm or conflict with the eggnog.)

Below are some possibilities for the rest of the menu. Don't offer it all: one or two of these selections will be adequate.

To determine how much food to provide, estimate the amount an "average guest" is likely to eat; serve one and a half times that amount for each guest.

Here are our menu suggestions:

A selection of *Christmas breads*, perhaps thinly sliced German stollen, small nut bread sandwiches, or a warm loaf of your favorite cinnamon bread.

Your selections may reflect Christmas customs from around the world, the best of your neighborhood bakery, or your own family specialties.

Flavored butters would be a fine addition to the breads. You may wish to offer honey, jam, or cream cheese as well.

A basket full of *hot miniature muffins or small biscuits*: put these in the oven just before the gathering and serve them warm to your eager guests. Again, offer butters, honey, jam, and/or cream cheese. You can fill cooled biscuits with thinly sliced ham and mustard sauce, or use a canapé gun to insert whipped cream.

Simple canape's: crackers, melba toast, or firm bread topped with softened cheese, butters, or other spreads. Mint jelly, pimento, parsley, and paprika make flavorful and colorful garnishes.

A tray of *holiday cookies: Brune kager*, *lebkuchen*, shortbread, and *springerle* are but a few of the delicious varieties from around the world. Thin slices of a holiday cake can also be good. (How about asking several guests to bring a dozen of their favorite light cookies?)

Whatever your choices, offer some bite-sized pieces of fresh fruits (with toothpicks for easy handling) and perhaps pretzels or roasted nuts. Guests will welcome coffee and tea after enjoying a cup or two of eggnog.

Once you've decided on your menu, refer again to the entertaining basics discussed in the beginning of this chapter. Selecting and inviting your guests, arranging your home for conversation, mingling, and assuming a festive attitude will be all-important in conveying your Christmas welcome.

⟨T⟩ Plan to have everything ready fifteen minutes before your guests arrive. Take time to relax: dispel any worries you might have about your party, and prepare to enjoy the celebration!

HOLIDAY EGGNOG

6 eggs, separated
½ c. sugar

¼ c. light rum or 2 tsp. vanilla
1 qt. half-and-half
½ to 1 c. whipping cream
nutmeg

1. In a large bowl, beat the egg yolks well with an electric mixer. Continue beating while you gradually add the sugar, beating about 10 minutes total. Slowly add the rum or vanilla.
2. Chill in a covered bowl for 1 to 24 hours. Midway through the chilling period add the half-and-half, stirring to blend.
3. Whip the cream to form soft peaks. Chill.
4. Just before serving, beat the egg whites until stiff. Use a wire whip to fold them gently into the chilled mixture.
5. Pour the eggnog into a punch bowl or individual cups. Top with whipped cream and sprinkle with nutmeg.

Makes 6 to 10 servings (just enough for an intimate evening!). For larger gatherings, make several batches, taking care not to overfill your mixing bowl. A gallon jar or bowl will hold a double batch.

⟨P⟩ You'll get the greatest volume from your beaten egg whites by having the eggs at room temperature. Be sure there is no trace of yolk in with the whites and that the bowl, beaters, and scrapers are absolutely spotless. And use a china or metal bowl—not plastic!

FLAVORED BUTTERS

Soften ½ c. (1 stick) butter or margarine (or some of each). Add your choice of the combinations below, mixing to blend well. Let stand at room temperature for two hours to blend flavors.

Lightly Cheesy
  3 oz. cream cheese,
    softened
  1 tsp. prepared mustard
  1 tbsp. grated Parmesan
    cheese

Honey Spice
  ¼ c. honey
  ½ tsp. cinnamon
  ⅛ tsp. allspice

Orange and Maple
  ½ tsp. finely grated fresh orange rind
  2 tbsp. maple syrup

Spicy Peanut
  ¼ c. peanut butter
  ½ tsp. garlic salt
  1 tsp. lemon juice

Herb
  1 tsp. dill, basil, or
    tarragon
  ½ tsp. lemon juice
  ⅛ tsp. white pepper

Expecting the Unexpected

Christmas visitors often come unannounced. Out-of-town travelers or friends you "bump into" while shopping can suddenly change your meal plans. A little foresight and a good attitude can help prepare you for impromptu celebrations and last-minute meals.

1. Plan not to panic! With creativity, confidence, and a sense of humor, you can graciously adapt your plans and skirt any calamity.

2. Try to always keep some emergency rations on hand for each course. You might use the supplies listed below as substitutions or extenders, or to create a last-minute meal.

Beverages: frozen orange juice, other canned or frozen juices; ginger ale, club soda, and colas; a bottle of chablis, rosé, burgundy; coffee, teas, cocoa.

Appetizers and snacks: plain crackers, some cheeses, peanut butter, hard-cooked eggs, olives, pickles, fresh fruit and crispy vegetables, popcorn, pretzels, nuts.

Salads: fresh or canned fruits or vegetables; lettuce or other fresh salad greens; dressing ingredients (mayonnaise, Italian dressing, cottage cheese, yogurt plus herbs, mustards, vinegars).

Breads: frozen French bread (slice horizontally or vertically for poor-boy sandwiches, garlic-and-herb bread, or crusty bread sticks); biscuit mix; a favorite muffin recipe with all ingredients on hand.

Entrees: frozen round steak or boneless chicken breasts (thawed twenty minutes in cold water, these will slice thinly for Stroganoff or stir-frying); spaghetti sauce (serve on pasta or pizza dough, use to stretch chili, or add to ground meat for sloppy joes); a canned ham, frozen fish fillets, or frankfurters; the makings for a favorite soup, casserole . . . or how about eggs and cheese for omelets?

Accompaniments: rice, noodles, and pasta; canned and frozen vegetables; fresh parsley and lemon; broth (canned or frozen); cream soups.

Dessert: frozen nut breads, cookies, cream puffs; ice cream or sherbet; fresh, canned, or frozen fruits (maybe a flaming dessert?).

And paper napkins and plates, candles, recorded holiday music . . .

Brunch: The In-Between Meal

A brunch offers a unique opportunity to entertain with a casual elegance that provides a natural setting for fellowship. Neither breakfast nor lunch, formal nor ordinary, rigid nor unplanned, brunch has a personality of its own.

The menu for a brunch can be more varied than for most meals. Since this might be the *first* meal of the day for some guests and the *main* meal for others, build a menu that is a hearty or elaborate version of breakfast. As you plan, remember what *you* most enjoy preparing, serving, and eating for brunch.

Provide a selection of foods that are attractive and perhaps a bit exotic (kiwi fruit, potato pancakes, shrimp creole . . .). The flavors, textures, and appearance should be contrasting but not conflicting.

Include some variations of typical breakfast foods: quiche, sausage, soufflés, waffles, scrambled eggs, coffee cake.

Serve a number of fresh fruits and vegetables, to complement the heartier fare and to add a fresh and colorful touch to the menu. Create fruit platters, relish trays, salads, compotes, juices, and garnishes.

Offer a choice of beverages, ideally something from each of these groups.

- fruit and vegetable juices
- champagne, sparkling cider, wine, or punch
- coffee, tea, or cocoa
- ice water

Have the beverages available throughout the brunch.

THE JUBILEE BRUNCH

Come, Jesus, glorious heavenly guest,
Keep Thine own Christmas in our breast;
Then David's harpstring, hushed so long,
Shall swell our jubilee of song.
    —"The Happy Christmas Comes Once More"
    Danish carol

The word *jubilee* draws its meaning from an Old Testament celebration: a year of jubilee came every fifty years as a time of legal and personal emancipation and restoration. Today jubilee means a time of rejoicing and is often an occasion for renewing friendships.

The Jubilee Brunch is designed as a celebration. You may have a specific event in mind—Christmas Day, a baptism, a homecoming, or a birthday—or simply some time spent with good friends. Most of the do-ahead menu is served chilled, so it is perfect for serving guests after an event. The menu is easily adapted; you could:

—initiate a potluck meal by asking guests to bring an appetizer, bread, or salad;

—make the meal more formal by serving a hot entree (perhaps a souffle);

—or pack it up and have a Jubilee picnic.

Whatever your chosen format, let your guests enjoy a cup of the sparkling punch while you extend your welcome and add the finishing touches to the meal. Then invite everyone to the buffet table. The grand finale dessert will make an exciting conclusion to the meal.

Menu
⟨*⟩ Jubilee Punch
Baked ham (hot or cold)
⟨*⟩ Deviled Egg Variations   Cheese cubes on pretzels
⟨*⟩ Spinach and Mushroom Salad   Fruit tray
⟨*⟩ Quick Cheddar Loaf   Warm dinner rolls or biscuits
Coffee, tea, milk
⟨*⟩ Cherries Jubilee

JUBILEE PUNCH

Two 10-oz. packages frozen raspberries
½ c. sugar
12-oz. can frozen lemonade concentrate
12-oz. can frozen orange juice concentrate
46-oz. can pineapple juice
26-oz. bottle club soda OR 1 bottle white champagne

1. 12 hours before serving, combine berries and sugar. Refrigerate.
2. Just before serving, press berries through a strainer. Discard seeds. Combine berry juice with other juices.
3. Add soda or champagne at the last moment. Keep cold with an ice block.
Makes about 14 cups.
⟨T⟩ Crepe paper makes a colorful throwaway tablecloth. Crisscross white streamers over a red background, or overlap several large sheets of red and pink paper for a geometric look.

A clear plastic table cover will keep this looking nice for the duration of the party.

DEVILED EGG VARIATIONS

• Decorate with black or stuffed olive slices, minced green onion, parsley, pimento, shrimp.
• Spice up the filling with chili powder, curry, Tabasco.
• Add ground nuts or grated cheese.
• Pipe filling into eggs with a canapé gun.
• Pack well-chilled deviled eggs for a picnic by setting them on top of crumpled waxed paper, or placing two filled halves "gooey sides" together.

SPINACH AND MUSHROOM SALAD

⅓ c. lemon juice
½ c. olive oil or
   salad oil
1 tsp. dried tarragon,
   crumbled
¼ tsp. each dry
   mustard, garlic
   salt, and pepper
2 c. thinly sliced celery

1½ lb. fresh mushrooms
2 tbsp. Parmesan cheese
1 bunch fresh spinach
1 head leafy lettuce
2 large or 3 small
   tomatoes, cut in
   wedges
1 or 2 avocados, sliced

1. The night before serving, mix lemon juice, oil, tarragon, mustard, salt, and pepper in a screw-top jar. Refrigerate. Slice celery. Refrigerate in tightly closed container.

2. Two to six hours before serving, slice mushrooms. Add with Parmesan cheese and dressing to celery. Mix gently, cover, and return to refrigerator.

3. Wash greens. Tear into bite-sized pieces. Refrigerate in a plastic bag or in a bowl covered with damp paper towels.

4. Just before serving, place greens in salad bowl. Drain mushrooms and celery, reserving marinade. Place mushroom mixture in center of greens. Arrange tomato and avocado in bowl. Pour dressing over salad.

Serves 12 to 15 generously.

QUICK CHEDDAR LOAF

2 c. flour
1½ tsp. baking powder
½ tsp. baking soda
1 tsp. salt
1 c. grated cheddar
   cheese

1 c. buttermilk
¼ c. oil
2 eggs
2 tbsp. honey

1. Combine cheese with dry ingredients in a large bowl. Set aside.
2. Beat remaining ingredients with electric mixer until blended. Add to cheese mixture and stir just until combined.
3. Pour into a greased 9″ × 5″ × 3″ loaf pan. Bake at 375° 50 to 55 minutes or until done. Cool in pan ten minutes, then remove loaf from pan and cool on a wire rack.

⟨P⟩ Breads made without yeast are usually easier to slice if made one day before slicing.

CHERRIES JUBILEE

1 quart canned pitted dark, sweet cherries
2 tbsp. cornstarch
¼ c. red currant jelly (or other jelly)
¼ c. brandy, kirsch, or cherry brandy
ice cream

1. Drain cherries, reserving juice. Measure juice, adding water to make 2 cups. Stir in cornstarch.
2. Place juice mixture in saucepan with jelly. Bring to a boil, stirring constantly. Simmer one minute or more. Add cherries and heat through.
3. Heat brandy. Ignite and pour over cherry mixture (see Flambé Fanfare, page 238).

⟨T⟩ Scoop ice cream into balls on a cookie sheet—or directly into individual bowls on a tray. Place in freezer until serving time.

A BIRTHDAY PARTY

Sometimes we forget that Christmas is a month-long birthday celebration. The guest of honor may be unseen, but his presence is assured at all our Christmas celebrations.

Invite friends of all ages to a birthday party for Jesus. The plan is childish (remember how he loved children!), with simple activities that make the wonder of the Christmas story come alive. "For it is good to be children sometimes, and never better than at Christmas, when its mighty Founder was a child himself." (Charles Dickens, *A Christmas Carol*)

In the invitations, ask guests to bring a gift for a shut-in, a foster child, or someone in the hospital. Specify whom the gifts will be for—age, sex, living situation—and a price range. The gifts may be placed under the Christmas tree as guests arrive.

Plan some activities to welcome your guests and share the party spirit.

Assemble brightly colored paper, glue, tape, and scissors on a table. Instruct guests to make a party crown to wear in honor of the King of Kings.

Give younger guests time for free play—a chance to check out the toy box and playroom. Watch for children who are uninterested or too bashful to keep busy. If arguments break out, entice some of the children into other play or steer everyone toward a more structured activity.

Work together to make a "Happy Birthday, Jesus" banner, with guests drawing a picture of what they would most like to give Jesus for his birthday. Use one long piece of butcher paper (approximately three by eight feet) or have guests work individually on smaller sheets of paper which are later strung together to form one long banner.

A favorite Russian game at Christmas is "Burial of the Gold." One player stands in the center of a circle made up of the others. A gold ring is passed from hand to hand around the circle as the center player tries to detect who has it.

In Spain, a merry occasion is made out of drawing messages from the "Urn of Fate." Friends gather at Christmas to learn, from the slips of paper, who fate has ordained shall be lovers and friends during the coming year. Adapt this tradition for your birthday celebration:

After the party seems to be moving along well, have everyone sit down together. Read a modern translation or paraphrase of the Christmas Story (Luke 2:4–20). Put the names of the main characters (Joseph, Mary, Angel, Angel Chorus, Shepherds) in your "Urn of Fate," one slip per person. Guests draw names to cast the dramatization of the Nativity. Give actors a few minutes (and some guidance) to prepare—then act out the story together.

Share a simple party meal.

Menu
⟨*⟩ Sandwich Cut-Outs
Fruit Kabobs (chunks of fresh fruit speared on toothpicks)
Hot Cider or Cocoa

SANDWICH CUT-OUTS

2 slices of bread per person
2 or more soft sandwich spreads:
    peanut butter and honey
    softened cheese (cream cheese-based or purchased spreads)
    egg salad, tuna, or other favorites
Decorations:
    banana or apple slices
    grated cheese
    chopped nuts, olives, parsley, tomato, chiles
    raisins, bacon bits, sprouts, lettuce
Cookie cutters:
    trees, snowmen, gingerbread characters, stars, hearts

1. Arrange all ingredients on a large table, with knives for spreading, plates, napkins, and a washrag. You may wish to cut crusts from bread slices, reserving scraps for bread crumbs,

croutons, or feeding the birds (another great project for the kids!).

2. Explain the procedure to your guests: each is to design a sandwich—open-faced or closed—using the ingredients you've set out. (Preschoolers may need some assistance.) Set a time limit of ten minutes, then award prizes for the most original, most artistic, most colorful, most seasonal. Have a prize for everyone.

3. When the sandwich spreading is completed (and everyone has admired the artistry), seat your guests and serve the kabobs and beverages. Leave the sandwich makings out for hungry artists who want a second helping.

4. After all have eaten, start some background music on the piano, guitar, or record player, and lead some carols. Record the songfest for your own enjoyment or for sharing with parents, grandparents, or shut-ins.

> Companions all sing loudly
>   In praise of Mary dear,
> Look up and bear each proudly,
>   The day of days is near.
>
> —traditional Spanish carol

Custom Inspection: Christmas Eve in Brazil

Brazilians celebrate Christmas Eve at their midnight *Missa de Galo*, or mass of the rooster. After worship, families return home for the *Ceia*, a traditional feast shared in the early hours of Christmas Day.

The Ceia menu often includes turkey stuffed with *farofa*—a mixture of farina, vegetables, and boiled eggs. Preparations for the meal begin a day or two earlier, when the turkey is put in the marinade and the stuffing is prepared and chilled. The Ceia's make-ahead format can be easily adapted for holiday meals.

THE BRAZILIAN CEIA

This two-part party plan centers around an evening out—maybe a concert, a Christmas pageant, or a caroling procession. Your guests gather for punch and light refreshments before departing together. A few hours later, everyone returns to the ready-to-serve Ceia.

Brazilian Ceia for Ten and Twelve
⟨*⟩ Brazilian Party Punch
⟨*⟩ Toast in Port   ⟨*⟩ Spicy Tomato Soup
⟨*⟩ Peru à Brasiliera (Roast Turkey, Brazilian Style)
Green Beans with Lemon
Punch, Juice, Wine.

Orange Sherbet
Coffee and Tea

⟨P⟩ For an enchanting flavor, break a stick of cinnamon into the ground coffee before brewing.

The roasting time you allot to the turkey should be based on your latest possible return time. Check the bird as soon as you get home; let it stand at least fifteen minutes before carving.

Fearing grease fires, electrical problems, or other disasters, some people are wary of leaving home while food is cooking. If you share these concerns, arrange for someone to stay home during the outing.

If this is impossible, you can roast the turkey, unstuffed, early in the day. Carve it, placing the slices on an oven-proof serving platter. Cover and refrigerate until just before the meal, when it can be reheated at 300° for fifteen minutes. The stuffing will need to be baked in a casserole dish for one hour (use the automatic timer on your oven) or heated in a microwave oven when you return.

If you plan to be gone two hours or less, you may leave the roasted turkey in the oven. Be sure the oven is off with the oven door slightly open. Return promptly and eat immediately. There's a risk of food poisoning if the turkey is left at room temperature more than two hours, so refrigerate leftovers promptly.

For a three-hour outing, time the roasting process so your departure is thirty to ninety minutes *before* the turkey is done. Turn the oven off as you leave; it will slowly cool, ideally allowing the turkey just enough time to finish cooking. *This is risky*: your entree may be slightly undercooked *or* too dry when you are ready to eat. Know your oven's rate of cooling and your time of return if you settle for this option.

Here is your timetable for preparing the food.

3 days ahead:

If the turkey is frozen, place it in the refrigerator to thaw. Check over the recipes. Do the necessary shopping.

18 to 36 hours ahead:

For the stuffings and marinade:
    chop 1½ c. onion and ½ c. celery
    mince 1 c. parsley
    grate ½ c. carrot.
Marinate and chill turkey.
Chill other ingredients until needed.

5 to 24 hours ahead:

Cook giblets and rice. Prepare farofa and bread dressing; refrigerate.

5 hours ahead:

Prepare and roast turkey.

2 to 24 hours ahead:

Prepare punch and garnishes. (Wash and cut lemon and parsley. Whip cream; refrigerate in a covered dish, or drop dollops on waxed paper and freeze overnight.)

1 to 2 hours before guests arrive:

For each guest, wrap a knife, fork, and spoon in a napkin. Place in a basket to set on the Ceia table.

Place water glasses and wineglasses on a tray. Set aside.

Lay out serving dishes and utensils.

Scoop balls of sherbet into individual dessert dishes or into a chilled serving bowl. Freeze.

Place coffee cups, spoons, creamer, and sugar on a tray (with dessert dishes if needed).

45 minutes before guests arrive:

Finish making punch.

Fill a pitcher with ice water for dinner. Refrigerate.

Set punch cups and napkins on a serving table or tray.

Make Toast in Port.

Tidy up kitchen.

15 minutes before guests arrive:

Cook rice.

Turn on porch light, and relax.

When guests arrive:

Place warm Toast in Port on platter. Serve with punch.

Just before leaving for the outing:

Gather up punch cups, napkins, and so forth. Put them in the dishwasher if you have time—or store them out of the way.

Pour leftover punch in a storage container and refrigerate.

Put snacks away and brush crumbs from the table.

When you return:

Prepare and serve soup.

Reheat/carve the turkey, enlisting help if needed.

Put stuffing in a shallow dish, cover with foil, and keep warm in the oven.

Complete meal preparations:

Cook beans.

Set plates, napkins, and basket of silverware on buffet table.

Dish up and garnish turkey, stuffings, beans, rice.

Call guests—offer beverages—say grace—eat!

BRAZILIAN PARTY PUNCH

2 lemons, 2 oranges, and 1 pineapple (or other fresh fruit)
⅓ c. sugar
3 liters rosé
two 12-oz. bottles ginger ale, chilled

1. Use a sharp paring knife to remove peel from lemons and oranges. Reserve orange peel. Cut fruit into ¼″ cartwheels.
2. Cut peel from pineapple. Quarter fruit lengthwise. Discard core and peel. Cut fruit into thin slices. Place in a punch bowl or large jar with lemon and orange.
3. Sprinkle fruit with sugar. Let stand 20 minutes.
4. Add wine and orange peel. Refrigerate at least 2 hours to "ripen."
5. Add ginger ale and ice just before serving. Replenish punch bowl with more juice, wine, and ginger ale if needed.

Makes about twenty 5-oz. servings.

TOAST IN PORT

(As strange as this sounds, it is delicious! It's quick and inexpensive, too!)

8 slices firm-textured white bread
¾ c. port
melted butter or margarine
cinnamon-sugar

1. Cut bread diagonally into quarters. Place on an ungreased cookie sheet and bake at 400° for about 10 minutes, until bread just starts to brown.
2. Generously butter a cookie sheet. Pour wine into a shallow dish. Dip both sides of bread into wine, then place on prepared pan. Brush with melted butter.
3. Bake at 400° for 10 minutes. Turn with pancake turner, sprinkle with cinnamon-sugar, and bake 10 minutes longer. Serve warm.

Makes 32 small appetizers.

Make a double or triple batch for your Ceia guests—or offer other breads and crackers as well.

SPICY TOMATO SOUP

four 10-oz. cans condensed tomato soup	2½ c. water ½ tsp. chili powder ⅛ tsp. black pepper
3 c. tomato juice	unsweetened whipped cream
2½ c. milk	

1. Combine all ingredients except whipped cream in a large soup pot. Stir over medium heat until hot but not boiling.
2. Ladle into mugs or bowls and top with dollops of unsweetened whipped cream.

Serves 12.

Make place cards for your Ceia guests by writing their names in red or silver on a clean holly leaf.

ROAST TURKEY, BRAZILIAN STYLE (PERU À BRASILIERA)

With contrasting textures and flavors, both farofa and bread dressings are distinctive side dishes that your guests are sure to enjoy. For a smaller dinner party, you may prefer to prepare just one of these two stuffings. Either recipe will make enough to stuff a 12-pound bird.

One 12-lb. turkey with giblets, thawed if frozen
Marinade:

3 cloves garlic, minced	½ c. coarsely grated carrot
¼ tsp. black pepper	
½ tsp. salt	½ c. chopped parsley
½ tsp. cloves	2 c. white vinegar
½ c. chopped celery	1 c. lemon juice
½ c. chopped onion	2 tbsp. oil

1. One day before cooking, remove the giblets from the turkey. Set aside. Rinse turkey and pat dry with paper towels.

2. Combine all marinade ingredients except oil (used in step 8). Place turkey breast-side down in a nonaluminum pan at least 3" deep. Pour marinade over turkey. Cover with plastic wrap and chill 12 to 30 hours, turning turkey over twice (or marinate in a large, tightly sealed cooking bag).

3. Cook giblets in lightly salted water until tender. Strain and refrigerate stock. Chop giblets and chill in covered dish.

4. Make *farofa* early on serving day (or one day in advance), chilling until needed:

Farofa

¼ c. margarine
½ c. chopped onion
¼ c. chopped parsley
1 c. peeled chopped tomato
half of the chopped giblets
¼ to 1 tsp. chili powder

¼ tsp. cumin
2 c. farina
   (cream of wheat)
   or cooked rice
½ c. sliced green olives
3 hard-boiled eggs

5. In a large skillet, sauté onion and parsley in 2 tbsp. margarine until onion is soft. Add tomato, giblets and remaining margarine. Mix to blend, then add seasonings and farina or rice. Stir constantly over medium heat for 5 minutes to combine flavors and heat through. Gently blend in olives and eggs. Taste and season if necessary. Chill while preparing bread dressing:

Bread Dressing

6 c. torn-up bread
¾ c. milk
3 strips bacon, cut up
½ c. chopped onion
¼ c. minced parsley

1 c. giblet broth
half the chopped giblets
½ tsp. salt
⅛ tsp. pepper

6. Pour milk over bread. Set aside while preparing other ingredients.

7. Sauté bacon, onion, and parsley over medium heat until onion is soft and bacon crisp. Add broth and bring to a boil.

Use a fork to mix in giblets, bread mixture, salt, and pepper. Refrigerate 30 minutes, or up to 12 hours.

8. Drain marinade from turkey. Strain into a saucepan. Add 2 tbsp. oil and heat to boiling. Cover and simmer 15 minutes.

9. Loosely stuff breast cavity with bread dressing, and neck cavity with farofa. Do not pack. Put unused stuffing in greased casserole dishes. Cover and refrigerate. (Serve as a side dish or with leftovers. Bake at 325° for one hour.)

10. Close and truss turkey. Baste with melted margarine. Roast at 325° until tender—about 4 hours for a 12-lb. turkey. Baste with heated marinade every hour or so.

11. After roasting, let turkey stand at room temperature 15 to 45 minutes. Remove stuffings and carve. Refrigerate leftovers promptly.

The Essentials for Any Sit-Down Meal:

• A neat, attractive, and comfortable table.
• A centerpiece that seated diners can see over.
• Salt, pepper, and all other necessary condiments placed within reach (one set per six to eight diners).
• A host who spends minimal time away from the other diners.
• Some special touches—
   —ice water
   —place cards
   —candles
   —the menu, written on a small card and placed on or near the table

MIDDAY DINING

A luncheon is an ideal way to entertain a few friends in a limited period of time. Freeing the majority of the day for other activities, these noontime gatherings are especially appreciated by busy holiday hosts and guests. The pace of the meal should be neither leisurely nor hurried, but smooth and welcoming.

To be able to greet, serve, and visit with your guests in two hours or less, you will need to make manageable plans. Do as much as possible before your guests arrive so just the last-minute touches are needed at mealtime.

Lunch is often considered a chance to cut calories, but your digestive processes are actually better able to handle rich or spicy foods midday than at the dinner hour. Whether plain or fancy, hearty or low-calorie, the main dish should be accompanied with a salad or light side dish, and followed with fruit or another light dessert.

The menu for this pasta luncheon is fairly simple to prepare and a pleasure to serve. The fresh flavors of the seafood salad make a perfect contrast to the rich and mellow pasta. Slightly spiced pears make a light do-ahead dessert.

Menu
⟨*⟩ Shrimp and Avocado Salad
⟨*⟩ Spaghetti Carbonara
Bread sticks
⟨*⟩ Caramelized Pears Almondine
Beverages of choice

SHRIMP AND AVOCADO SALAD

leafy greens, washed and drained well
1 large or 2 small ripe avocados
1 orange and/or tomato, sliced or cut in wedges
1 can (5 oz.) baby shrimp, drained

Dressing:

⅓ c. tarragon or cider vinegar	⅛ tsp. pepper
	⅛ tsp. paprika
½ c. honey	½ tsp. basil
¼ tsp. dry mustard	½ tsp. marjoram
1 tsp. garlic salt	1 c. salad oil

1. In a blender jar, combine all dressing ingredients ex-

cept oil. Keep the blender running and add oil in a slow stream. Blend 1 minute. (Or combine ingredients in a quart jar, cover tightly, and shake for 2 minutes.) Refrigerate.

2. Arrange greens on salad plates. Peel and slice avocado. Arrange with orange and/or tomato on top of greens. Sprinkle with shrimp.

3. Shake dressing well. Pour into a small pitcher for diners to add—or pour over salads just before serving.

Serves 6.

SPAGHETTI CARBONARA

1 tsp. salt
1 tbsp. oil
8 oz. pasta (spaghetti, fettucini, or other)
2 eggs, beaten well
½ c. Parmesan cheese (preferably freshly grated)
freshly ground pepper
4 strips of bacon, fried crisp and crumbled OR ½ c. chopped
    ham (optional)
2 tbsp. minced fresh parsley

1. Place an oven-proof serving bowl in a 200° oven. Turn off oven.

2. Bring a large kettle of water to a boil. Add salt and oil, then pasta. Cook, uncovered, 5 to 15 minutes until pasta is soft to bite, not mushy. Drain well.

3. Put pasta in the heated bowl. Immediately stir in eggs, using 2 forks or chopsticks to "toss" pasta and eggs. The egg will cook almost immediately.

4. Sprinkle with cheese, pepper, bacon, and parsley. Toss lightly.

5. Serve immediately, using two forks to lift pasta onto plates.

Serves 4 to 6.

⟨T⟩ For luncheon entertaining, place empty bowl in the oven and boil the water before guests arrive. Add pasta after welcoming everyone. Toss the pasta at the table as guests enjoy their salads.

CARAMELIZED PEARS ALMONDINE

6 pear halves, canned or fresh (Fresh pears should be peeled
     and cored, then sprinkled with lemon juice.)
⅓ c. slivered almonds
1 tbsp. margarine
⅓ c. granulated sugar
sweetened whipped cream, optional

1. Place well-drained pear halves cut sides down in individual dessert dishes. Set aside.

2. Melt margarine in a small skillet or saucepan. Add sugar
and stir constantly over medium heat until mixture turns light
brown. Immediately pour over pears and sprinkle with slivered almonds.

3. Serve at room temperature, topped with whipped
cream if desired.
     Serves 6.

Family Ties

It's hard to believe how fast the years go by—especially the
years of raising children. As the children grow, their interests
and abilities change, as do family activities. Those excursions,
projects, and activities that are shared by a family often become cherished memories and may be building blocks for traditions of future generations.

Entertaining can be a delightful family activity. The Scandinavian *Julbörd* (page 275) includes plans that all family members may enjoy. A "just us" celebration can be held anytime:
maybe a formal dinner with candles and crystal, a bountiful
picnic, a festive meal from another culture.

Most of the menus in this book can be used for just such
special occasions. You might ask each family member to be
in charge of one Christmas-season meal. This person need not
do all the work alone, but can create the menu and organize
preparations.

Do some research to learn how your ancestors—even your

parents—celebrated Christmas. Ask for menus and recipes and incorporate these traditions (or adaptations thereof) into your own holiday meals.

Some chaotic evenings can be turned into spontaneous celebrations by having a no-cook supper (perhaps fresh fruit and cheeses, take-out food, or leftovers) in front of the fireplace. Sing a carol or tell a story.

Have a fondue party around the family dinner table. Tradition dictates that anyone dropping bread or meat into the fondue pot must forfeit a kiss!

Here are some ideas for family entertaining.

• Have a Christmas potlatch. Ask families to prepare a Christmas recipe that is part of their ethnic tradition. As host, you may want to coordinate the meal by asking what each family plans to bring; round out the meal with your own favorites. Decorations, music, games, and activities can come from the traditions of your guests.

• Have a dollar dinner, caroling party, or one of the other "going places" parties described on page 216.

• Enjoy the tradition of visiting that marks the Feast of St. John the Evangelist (December 27 on the Christmas calendar, beginning on page 198). Invite several families over for some post-Christmas fun. Help your children set out some new toys to share (assist them in deciding if some need to be put away for the duration of the party), and plan activities for everyone to enjoy.

• Plan to put out the welcome mat after the school Christmas concert or church pageant. Make the arrangements as a family: each child might invite the families of some friends and a teacher or other favorite adult.

> With faces gleaming, and happy laughter,
>   The children gather 'round the tree.
> To them the tree speaks of the Savior,
>   And thro' their eyes we heaven see.
> —"'Tis the Eve of Christmas"
> German carol

Stretching Resources

". . . our Diner concisted of pore Elk, so much spoiled that we eate it thro' near necessity, some spoiled pounded fish and a few roots."

Captain William Clark thus described his 1805 Christmas dinner.[4] Modern entertaining efforts pale in comparison to the work required to create a festive meal from foods available to those exploring the Far West in the eighteenth and nineteenth centuries. Mule, venison, buffalo, and rabbit (dried, stewed, or boiled) were served with whatever accompaniments could be found. For a Christmas party in Utah in 1840, the featured dessert was "boiled flour pudding prepared with dried fruit accompanied by four quarts of sauce made of the juice of sour berries and sugar."[5]

Making the most of what is at hand is always a key to hospitality. Your resources have their limits—but if spoiled meat and boiled flour pudding can be made a feast, anything is possible!

PINCHING PENNIES

Finances may seem to be an obstacle to entertaining. But if you carefully think through the options, plan wisely, and work resourcefully, you can look forward to entertaining without compromising yourself or your budget.

A major cost of entertaining is the food and drink. Serving a full meal is more expensive than serving snacks or dessert. $ Whether you serve light refreshments or a full meal, choose your menu carefully. $ Don't attempt new recipes or unusual menus that may not be successful. $ Always purchase the best you can afford: in-season produce and current bargains will

[4] John E. Baur, *Christmas on the American Frontier 1800–1900* (Caldwell, Idaho: The Caxton Printers, 1961), p. 78.
[5] Ibid. p. 106.

give you more for your money and are worth planning around. $ Don't limit your menu to meat and potatoes (or turkey and stuffing). Build your meal around casseroles, grains, vegetables, cheeses, and eggs instead of roasts or steaks. $ Stretch small portions of an expensive entree by serving an additional course in the meal. A flavorful soup, a simple pasta dish, or a plate of fruit and cheese are classy first-course selections that take minimal work. $ Serve a punch instead of soft drinks, champagne, or other beverages. Always offer ice water, perhaps with a thin slice of lemon or a mint leaf. $ Don't be stingy. Plan carefully but always have enough food to offer your guests.

> It is not the basic cost of the food but the care with which it is selected and prepared that makes it gourmet rather than pedestrian.
> —James Beard
> *How to Eat Better for Less Money*

Party decorations may also strain your budget. Here are some quick and low-cost ways to create a festive atmosphere.

• Concentrate on mood enhancers: a fire in the fireplace, carols playing on the stereo, lighted candles, the scent of pine. (Try a pine-scented candle, or boiling a pine branch, page 168.)

• Display family favorites: ornaments hanging on the tree or arranged among greens, a small ornament at each place setting at the table for a sit-down dinner, a book of carols on the piano, jingle bells tied to doorknobs.

• Use children's decorations: chains cut from construction paper, cotton ball snowmen, and other holiday artwork.

• Arrange an edible centerpiece using grapes, tangerines, small apples, cheeses, shaped breads, nuts, and so forth. Don't make it too formal if you want guests to sample it.

• Display your Christmas cards.

• Wrap gifts (or empty boxes) and display them under the tree. You might want to give a small gift to your guests as they leave.

• Decorate your table with *Julgranskaramell*—festively wrapped gift tubes filled with small surprises for your guests. Make one for each guest, enclosing nuts, candies, toys, stickers, and a miniature note card with a special holiday greeting.

You have many options for cutting costs at each stage of planning. Invitations may be by telephone, postcard, engraved note, or telegram. Activities may be conversation, meal preparation, rented movies, or a string quartet comprised of your guests. Keep your budget in mind as you evaluate the options, and be creative in making your dollars go far.

Lack of funds is a poor excuse for not entertaining. Your friends will appreciate the warmth of your welcome and your contagious enthusiasm for Christmas more than the finest food, drink, and decor imaginable. Your careful planning of a simple, elegant celebration will result in an event deserving of fond memories.

CREATING COLD STORAGE

Holiday dinners, entertaining, and vacations from work and school put stress on any refrigerator. With ingenuity and planning, you can expand your cold storage space for special events.

1. First, clear your refrigerator of everything you will not need immediately: horseradish, yogurt, bologna . . . Items not needing constant refrigeration (catsup, unopened soft drinks, pickles, produce) may be stored in a cardboard box for a few hours. Be sure to place it where it won't freeze, get wet, or be discovered by pets, insects, or rodents.

2. Put perishables (dairy products, eggs, leftovers) in an ice chest with plenty of ice. Store it out of sight.

3. Fill an ice chest, dishpan, laundry sink, even a wheelbarrow, with ice and add individual containers of the beverages you plan to serve. Keep this in the kitchen (or out of sight) for your own convenience, or with the other refreshments, where it's available for your guests' self-service.

WORKING TOGETHER

During the rugged and unpredictable days of the gold rush, festive meals often required creative cooperation. One group of gold seekers pooled resources for a meal that included the loin of a grizzly bear, six bottles of wine, and two pounds of raisins. Their festive spirits and cooperative efforts made it a celebration.

> . . . each member of the mess undertaking that portion of the preparation he was best prepared to deal with; one agreeing to bake, another to roast the venison, another to boil the bacon, one gentleman taking in charge the manufacture of short and sweet bread, a second choosing for his department the pies, made from preserved apples . . .
> —John E. Bauer
> *Christmas on the American Frontier 1800–1900*

Creative cooperation can take many shapes. You may not wish to do it like the gold seekers, but asking your guests to contribute something will give them an opportunity to invest their own resources in the celebration.

    • Hors d'oeuvres, rolls, salads, and desserts are easy-to-transport basics in any meal. Asking guests to bring accompaniments can free you for preparing the rest of the meal and party. The Scandinavian *Julbörd* (beginning on page 275) is an example.

    • Consider the meal you could host if you had several chefs working together. Wouldn't *that* be the Ultimate Potluck!

For best results when planning a potluck:

1. Make up a master menu that will provide a general or specific outline for the meal:

    • A feast of family favorites (ask guests to bring an

entree, salad, and/or dessert that is traditionally featured at their family's holiday meals).
- A red and green dinner (see the list of possibilities on page 232).
- A Seafood Buffet, Mexican Brunch, or Pennsylvania Dutch Christmas Dinner (see page 267 for the menu for this one).

2. Be gracious as you communicate your expectations to your guests. Avoid a hodgepodge meal by being specific about:

- The theme for the meal (Pennsylvania Dutch dinner).
- What you would like them to bring (mince pie).
- How much you would like them to bring (How many guests will there be? Will there be other desserts?).
- What else you'll be serving (roast goose and accompaniments).

3. Prepare to "cover the basics." Have garnishes, serving dishes, utensils, and backup supplies ready in case some part of the meal doesn't arrive as planned.

- Try a progressive dinner. Several people cohost the meal, with each course served at a different home. The Posada Procession on page 284 is based on this idea.
- Make a pot of "stone soup." Ask each guest to provide a vegetable for the soup pot, fruit for the compote, or cake for the dessert tray.

There's an old story about a clever but hungry woman who invited a few friends over for some homemade soup. "I've everything I need," she told each guest, "except . . ." Potatoes, beans, chicken, bread—everybody was told something different.

The woman placed one well-washed stone and plenty of water in her soup kettle. As the guests arrived, their contributions were added: two potatoes, half pound of beans, a chicken, and so on. The aroma soon reached neighbors and passersby, many of whom joined the festivities. And no one went away hungry!

Custom Inspection: The Pennsylvania Dutch

The Pennsylvania Dutch tradition of living off the land has changed little with the passing of time. Christmas involves a meshing of superstition, family gaiety, religious observances, and community events that involve all ages.

Christmas Eve marks the arrival of Belsnickel and Santa Claus, and a special midafternoon "lovefeast" held for children at the local church. Candles burn to commemorate the coming of the "Light of the World."

For the Pennsylvania Dutch, Christmas Day is a bad time to bathe, to take on a job, even to change your underwear. It's a great day to gather for the memorable worship services and then return home for a festive meal.

In the years when Christmas was strictly a religious holiday, the day after Christmas was a day just for pleasure. Many Pennsylvania Dutch folks still enjoy spending the day in the city or at home, participating in outdoor activities. A "second Christmas dinner" may rival that served the day before, as cooks prepare a new round of favorites to add to the abundant leftovers.

The strong similarity between Pennsylvania Dutch and German cultures is more than incidental. The *Deutsch* in Pennsylvania *Dutch* means "folk" and "German," two appropriate descriptions of these people from the heart of Europe.

A PENNSYLVANIA DUTCH CHRISTMAS DINNER

This version of the Pennsylvania Dutch Christmas meal is based on foods native to German and Lancaster County cuisine. Both pork and goose are favorites, but the meal's many side dishes make it bountiful even without a meat course.

Typical of all Pennsylvania Dutch meals are a number of "sweets-and-sours": preserves, jellies, and cakes, and a colorful variety of pickles and relishes. The entire table is filled with these accompaniments at a feast. Add your own touches to this meal by including your favorites: perhaps a recipe that your family has enjoyed for generations, or some selections from the delicatessen.

Menu
⟨*⟩ Roast Goose or ⟨*⟩ Pork with Apples and Onions
⟨*⟩ Potato Filling
⟨*⟩ Purple Cabbage   Hot buttered corn
⟨*⟩ Pepper Relish
⟨*⟩ Pickled Red-Beet Eggs
Fresh bread
Butter, apple butter, jellies, and jams
Cider and water

Mincemeat Pie and Coffee

Custom Inspection: The German Christmas Meal

German children's search for hidden gifts precedes a festive dinner on Christmas Day (see page 96). Roast duck is often served, but goose, pork, chicken, and beef may be a family's traditional favorites.

Whatever the main course, the accompaniments are sure to include apples, reminders of the tree of knowledge, and nuts, symbols of life's mysteries and difficulties. "God gives the nuts, but man must crack them by himself," notes an old proverb.

God bless you, young and old and weary,
God bless you, little children all!

May Christmas blessings bright and cheery
   To-day on brown and gray hairs fall!
              —"Christmas Message"
              German folk song

Children can help decorate your Pennsylvania Dutch table by making candle holders from shiny red apples. From the blossom end of each apple cut a one-inch-deep plug just wide enough to hold a small white candle. You may wish to set one at each diner's place at the table.

PORK WITH APPLES AND ONIONS

Loin of pork (allow 4–6 servings per pound)
5 baking apples, cored and cut in half-inch slices
5 medium onions, peeled and halved crosswise
butter or margarine
apple jelly

Roast pork at 325°, 30 minutes per pound. One hour before the roast is done, place onions and apples around the pork. Dot onions with butter. Baste roast with melted apple jelly.

ROAST GOOSE

1 roasting goose (choose a young goose that has been freshly slaughtered or commercially frozen; a 12–14–lb. goose serves 6)
2 large cooking apples
1 lemon
1 onion

1. Thaw goose if frozen. Rinse thoroughly inside and out with cold water. Use a small knife to trim off all visible fat. Reserve the giblets. Salt the cavity.

2. Use a sharp fork to prick the skin all over so the fat will drain out during cooking.

3. Core and quarter apples. Cut lemon in half. Peel onion and cut in ¼" slices. Place in cavity of goose. Truss.

4. Place goose breast side up on a rack in a large roasting pan. Insert roasting thermometer into meaty part of thigh, not touching the bone.

5. Roast at 400° one hour. Reduce heat to 325°. Roast 2½ to 3½ hours longer, until thermometer reaches 185°.

6. Lift goose onto platter or carving board. Discard drippings and stuffings.

Pennsylvania Dutch farmers take great pride in their *grumbeera*, that is, groundberries (or potatoes). The potato crop is stored for year-round enjoyment, and potatoes appear in most menus. Fried potato cakes, potato dumplings, mashed potatoes . . . there are infinite variations!

Potato Filling is a Pennsylvania Dutch standby, an easy and delicious way to prepare potatoes in advance. The casserole may be refrigerated up to 24 hours and baked just before serving. Add 15 minutes to the baking time.

POTATO FILLING

8 medium-sized
   potatoes*
¼ c. butter or
   margarine
1 c. finely chopped
   onion

½ c. finely chopped
   celery
½ c. milk
1 egg, slightly beaten
⅛ tsp. pepper
salt

4 slices bread, cubed (2 c., slightly packed to measure)

1. Peel and quarter the potatoes. Place in a pan with cold water to cover. Bring to a boil, then add ½ tsp. salt. Cover and cook over low heat until soft.

2. Drain potatoes, reserving ½ c. broth. Mash without adding milk or broth.

3. In a large skillet, sauté onion and celery in butter until soft. Add bread cubes. Sauté until lightly browned.

* For best results, use long white, round white, or russet potatoes.

4. Gently mix all ingredients together, including reserved broth, and salt to taste.

5. Butter a 9″ × 13″ baking dish. Fill with potato mixture and cover with foil.

6. Bake at 350° one hour. Uncover after 30 minutes.
Makes 16 servings.

Nearly every conceivable vegetable—garden-fresh or canned—is enjoyed in Pennsylvania Dutch cooking. Leftover vegetables are chopped to be made into delicious relishes.

Make a colorful and unusual centerpiece with fresh vegetables. Focus on Christmas colors: use red and green bell peppers, tomatoes, zucchini, broccoli, kale, parsley, radishes, okra, beets, and so on.

PURPLE CABBAGE

2 strips bacon, diced (or 2 tbsp. butter or margarine)
1 medium head red cabbage, cut in ⅛″ strips
2 cooking apples, pared, cored, and cut in ⅛″ slices
½ c. thinly sliced onion
½ c. red wine vinegar
2 tbsp. honey
½ tsp. salt
⅛ tsp. pepper

1. In a large skillet, partially cook bacon over medium heat (or melt margarine). Add cabbage, apple, and onions. Sauté 5 minutes.

2. Combine remaining ingredients and pour over vegetables. Bring to a gentle boil, then cover and simmer 30 minutes or until cabbage is tender.
Makes 8 to 12 servings.

PEPPER RELISH

1 red pepper
1 green pepper

1 medium white onion
2 stalks celery

½ c. sugar   1 tsp. salt
½ c. water   1 tbsp. mustard seed
¼ c. cider vinegar   1 tsp. celery seed

1. Clean, trim, and finely chop vegetables. Place in a 2-qt. pan with other ingredients.

2. Stir over medium heat until mixture comes to a gentle boil. Cover and simmer until vegetables are tender but crisp, about 15 minutes.

3. Pour into a glass container. Cover and let cool at room temperature one hour. Stir or shake gently and refrigerate.

4. Serve cold with meats, cheeses, and breads.

Makes about 3 cups.

PICKLED RED-BEET EGGS

two 16-oz. cans small   ½ c. sugar
    whole beets   6 whole cloves
1 medium white onion,   1 tsp. salt
    thinly sliced   1 dozen hard-cooked eggs
1 c. cider vinegar

1. Drain beets, reserving juice. Add water to make 2 c. liquid. Heat beet juice, vinegar, sugar, salt, and cloves to boiling.

2. Place beets and onion in a shallow glass bowl. Add hot marinade. Cover and refrigerate 12 to 36 hours.

3. Shell eggs. Place in a gallon glass jar or deep dish. Use a slotted spoon to lift beets onto a plate. Pour marinade over the eggs, gently tilting jar to be sure marinade reaches each egg. Place beets on top. Cover and chill 12 hours.

4. Serve eggs whole, sliced, or quartered. Arrange on a bed of curly greens such as escarole or parsley.

MINCEMEAT

Mince pie is one of the oldest Christmas traditions. When the Crusaders returned from the Holy Lands with many Oriental spices, it seemed appropriate that these ingredients "from Jesus' homeland" be used in a dish honoring his birth. The first mince pies contained so many combinations of these spices that they were said to symbolize the variety of the Magi's gifts. The resulting flavor was so complex that the English claimed, "The devil dares not show himself at Christmas time lest he should be baked in a pie."[6]

With time, recipes for mincemeat became more subdued. They still required a number of ingredients, but in more harmonious combinations.

A Minc't Pie
Take a Leg of Mutton, and cut the best of the flesh from the bone, and parboil it well: then put to it three pound of the best Mutton suet, and shred it very small: then spread it abroad, and season it with Pepper and Salt, Cloves and Mace: then put in good store of Currants, great Raisins and Prunes clean washt and pickt, a few Dates slic't, and some Orange peels slic't: then being all well mixt together, put it into a coffin,* or into diverse coffins, and so bake them: and when they are served up open the lids, and strew store of Sugar on the top of the meat, and upon the lid. And in this sort, you may also bake Beef or Veal; only the Beef would not be parboiled, and the Veal will ask a double quantity of suet.

—Gervase Markham
The English House-Wife, 1611

The shape of the pie was as significant as the ingredients. For centuries, oblong or oval pastries were baked to denote the manger, and a slight depression in the center sometimes held a small figure of the Christ Child. Puritans loudly ob-

[6] T. G. Crippen, *Christmas and Christmas Lore* (New York: Dodge Company, 1928) p. 123.
* coffin = crust

273

jected to the symbolism and made mince pie illegal during their term of power.

Persistent Catholics and Anglicans disguised the pies by baking them in circular pans. Superstitions bolstered the pie's popularity. Some said that refusing a piece of mince pie at Christmas brought bad luck for the coming year, others that eating mince pie each of the Twelve Days of Christmas assured twelve happy months in the New Year.

Today's mincemeat often comes from a box or jar, though countless homemade variations feature green tomatoes, venison, cranberries, and whatever else might be in plentiful supply. It's a special favorite with Pennsylvania Dutch cooks, who always enjoy using bits of "this and that."

Custom Inspection: Scandinavian Countries

Winters in Scandinavia are lengthy and cold. In the days when the population depended upon fishing and agriculture for their way of life, the icy seas, frozen fields, and short days severely limited work time and food supplies. Even today, the constant wind and cold can make residents long for spring.

On one of the darkest days of the year, Sweden's St. Lucia brings light, hope, and the first of the Christmas festivities. December 13, the shortest day on the unreformed calendar, is the feast day for St. Lucia, a young Sicilian woman who was martyred for refusing to marry a pagan. Missionaries brought her story to Sweden, where it is believed that her presence has saved people from famine and need.

St. Lucia's day now begins in Swedish homes hours before sunrise. The oldest daughter, dressed in a long white gown and wearing a crown of evergreens and candles, serves coffee and buns to her family while they are still in bed. Later in the day, parades, pageants, and church services are held in honor of St. Lucia. Many communities select a young woman as their Lucia Queen to preside over the day's festivities. A ballad dedicated to "Santa Lucia" promises the return of lighter and better days, and marks the beginning of Yuletide celebrations.

Scandinavian Christmas celebrations intertwine family and community ties. Christmas dinner is prepared in amounts ample enough to serve everyone, with baskets of holiday foods delivered to the village poor.

THE SCANDINAVIAN JULBÖRD

This is a two-phase party for all ages. On December 13 (or thereabouts) a plate of freshly baked Lucia Buns accompanies a *Julbörd* recipe and an invitation for a festive gathering one or two weeks later. That gathering will feature a potluck smorgasbord of traditional Scandinavian foods, a ceremony of well-wishing, and some surprise activities for everyone. Here's the suggested timetable.

December 10–13:
    Plan the party.
    Copy recipes for distribution.
    Make ⟨*⟩Lucia Buns.
December 13:
    Deliver invitations, recipes, and Lucia Buns.
One day before the party:
    Prepare ⟨*⟩Hot Cranberry Glög. Refrigerate.
    Prepare fresh ham (or purchase a ready-to-eat ham).
    Complete shopping. Review planning notes.
Party day:

morning	Make ⟨*⟩Christmas Porridge.
	Set up eating area, decorations, and so forth
3:30	Prepare ham. Bake.
4:00	Welcome guests!
4:15	Dipping Day ceremony (see page 277)
4:30–5:30	Children decorate a tree; the adults can't see it until it's finished!
	Adults complete dinner preparations, enjoy conversation, singing . . .
5:45	Eat!
7:30	Santa can't come!

The children must dress up in old clothes and be "elves" to hand out gifts. (Guests may be asked to bring a gift to exchange, or hosts may make or purchase a small gift for each guest.)

End the evening with carols and a reading of Luke's Christmas Story (Luke 2).

Menu for the Scandinavian Julbörd:
⟨*⟩Hot Cranberry Glög
Ice-cold lemonade, optional
Crisp crackers or thin slices of bread
Pâté   Pork sausage   *Lutfisk*
⟨*⟩Pickled Fresh Cucumbers
⟨*⟩Sardines with Apples
⟨*⟩Ham in Mustard Crust
Mashed or boiled potatoes   ⟨*⟩Vegetables au Gratin
⟨*⟩Christmas Porridge
Spritz or cut-out cookies
Coffee, tea, milk

Host provides: Glög, lemonade, ham, potatoes, Christmas Porridge, coffee, tea, and milk

Guests prepare: crackers or bread, pâté, pork sausage, *Lutfisk*, Pickled Fresh Cucumbers, Sardines with Apples, Vegetables au Gratin, cut-out cookies

LUCIA BUNS

These rolls have the texture of a tender bagel, with spices, almonds, and raisins adding a festive flavor.

½ c. warm water   ½ c. sugar
1 c. milk   1 tsp. salt
½ c. margarine or   5 to 6 c. flour
  butter   1 egg, beaten
2 packages active   ¼ tsp. saffron or
  dry yeast   1 tsp. cinnamon

½ c. ground almonds   2 egg yolks
  (not blanched)   1½ tbsp. water

1. Measure water, milk, and margarine into a saucepan. Heat over medium heat until very warm, 115° to 125°.

2. In a large bowl combine yeast, sugar, salt, and 2 c. flour. Add warm liquids and mix well. Add egg and beat 3 minutes.

3. Stir in saffron or cinnamon and almonds. Add enough flour to make a stiff dough.

4. Knead dough on a lightly floured counter until smooth and no longer sticky, 8 to 10 minutes, adding more flour if necessary.

5. Place dough in a large greased bowl. Flip dough once to grease top. Cover with a clean towel and let rise in a warm place for one hour. Grease two baking sheets.

6. Punch down dough. Break off 1½" pieces of dough, rolling each into a 10" rope. Place on baking sheet, shaping into a tight S.* Poke a raisin deep into the center of each coil.

7. Cover baking sheets with a clean towel. Let rise until double—about 25 minutes. Preheat oven to 350°.

8. Combine egg yolks and 1½ tbsp. water. Brush evenly over entire surface of rolls.

9. Bake about 20 minutes. Cool on wire racks. Best served warm, these also may be wrapped tightly and frozen before serving. (Reheat at 350° 15 to 20 minutes.)

Makes 3½ dozen rolls.

DIPPING DAY

Years ago a particularly harsh winter created a famine in the Northlands. Many households had only thin broth and black bread available for the usually bounteous Christmas Eve supper, but shared the simple fare with a spirit of hope and celebration.

"Dipping Day" is a Swedish reminder of that long-ago

---

* Another time shape dough to make cinnamon rolls.

Christmas, and a family ceremony of sharing. Families stand around a pot of broth (often the stock from cooking the Christmas ham or sausages). Each person in turn dips a chunk of bread into the broth to ensure good luck for the coming year.

To share this custom with your guests, prepare a pot of broth. If you've simmered a fresh ham, you may wish to use its spicy stock.

Place a loaf of unsliced bread nearby. Each guest can take a turn at breaking off a chunk of bread and dipping it into the broth. You might offer fondue forks or long-handled carving forks to spear the bread for dipping. Cheer your guests on with toasts and compliments. Share your dreams and hopes.

HOT CRANBERRY GLÖG

1 qt. cranberry juice
2 c. water
6-oz. can lemonade
    concentrate
1 c. grape juice

1 tsp. cinnamon
½ tsp. cloves
¼ c. raisins
1 lemon, thinly sliced
1 c. vodka, optional

1. In a saucepan combine cranberry juice, water, lemonade, grape juice, spices, and raisins. Heat to a boil, then simmer 10 minutes or more.

2. Serve warm, adding vodka and lemon slices ten minutes before serving.

Makes 8 to 9 cups.

⟨T⟩ Punch may be refrigerated up to 12 hours. When ready to serve, add vodka and lemon slices, then warm over low heat.

PICKLED FRESH CUCUMBERS

4 medium cucumbers
¼ c. granulated sugar
1 tsp. salt
⅛ tsp. white pepper

1 c. white vinegar
¼ c. water
¼ c. chopped parsley

1. Peel cucumbers lengthwise, leaving alternate strips of peel intact. Cut thin slices of cucumber into a bowl with a tight-fitting lid.

2. Mix sugar, salt and pepper. Sprinkle over cucumbers.

3. Combine vinegar and water. Pour over cucumbers. Add parsley. Cover and shake to mix.

4. Refrigerate 2 to 24 hours. Drain. Serve with sausages and meats.

Makes about 3 cups.

SARDINES WITH APPLES

One head leafy green lettuce, washed and drained
3 or 4 shiny red apples, washed
1 can (3¾ oz.) Norway Brisling sardines, slightly smoked, in
   olive oil
2 hard-cooked eggs
⅓ c. lemon juice
⅓ c. olive oil
¼ tsp. dry mustard
⅛ tsp. pepper

1. Line a salad platter (12″ square or round) with lettuce.

2. Core apples but do not peel. Slice thinly. (If salad is made ahead, sprinkle apple slices with additional lemon juice.) Place in an attractive layer on top of lettuce.

3. Drain sardines, reserving oil. Arrange sardines over apples—like the spokes of a wheel, or in a crisscross pattern with apple slices. Decorate with sliced egg.

4. Combine lemon juice with oil from sardines, olive oil, dry mustard, and pepper. Pour over salad just before serving.

Before modern transportation and processing transformed the marketplace, preserved fish, meats, and poultry were the Scandinavian specialties that filled the Christmas table. Holiday foods were prepared weeks ahead by tradition-minded cooks who followed recipes handed down from generation to generation.

It was customary to fast in preparation for Christmas religious observances. That first meal was sure to include *lutfisk*, a fish that had been soaking in a lye solution for all of Advent.

Lutfisk, or lyefish, is still a part of the Christmas meal. Its preparation begins on November 30, St. Ander's Day, when a fisherman's finest catch is placed in the customary marinade.

Lutfisk is readily available in Scandinavian markets and may be found in American supermarkets as well. Purchased lutfisk needs only to be boiled before serving; adding salt at the last minute somehow ensures the "characteristic quiver" of this traditional dish. It's often served with a peppery mustard sauce and boiled potatoes.

The pig, fattened and butchered expressly for Christmas, is perhaps akin to the sacred boar served to the heroes of Norse legends. Commercial and family farms today provide the meat essential for the holiday meals: ham, short ribs, sausages, head cheese, and pâté.

The Christmas ham traditionally goes into its spicy brine on the day of Anna, December 9. After the curing process, the ham may be boiled or baked and is often wrapped in crust. It may be served hot or cold, accompanied by fresh cucumber pickles, spiced cabbage, rutabagas, turnips, and potatoes.

Sausage is popular enough to be enjoyed year-round, but the best-quality pork is made into the Christmas sausage. Since the process is time-consuming and requires a meat grinder and sausage tubes, most homes now purchase their sausage links.

Liver pâté, a favorite on the Christmas smorgasbord, is also an all-season delicacy, but home recipes take priority during the holidays. Traditional Swedes will shape the pâté in a square and coat it with pork fat. Modern versions are leaner and require less work. Garnished with lettuce, tomatoes, and pickled beets, it is an elegant buffet dish.

HAM IN MUSTARD CRUST

1 fresh ham, 10 to 12 lbs.
2 bay leaves

½ tsp. whole peppercorns
½ tsp. whole cloves
½ tsp. whole allspice
1 tsp. marjoram
1 onion, chopped
crust (recipe follows)

1. Place ham, fat side up, in a large kettle. Add cold water to cover. Bring to a boil. Skim fat off surface and add spices and onion. Cover and simmer on very low heat for 4 hours.

2. Remove ham from stock. Discard skin and all surface fat. Wipe ham with a cloth, return to stock, and refrigerate overnight. Drain well.

3. Prepare crust:

1 egg white   1 tbsp. sugar
1 tbsp. dry mustard   ¼ c. fine dry bread crumbs

4. Beat egg white until foamy. Sift in mustard and sugar, folding gently to blend.

5. Brush mixture over the ham. Sprinkle with bread crumbs.

6. Bake at 325° 2½ to 3 hours or until surface is browned and ham is fully heated.

⟨T⟩ Save time by using a 10–12–lb. ready-to-eat ham. Prepare and apply crust as directed and bake until ham is heated through.

VEGETABLES AU GRATIN

1 medium head cauliflower   1 c. light cream or milk
1 bunch broccoli   1 tsp. salt
   (1½ lb.)   ⅛ tsp. white pepper
¼ c. butter or   4 large, firm tomatoes
   margarine   1 c. dry bread crumbs
¼ c. flour

1. Wash and trim the cauliflower and broccoli. Break into flowerets. Steam in a tightly covered saucepan for 10 minutes. Drain.

2. Melt butter or margarine in a saucepan over medium heat. Add flour and cook for two minutes, stirring constantly. Add milk, salt, and pepper. Continue to cook and stir for about three more minutes, until mixture is thick and bubbly.

3. Peel and core tomatoes. Cut into ¾" cubes. Combine with steamed vegetables in a large buttered baking dish (or two smaller ones). Pour cream sauce over vegetables and sprinkle with crumbs. Bake at 450° 12 to 15 minutes, or refrigerate 2 to 12 hours and bake 375° 15 to 20 minutes.

Makes 12 ample servings.

Scandinavia is populated year-round by spirits that acquire a new importance at Christmastime. Although no longer feared as spirits of the dead, these mischievous critters continue to play a role in the Christmas activities.

Most resembling the spirits of old are Norway's *oskerien*. These are especially frightful on Christmas night, when they speed through the dark to seize any imprudent person who dares to go out. A share of the Christmas feast is left out by superstitious celebrants; the hungry oskerien are appeased by dining on the "spirit of the food," and leave it looking just the same the next morning.

Norway also hosts the *Julnisser*, white-whiskered elves who spend most of the year hidden in the stable. For Christmas activities, they don red suits with pointed caps, and ride around on the *Julbuk* (Christmas goat), which has been known to butt naughty children.

Danish Christmas festivities of years ago included many supernatural beings. Now, only the *Nisser* are left to help with celebrants. Dressed in gray homespun outfits with bonnets, long red stockings, and white clogs, they enjoy tolling the church bell that announces the arrival of Christmas. The helpful Nisser become pranksters when teased, and may hide shoes, upturn chairs, and cause milk to sour. Children are careful to leave them a dish of Christmas porridge and a bit of codfish, doing their best to keep the little folks in good humor for the holiday.

Swedish homes are inhabited by little gnomes called *tomten*. They live in dark corners of the house, coming out late at night to eat and check on the state of the household. They especially enjoy Yule festivities, which they watch unobserved from a corner.

Throughout Scandinavia, rice porridge is a must on Christmas Eve. Served as a first course in some homes and a dessert in others, it is also a delicious breakfast—and essential for charming the Nisser! The custardlike porridge is traditionally served warm, but could be made ahead and gently reheated to serve.

One lucky almond adds a touch of mystery to the porridge. The almond may represent a guarantee of good luck in the coming year—or may announce who is to receive a special prize from the host.

CHRISTMAS PORRIDGE

1 tbsp. margarine or butter	½ tbsp. vanilla
¾ tsp. salt	1 c. heavy cream
1 tbsp. sugar	1 blanched almond
1 c. long-grain white rice	two 10-oz. packages
1 qt. milk	frozen sweetened
½ c. sugar	raspberries
½ tsp. cinnamon	2 tbsp. cornstarch
	2 tsp. lemon juice

1. Boil 1 c. water. Add butter, salt, and 1 tbsp. sugar. Stir in rice. Cover and cook over low heat until water is absorbed— don't peek for 10 minutes!

2. In a large saucepan (not aluminum) combine milk, ½ c. sugar, cinnamon, and vanilla. Heat to simmering. Gradually add rice mixture. Cover and cook over lowest possible heat for two hours. Take the pan off the stove and set in a warm place until serving time. The pudding is traditionally served warm.

3. Whip cream to form soft peaks. Just before serving, add one whole blanched almond and the whipped cream. Fold in to blend. Top each serving with *RASPBERRY SAUCE*: Mix cornstarch and lemon juice in a small saucepan. Stir in rasp-

berries. Cook, stirring, over medium heat until sauce thickens. Let sit 10 minutes or more before serving.

⟨P⟩ Aluminum pans and utensils give a metallic gray color to cream sauce and puddings. When preparing these foods, use glass, enamel, or stainless steel pans and plastic or wood utensils.

Custom Inspection: Las Posadas in Mexico

Posada is Spanish for "inn"—a simple name for a lengthy and complex celebration. In their efforts to convert the Indians to Christianity, missionary priests designed a religious ceremony around the natives' love of drama. *Las Posadas* is now a popular tradition in Mexico, parts of Spain, and the American Southwest. The celebration most often involves nine families, who meet at a different home each night. Beginning December 16, the participants become pilgrims and innkeepers for the reenactment of the Holy Family's search for a place to rest. Two children carry replicas of Mary and Joseph and lead the candle-carrying procession of "pilgrims" to the "innkeepers," who deny them entry. On the ninth night, a child is chosen to carry the Holy Infant. The procession is admitted to an altar room, where prayers and hymns befit the occasion. Piñatas, festive treats, dancing, and fireworks add to the party. At Midnight there's an intermission for Christmas Eve Mass— after which the festivities resume till dawn.

THE POSADA PROCESSION

We adapted this dramatic celebration into a unique progressive dinner party. Each of the four courses includes a festive activity as well as one or more of Mexico's traditional Christmas foods.

This party is especially fun when hosting responsibilities are shared with several friends. The party can be arranged in several homes, with the procession traveling from one home to another for each course. Or the celebration can be set up under a single roof, with each course in a different room of your home (or church).

Here's the plan.

First Course
⟨*⟩ *Menudo:* a spicy beef soup (or offer a broth garnished with slices of avocado)
Soft tortillas with butter

(1) Greet guests. (2) Have yarn scraps and small sticks ready for making "God's Eyes," a favorite Mexican decoration. See page 122 for some history and instructions. (3) Tell the story of Las Posadas. (4) Serve refreshments. (5) Have an unassembled crèche with the same number of pieces as you have diners. Ask everyone to choose one piece, then assemble the Nativity scene together. After each course, guests carry their crèche character to the next stop, where the nativity scene is reassembled.

Second Course
⟨*⟩ *Ensalada de Noche Buena*
Iced water with lemon or lime wedges

(1) Reassemble the crèche. (2) Read Matthew 1:18–23. (3) Eat. (4) Sing some carols. (5) Disassemble the crèche and move to the next course.

Third Course
⟨*⟩ *Guajolote Relleno* (Stuffed Turkey)
Rice   ⟨*⟩ *Legumbres Mexicana*
White wine, champagne, or sparkling white grape juice

(1) Reassemble the crèche. (2) Fill glasses for each guest and offer toasts to friendship, children, peace. (3) Enjoy the meal together. (4) Disassemble the crèche and move to the next course.

Fourth Course

Light the walkway to the final course (see page 183). The house should be darkened.

⟨*⟩ *Bañuelos*
Coffee and Hot Chocolate
(whipped cream and liqueurs, optional)

(1) Hand an unlit candle to each guest as he or she enters. (2) Read John 1:1–5. Light one candle, then have each guest share the flame with another guest. (3) Reassemble the crèche. (4) Enjoy *bañuelos* and beverages. (5) After dessert, usher your guests into a family room, garage, or other large cleared area where you've hung a piñata.

Throughout Mexico, small market stalls announce the coming of Christmas. These *puestos* display colorful decorations and delicious treats which lure passersby to take a closer look. Among the wares are tissue-covered clay pots shaped like stars, lambs, and donkeys. These are the piñatas, ready to be filled with treasures for Christmas parties.

To the Aztecs of ancient Mexico, the piñata was an annual sacrifice to the war god Haizilopochtli. A clay pot filled with gifts was decorated with feathers and plumes, then placed on top of a pole in the temple. On the New Year, the pot was knocked from its precarious perch, spilling the contents before their idol. Franciscan missionaries to Mexico chose to make the piñata a secular custom, and it frequently is the finale to Las Posadas.

Your piñata may be made from papier-mâché or clay, but must be fragile enough to crack when hit with a stick. Purchase it at an import store or make your own. Fill it with plastic toys, erasers, nuts, candies, and other small, unbreakable souvenirs (plenty for everybody) and hang it from the ceiling with a small rope or wire. Have a broomstick-sized pole handy for striking the piñata.

Everyone should have a chance to try to break the piñata. (You might have guests draw numbers to determine the "batting order.") Blindfold the batter, then give the piñata a bit of a swing to make it even harder to hit. Limit the batting to thirty seconds per person. Lively music, a cheering crowd, and an assortment of fascinating treasures make the piñata a celebration in itself!

> Perhaps it simply means—this symbolic "posada"— that after the hard days, the long months (maybe even the bitter years), there comes somehow to everyone the clean white snow, the sparkling tree, the gifts, and the new birth of friendship and life that is Christmas, holiday of the newborn child.
> —Langston Hughes
> "Memories of Christmas"
> *Christmas Gif'*

MENUDO

Widely popular all year, this soup is a Mexican favorite on Christmas Eve. The generous amount of hot pepper makes it a preferred remedy for hangovers.

Menudo is traditionally made with tripe (the muscular lining of a cow's stomach) and veal knuckle. This recipe is much simpler, but flavorful and hearty. If you prefer a more authentic version, make the stock by boiling 1″ pieces of tripe and a veal knuckle for 3 to 6 hours until the tripe is tender. Discard all bones.

2 tbsp. oil or rendered beef fat	1 c. thinly sliced carrot circles
2 c. chopped onion	15-oz. can hominy
4 cloves garlic	½ c. chopped fresh cilantro or mint
2 qts. beef bouillon, canned or homemade	2 tbsp. dried or fresh minced parsley
1 tsp. salt (or to taste)	1 c. chopped fresh tomato
¼ tsp. pepper	2 limes, cut in thin wedges
4-oz. can seeded green California chiles, chopped	

1. In a large soup pot, sauté onion and garlic in oil. Add bouillon, salt, pepper, chiles, and carrots. Bring to a boil, then cover and simmer 30 minutes.

2. Add hominy, cilantro or mint, and parsley. Simmer 15 minutes longer. Add tomato 5 minutes before serving.

3. Garnish individual bowls with salted lime wedges. Makes 10 first-course servings.

SOFT TORTILLAS

Wrap 8 to 10 tortillas in foil. Heat in a 300° oven 10 minutes. Keep them soft and warm in a cloth-lined basket.

To eat, lay a warm tortilla in the palm of your hand. Spread with butter and roll . . . *delicioso!*

ENSALADA DE NOCHE BUENA

green leafy lettuce
1 fresh pineapple or 1 large can pineapple chunks, drained
3 bananas, cut in ½" slices
2 or 3 oranges, peeled and sectioned
1 or 2 red apples, cored and sliced
1 lime, peeled and sectioned, membrane removed
16-oz. can sliced beets, drained
2 pomegranates, separated into seeds
½ c. chopped peanuts
⅓ c. mayonnaise
⅓ c. orange juice
2 tbsp. wine vinegar
1 tbsp. sugar

1. Arrange lettuce leaves around the edges of a large, circular platter (16" or 20" diameter).

2. Place prepared pineapple, bananas, oranges, apples, and lime in a large bowl. Gently toss to distribute juices over apples and bananas.

3. Arrange beets and fruits in a decorative pattern on top of the lettuce. Sprinkle with pomegranate seeds and peanuts.

4. Combine mayonnaise, orange juice, vinegar, and sugar until smooth. Pour over salad just before serving.

5. Provide small plates for guests to fill with their selections from the platter.

GUAJOLOTE RELLENO (STUFFED TURKEY)

4 slices bacon or
   3 tbsp. vegetable oil
1 c. chopped onion
1 clove garlic, minced
2 lbs. ground pork
2 tart apples, peeled,
   cored, and coarsely
   chopped
3 carrots,
   peeled and sliced
4-oz. can diced green
   chiles
½ tsp. cinnamon
½ tsp. salt

2 green-tipped bananas
¼ c. coarsely chopped
   blanched almonds
12-lb. turkey
2 tbsp. lemon juice
melted margarine
⅓ c. flour
½ c. white wine
   or water
8-oz. can stewed
   tomatoes

1. Cut bacon into 1″ pieces. Fry over medium heat until crispy. Drain, reserving drippings.

2. In a large skillet, sauté onion and garlic in bacon drippings or oil until soft. Add ground pork. Cook until meat is lightly browned. Drain and discard fat.

3. Add bacon, apples, carrots, tomatoes, chiles, salt, and cinnamon. Stir gently to combine all ingredients. Cover and simmer 10 minutes.

4. Cut bananas into ¼″ slices. Add with almonds to stuffing. Refrigerate 30 minutes or overnight.

5. Wash turkey inside and out with cold water. Drizzle the cavity with lemon juice. Stuff, close, and truss turkey.

6. Place the turkey on a rack in a shallow roasting pan. Baste with melted margarine, then cover loosely with foil. Roast at 325° until tender (about 4 hours for a 12-lb. turkey). Baste with margarine several times during the roasting period.

7. Place turkey on platter or carving board when it is finished roasting. Measure the drippings, adding turkey or chicken broth to make 3 cups. Heat in a saucepan to boiling. Mix flour with wine or water. Stir into hot drippings. Continue stirring over medium heat until gravy becomes thick and bubbly. Add salt and pepper to taste, if desired.

⟨T⟩ For tips and ideas on making the most of leftover turkey, see "Using the Remnants," page 306.

LEGUMBRES MEXICANA

16-oz. can tomatoes, whole or sliced	1 tsp. oregano
	1 tsp. salt
10-oz. pkg. frozen corn	½ tsp. pepper
4 medium zucchini, in ¼" slices	
1 green pepper, trimmed and diced	

1. Use kitchen shears or a sharp knife to cut tomatoes into bite-sized pieces.

2. Combine all ingredients in a saucepan. Heat to boiling. Cover and simmer until zucchini is tender, about 15 minutes. Serves 10 to 12.

In Oaxaca, Mexico, irregular pieces of pottery are collected year-round for a unique Christmas Day celebration. The odd dishes are used by street vendors to serve *bañuelos*, a sticky holiday pastry. After enjoying the treat, celebrants customarily smash the pottery in the streets, so that by Christmas morning, stacks of shattered dishes litter the town square.

BAÑUELOS

3 c. flour	¼ c. margarine
1 tsp. salt	or butter,
1 tsp. soda	melted and cooled
1 tsp. baking powder	½ c. milk
1 tbsp. sugar	2 eggs
	oil for frying
	honey or cinnamon-sugar

1. Combine the dry ingredients in a medium bowl. Add margarine, milk and eggs. Mix to form a heavy dough.

2. On a lightly floured board, knead dough about two minutes or until smooth. Form into balls the size of a walnut. Set aside for 15 minutes.

3. On sheets of waxed paper, flatten each ball into a 4-inch circle. Store between layers of waxed paper until ready to cook—a few minutes or several hours.

4. Fry in hot oil (375°) until puffy and brown. Drain on paper towels. Drizzle with honey or sprinkle with cinnamon-sugar.

Makes about 2 dozen.

Buying Time

> Dame, get up and bake your pies
>   bake your pies, bake your pies
> Dame get up and bake your pies,
>   On Christmas Day in the morning.
>   —traditional Old English song

There never seems to be enough time to do everything, especially when it comes to entertaining. The invitations can always be a bit more creative, the decorations more elaborate, the food more gourmet. Setting priorities, making plans early, and following a schedule help you make the most of your time. And "Buying Time"—e.g., paying for a convenience or hiring some assistance—can make the difference between relaxed success and chaotic disappointment. You can, for example, purchase some ready-made specialties from a caterer, bakery, deli, or grocer. Or hire a student or homemaker to help with baby-sitting, housekeeping, or kitchen jobs—before, during, or after the party. There are all kinds of experts available ready to assist you. All you have to do is call them.

CATERERS: PARTY PROFESSIONALS

Hiring the services of a caterer is like bringing home the ease and elegance of a fine restaurant. A good caterer is an expert at preparing food for guests. This expertise includes designing unique plans for each occasion and selecting refreshments that are distinctive and appropriate.

The cost for these services is usually three to four times the actual price of the food. You will be paying for food, service, and freedom from some of the trickier responsibilities of entertaining. For an added fee, some catering services will do more, such as provide equipment, entertainment, photography, or decorations.

If your time is shorter than your budget, you may want to consider using a party-planning service. These professionals will make all the arrangements but still let you consider the event Your Party.

Always start early when looking to hire a caterer or party planner: six months to a year in advance of a large party, one month before a small gathering. Expect that holiday times will be busiest and dates may fill far in advance.

When working with a caterer, follow this plan:

1. Know what your "givens" are: the *how many, where, when,* and *why* of your celebration. Write down these details. Try to be specific ("There are seventeen members of the choir, and each is likely to bring a spouse or escort")—but not limiting ("A prime rib buffet might be nice, but maybe the caterer could suggest something even better. . . .").

2. Determine your catering budget. If it looks like you can't afford a catered party but would appreciate some professional help, consider your alternatives.

—You may choose to hire servers to assist you with your own well-prepared menu.

—Perhaps changing the style of the celebration (a catered dessert? a snack buffet?) would make catering a more affordable option.

—Some caterers prepare gourmet "take-out" foods. These may be ready to serve, or may only need to be defrosted and/or heated. You could spend your time and energy preparing the buffet table and readying your home while investing your money in fancy foods to share.

3. Investigate the catering businesses in your area. Begin with the yellow pages of the local telephone directory. Note the locations, services offered, and specialties of the caterers listed. You'll also want to ask your friends and associates for recommendations and references.

4. Continue your investigation by telephone. Before you call, write down notes and questions about the event you have in mind: where, how many guests, the date, time of day, special commemoration.

Assume a friendly, confident attitude on the telephone. Mention that you are still shopping for a caterer and you have some questions you'd like to ask. Those questions may include:

—Would they be available on the date/time you have in mind?

—How much do they charge? Does this include delivery?

—Decorations? Service? Tableware? Cleanup?

—What about a contract? When do you pay?

—Will they visit the location of the event before the party?

—Could you sample menu items before the party?

—How soon do you need to confirm?

Remember—the only dumb question is an unasked question!

Respect the caterer's ideas and opinions, and expect courteous and professional answers. Don't be long-winded. Find out what you need to know, then thank them and say you'll call back when you've come to a decision.

5. Once you select a caterer, give that person all of your cooperation. Provide details about the facilities, number of guests, and your personal preferences. Be firm about your own expectations, yet consistently courteous and flexible as you allow the caterer to be the authority. Should there be a change of plans, contact the caterer immediately and expect to pay for any last-minute requests.

The expense of a caterer may make all the difference in your entertaining plans. Even with these professional services, though, it is up to you to be the host, to provide the attitude of acceptance and festivity that makes your party a celebration for each of your guests.

TIPS FOR PARTYING AT A RESTAURANT

• If possible, select a restaurant where you are familiar with the accommodations, menu, and service.

• Telephone the restaurant several weeks before the party to ask preliminary questions. Then visit the restaurant in person.

1. Examine the facilities (parking, size and arrangement of the banquet room, tables, chairs).

2. Look over the menu. Will guests have free reign on the menu, or would you prefer to order in advance? Perhaps you can select two entrees for your guests to choose from. Is a buffet or family-style dinner possible? Will alcoholic beverages be available? If so, will you choose a specific wine or will there be an open bar?

3. Talk with the staff. How many servers will you have (including waiters, bus help, bartenders)? What is the expected gratuity?

4. Schedule a second visit to finalize the arrangements.

• Make two copies of all specifics: one for yourself and one for the restaurant staff.

• Specify in the invitations who pays for the meal: "a no-host meal" or "dinner is on us."

• Avoid last-minute problems by calling the banquet manager or maître d' the day before the party. Check arrangements, verify party size, confirm menu.

• Be the first to arrive at the celebration. Bring candles, flowers, nut cups—some little extras to personalize the meal. Write out a seating chart and bring place cards.

• Assume a contagiously festive attitude. Greet guests individually, make introductions, and initiate conversations. Don't be preoccupied with details, but do what you can to make it an enjoyable experience for your guests *and* the restaurant staff.

RENT IT, RETURN IT!

A quick call to a rental service may give you some surprising news: there, you may find a great variety of items at a price

lower than you'd expect. And renting what you need to entertain twenty guests at once may be more affordable and less exhausting than using your own supplies to host two parties for ten.

To get the best rental service, start a minimum of two weeks before the event. A month or more is wise if you need to rent items on a holiday weekend or if the rental services in your community tend to be extremely busy during the holidays. List what you'll need, then do some comparison shopping by telephone. Find out what's available, how much it will cost, and what the deposit fee is. Then visit the rental outlet to take a look at what you will be paying for. Find out when (date and time) you can pick up the items, and the return date. If all arrangements meet your approval, sign a contract to guarantee both cost and availability.

When you arrive to pick up your order, check each item before taking anything out of the rental outlet. Exchange any unsatisfactory items.

At home, wash each piece before and after using it. Take loving care of all that you've rented. If you should notice any damaged pieces before you use them, call the rental outlet and report the problem.

After you've finished with the rented items, package them carefully (and cleanly) and return them promptly. Let the rental outlet know of any problems you encountered, and be prepared to pay for any missing or damaged items.

'SPECIALLY QUICK FINDS

All of your Christmas comings and goings may find you in need of a ready-to-eat meal that doesn't come from a burger stand or pizza parlor. Whether it's a meal on the run or a picnic just for fun, you can depend on a number of sources for a complete and delicious no-cook meal.

Many restaurants will prepare some (if not all) of their specialties to take out. Besides pizza, burgers, and fried chicken, you might consider

—Chinese egg roll, barbecued pork, sweet-and-sour shrimp

—Mexican nachos, guacamole, gazpacho, tortillas
—ice cream cake, whole pies, cheesecakes, giant cookies

You may be surprised at what your grocery has to offer for quick meals, including a wide selection of everyday and specialty foods. Meat and deli departments are sure to have cheeses and cured meats, and possibly roasted chicken, freshly cooked shellfish, and other ready-to-eat entrees. Look for an in-store bakery for fresh breads, pastries, cakes, and cookies. The produce department offers all kinds of fresh additions to your meal. And for a quick at-home meal, check the supermarket freezer. For entrees, accompaniments, desserts, and snacks—all ready to heat in their own cooking dishes.

A delicatessen can provide a full meal that's tasty, interesting, and affordable. Cheeses and meats, crackers, breads, salads, imported olives, and a wide selection of beverages may all be found at a deli. The staff can help you make your selections as well as prepare sandwiches, lunch boxes, or snack trays to order.

THE DELI DINNER

The selections and convenience of a delicatessen—plus some homey touches from your own kitchen—are a combination that makes a quick, versatile, and delicious meal. Of course, this menu can easily be adapted to include favorite items from the take-out department of your supermarket or a favorite restaurant.

You may wish to do all the shopping prior to the party, or visit the deli with a group of celebrants en route to a special outing. Either way, this is a meal that can be prepared quickly for last-minute entertaining.

If you're taking this meal on the road, prepare your picnic basket with some basic supplies and accompaniments:

tablecloth   napkins

salt and pepper
a damp washcloth or
    moist towelettes
glasses/cups
plates
forks and spoons
garbage bag

cheese board and slicer
vacuum bottles
    (full or empty)
bottle opener/corkscrew
knives/spreaders
insulated container of ice

Lettuce, sandwich spreads, coffee, and other menu items may
also be brought from home.

Menu
Fresh fruits
Salad selections

Make-your-own sandwiches:
Breads, cheeses, meats
Lettuce, sprouts, sliced tomatoes, sliced onions
Mustards, jellies, butter, mayonnaise
Juice, wine, tea, coffee
Chocolate truffles or other desserts

Quick Snacks for Drop-In Guests

Roast chestnuts at 425° (prick the shells first) for 15 to 20
minutes. Or roast peanuts in the shell at 250° for about 20
minutes. The wonderfully warm smell will let you know when
they are ready!

One of James Beard's favorites: make a quick batch of biscuits
from a mix or from scratch. Serve them hot with butter and
red jam.
    (Cream Cheese + Raspberry Jam = A Delectable Treat!)

Over a block of cream cheese, sprinkle
    —onion flakes from a package of dry onion soup mix (use
a fork to lift the flakes from the package);
    —drained shrimp in cocktail sauce; or

—crumbled bacon, minced green onion, sauteed mushrooms.

Serve with crackers.

Set out slices of crisp apples, wedges of one or two favorite cheeses, and some crackers. Place a cutting board and knives within easy reach.

Top crackers, fill celery, or spread sandwiches with
    —cottage cheese plus walnuts, raisins, chives, and/or bacon bits,
    —egg salad (add sunflower seeds and chopped olives . . .);
    —flaked tuna mixed with mayonnaise and grated cheese; or
    —peanut butter with sesame seeds and chopped dates

Sandwich cream cheese, butter, peanut butter, even ice cream between thin slices of nut breads.

⟨T⟩ Nut breads (unsliced) will keep up to four months in the freezer, and need only minutes to thaw before they are sliced. It's handy to have several varieties on hand for breakfast, snacks, or dessert.

Easy Eating: Coping with Stress

The high pace of the holiday weeks often takes a toll on our physical well-being. Stress affects the body's functioning and may lead to elevated blood pressure, headaches, and digestive problems.

An important part of coping with stress involves your eating habits. Slight changes in your diet can make an important difference in how you feel, especially during tense times. Here are some helpful hints.

Make preparations easier by planning ahead. Fix simplified menus that take a minimum of time and mental energy to get on the table. As you do your regular grocery shopping, purchase the ingredients needed for some favorite quick meals. See the suggestions on page 297.

Eat less. Instead of heaping your plate with full-sized servings, sample miniature portions. Stop eating *before* you are full, even if it means leaving food on your plate. Chew each bite slowly.

Reduce the amount of fats you eat. Butter, cream, fatty meats, and fried foods are hard to digest. Cut down on or eliminate caffeine, sugar, and alcohol.

Get some exercise daily. Walk, jog, swim, jump rope—physical activity is essential in maintaining optimum physical and mental health.

Conscientious Celebrations

Concerns about personal health, world hunger, and our endangered planet have prompted many conscientious eaters to reassess their diets. The response often involves "eating lower on the food chain"—that is, consuming more grains, fruits, and vegetables, and less meat, salt, sugar, fat, and processed food.

Generations ago, people had other reasons for assuming a vegetarian diet. During the dark Yule season, Norwegians longed for the sun's return. They hoped that by letting their world rest, they would hasten the sun's reappearance, so even traps and fishnets remained untouched for the twelve-day festival.

The Catholic church declared Christmas Eve a meatless day, intending it as a time to prepare both mind and body for Christ's birth. In many Catholic countries, Christmas Eve Mass is followed by a festive meal based on elaborate fish dishes, fancy breads and pastas, and seasonal produce.

Many holiday meals can be easily adapted for vegetarian diets. Eliminating the roasted meat or poultry is the first step, leaving a wonderful assortment of other dishes to enjoy. Check recipes and labels for chicken broth, bacon bits, beef fat, and

other meat products that may throw your vegetarian intentions out of line.

Custom Inspection—II CENONE: A Sicilian Christmas Eve Meal

Il Cenone, the meatless feast served on Christmas Eve in Sicilian homes, is often a family potluck affair with as many as twenty fish dishes. The meal traditionally follows a 24-hour fast, making the delectable foods taste even better.

We suggest a much simpler meal. The menu here includes a snack that can be served a few hours before or after the main meal.

Menu
⟨*⟩ Holiday Fritters
Fresh fruits, roasted nuts
(place in baskets, adding tiny satin bows so
the snack doubles as a decoration)

⟨*⟩ Sicilian Orange and Onion Salad
⟨*⟩ Homemade Pasta with Butter and Grated Cheese
(or your favorite pasta sauce)

⟨*⟩ Baked Fish in Sesame Sauce (optional)
Steamed broccoli or zucchini

Spumoni or vanilla ice cream
Hot coffee (with liqueurs if desired)

Use pinecones to hold the place cards for your table. A small ribbon glued to the corner of the place card will be a festive touch.

HOLIDAY FRITTERS

2 c. flour	¼ c. sugar
1 tsp. baking powder	2 eggs

1 c. milk
oil for frying

powdered sugar or
cinnamon-sugar

a selection of fritter fillers: apples (peeled, cored, and cut
 in ¾″ chunks), dried figs, prunes, dates (halved and
 pitted), banana chunks, pineapple (in ¾″ chunks),
 cheese cubes, and so on.

1. Mix dry ingredients together in a large bowl. Combine
eggs and milk, then add to dry ingredients. Mix to make a
thick batter.

2. Heat two inches of oil to 375°. Drain prepared fruits.
Dry thoroughly with paper towels.

3. Use a fondue fork to dip individual pieces of fruit into
the batter. Carefully drop into the oil, a few at a time. Fry
until golden, turning to brown evenly.

4. Use a slotted spoon to lift fritters out of the oil and onto
paper towels to drain. Serve hot, dusted with powdered sugar
or cinnamon-sugar. (These are best when hot and fresh, but
may be reheated at 250°.)

SICILIAN ORANGE AND ONION SALAD

Traditionally prepared with Mediterranean blood oranges,
navel oranges make this a superb dish. And so colorful! Use
the brightest oranges, the reddest onions, and the freshest
greens you can find.

Prepare 45 minutes before serving.

4 to 6 navel oranges, chilled
1 medium red onion
about ⅓ c. olive oil
salt and freshly ground black pepper
8 leaves Romaine lettuce

1. Use a sharp paring knife to remove the skin and white
membrane from oranges. Cut out sections or cut horizontally
into cartwheels.

2. Peel the onion. Slice horizontally into rings and mix

with oranges in a salad bowl. Drizzle with oil. Sprinkle generously with salt and pepper. Gently mix to distribute dressing.

3. Let salad sit at room temperature for 30 minutes. Serve on fresh Romaine.

Serves 8.

HOMEMADE PASTA WITH BUTTER AND GRATED CHEESE

3 c. sifted flour
½ tsp. salt
3 large eggs
1 tbsp. olive oil

⅓ to ½ c. water
¼ to ½ c. butter or
    margarine, melted
1½ c. grated cheese*

1. Combine flour and salt in a large bowl. Drop the eggs and oil into the center of the flour and mix well.

2. Gradually pour in the water, stirring until dough leaves the sides of the bowl and forms a ball.

3. Turn dough onto a lightly floured board. Knead with the back of your hand for about 10 minutes, until dough is smooth and satiny. Cover and refrigerate for about 15 minutes. Tidy up the kitchen while you wait!

4. Divide dough into four equal parts. Roll each part into ⅛" thickness. Cut into long strips. Let strips dry on wooden or wire racks.

5. Cook noodles in a large kettle of boiling salted water just until tender. Drain well. Put the pasta in a serving bowl, toss with butter, then mix in the cheese. Serve immediately. Makes 1½ to 2 lbs. pasta.

BAKED FISH IN SESAME SAUCE

2 lbs. white fish
    steaks or fillets

¼ c. minced fresh
    parsley

---

* Parmesan (freshly grated, of course) is just one of dozens of great pasta cheeses! Among the choices are Fontina, Jarlsberg, mozzarella, Colby, Edam, and Gorgonzola. Soft cheeses (such as farmer cheese or Brie) should be cut into small pieces, not grated. Try combining two or three favorites: Parmesan, Romano, and Gruyère.

½ c. lemon juice
¼ c. olive oil
¼ c. margarine, melted
½ c. sesame seeds
2 tbsp. grated fresh
   onion

½ tsp. cayenne pepper
   (or to taste*)
1 tsp. salt
garnish: lemon wedges,
   tomato slices, and
   parsley sprigs

1. Prepare fish for baking. Place in a lightly greased shallow baking dish.
2. Combine other ingredients (except garnish) and pour over fish.
3. Bake in a 300°–350° oven until fish flakes easily with a fork, 20 to 30 minutes. (Use the lower temperature for thicker pieces of fish.) Baste fish with sauce several times during baking.
4. Garnish with lemon, tomato, and parsley.
Serves 8.

Custom Inspection: The French Christmas Eve Meal

In France, Christmas is a religious holiday that centers around the midnight mass on Christmas Eve. Many families gather after worship for *Le Réveillon,* literally "The Awakening"—a peaceful gathering that welcomes Christmas.

People on the road
   Carry lighted lanterns;
See their bobbing lights
   Lead the way to church.
There they will keep watch
   'Till the hour of midnight,

* This amount of cayenne pepper makes a spicy sauce! Use ¼ tsp. or less for sensitive tongues!

When the bells will ring
Joyous melodies.

—"Voici le Noël"
French carol

LE RÉVEILLON

This version of Le Réveillon is a light meal, one that would be easy to digest even in the wee hours of Christmas morning. The dessert is a variation on *Le Bûche de Noël*, the elegant Yule log dessert that symbolizes Christ as the Light of the World.

Menu
⟨*⟩ *Potage Noël:* a chicken bisque
French bread (preferably baquette)
Cheese tray: Brie, Muenster, raclette, and other favorites
Fresh fruits
⟨*⟩ *Bûche de Noël*

POTAGE NOËL

½ c. butter or margarine
¼ c. minced onion
1 c. flour
8 c. chicken stock
1½ c. finely chopped cooked chicken or turkey

½ c. minced green pepper
½ c. grated carrot
½ tsp. basil
½ tsp. pepper
½ tsp. curry powder
salt
garnishes

1. Sauté the onion in butter in a small pan. Stir in flour. Cook and stir over medium heat 3 to 5 minutes. Remove from heat.

2. Pour stock into your soup pot. Heat to a gentle boil. Add roux (flour mixture), stirring until smooth. Simmer 10 to 15 minutes.

3. Add other ingredients and simmer 10 minutes longer.

Garnish with color: grated carrot, parsley, minced green pepper, paprika.

Serves 4 to 6 generously.

⟨P⟩ Make this a vegetarian bisque by substituting vegetable broth for the chicken stock. Chop 8 oz. fresh mushrooms and sauté with onion. Omit chicken.

BÛCHE DE NOËL

⅔ c. flour
1 tsp. cinnamon
½ tsp. nutmeg
1 tsp. baking powder
½ tsp. salt
3 eggs, separated

½ c. granulated sugar
1 tsp. almond flavoring
⅔ c. canned pumpkin
confectioners' sugar
1 qt. vanilla or almond
   ice cream

1. Combine flour, spices, baking powder, and salt. Set aside.

2. In a large mixing bowl, beat egg yolks at high speed for 5 minutes or until thick. Continue beating at medium speed while gradually adding sugar, then almond flavoring and pumpkin. Fold in dry ingredients.

3. In a separate mixing bowl, beat egg whites until stiff. Fold into batter.

4. Grease a 10″ × 15″ jelly roll pan. Line with waxed paper. Grease paper. Spread batter smoothly in pan.

5. Bake at 375° 15 minutes or until top springs back when lightly touched. Do not overcook. Immediately (and carefully) invert cake onto a tea towel dusted with confectioners' sugar. Remove waxed paper. Roll cake and towel together into a 15″-long cylinder. Cool rolled cake completely on wire racks.

6. Unroll carefully. Trim crusty edges. Spread cake with slightly softened ice cream. Reroll (without the towel). Wrap cake in plastic wrap or waxed paper. Freeze at least one hour. Let stand at room temperature 10 to 15 minutes before serving—then dust with confectioners' sugar, decorate with holly . . . voilá!

Decorate the Réveillon table with evergreens and a cluster of candles.

Leftovers

Many cooks would feel lost on December 26 without a refrigerator filled with leftovers. Dinner on the "day after" often takes minimal preparation time, with yesterday's delicious dishes tasting just as good the second time around. But a few days later, those leftovers are apt to have lost their appeal.

Making the best use of holiday leftovers takes some thought and a little extra work:

ALWAYS handle leftovers wisely to minimize the growth of germs and bacteria, and prevent spoilage. Hot dishes should be quickly cooled in ice water or the refrigerator, then covered or wrapped and chilled. NEVER reheat leftovers more than once.

Be realistic in what you keep. Does it make sense to keep that dab of mashed potatoes? How might you recycle the rest of the broccoli? How much ham can you use in the next three or four days?

Share the bounty with your guests, particularly if they contributed to the meal. Fix up a dinner box for a friend with the flu, a busy single parent, or someone who lives alone. Include garnishes and instructions for storing, preparing, and serving.

USING THE REMNANTS

1. Assess what you have. Leftovers aren't what they once were!

• Flavors have blended, perhaps becoming stronger or more subtle. A complementary sauce or seasoning can renew the appeal.

• Textures have changed. Cheeses, eggs, and meats are apt to be tougher. Cut meats in small pieces to minimize their toughness. Fruits, vegetables, grains, and casseroles will be softer. Crisp bacon, water chestnuts, raisins, or fresh produce will add some texture.

• Colors may have run together (fruit salads), dulled (a stew) or changed in hue (red cabbage). An interesting garnish, fresh ingredients, or a disguising sauce may make the difference.

2. Combine leftovers conservatively. The dump-and-stir-it-all-together method seldom produces a classic! You'll be wise to use only a few remnants in any one dish and to keep the final product in mind as you create. A "mathematical approach" will help you think it through.

beef strips + teriyaki sauce + skewers = teriyaki strips
cream soup + pureed vegetables = cream of vegetable soup
cookie crumbs + pudding + fruit compote = parfaits

3. Use some leftovers to make your own "convenience foods"—sandwich fillings, turnovers, soups and stews, stock, marinated salads, bread crumbs, croutons, fritter-fillers.

4. Freeze some leftovers for future use. Refer to your freezer manual or cookbook to learn which foods freeze best and the maximum cold-storage time. Refrigerator-freezer compartments are only suitable for short-term freezing.

• DO FREEZE: nonalcoholic punch; breads; unfrosted cakes and cookies; pie crust; cooked ham, turkey, or meat; broth; gravy; some sauces and casseroles.

• DON'T FREEZE: mayonnaise, eggs, most salads, pasta or potato dishes.

• Freeze foods in usable quantities, but remember that small containers and small pieces have more exposure to the drying effects of cold air.

• Prevent moisture loss and freezer burn by squeezing out all the air. Package foods snugly, using freezer containers or a double wrap of foil or plastic.

• Label each package with the date, a description of the contents, and the quantity.

• Keep track of what you've frozen. Make a written inventory. Tape one copy to the freezer door and another inside your recipe box or cookbook.

ELEGANCE FROM EXTRAS

This menu makes delicious use of leftovers. Most of the preparations are done several hours in advance—or even the night before.

Menu
⟨*⟩ Jellied Apple & Apple Salad
⟨*⟩ Italian-Style Turkey Pie
Steamed vegetables with butter
Bread or rolls (optional)
⟨*⟩ Quick Parfaits

JELLIED APPLE & APPLE SALAD

3 c. apple cider
2 envelopes unflavored gelatin
6-oz. can frozen limeade concentrate
1 c. diced red apple*

¼ c. chopped celery
¼ c. chopped walnuts (optional)
greens, mayonnaise
cinnamon

1. Combine 1 c. cider with gelatin in a small saucepan. Let stand five minutes. Stir over low heat until gelatin is dissolved.

2. Add remaining ingredients. Refrigerate until thick (about 1 hour).

---

* Orange segments or drained canned pineapple may be used in place of all or part of the apple.

3. Stir to distribute all ingredients. Pour into one 6-c. mold or 8 individual molds. Chill until firm.

4. Unmold by dipping mold(s) into a bowl of hot water for about 5 seconds (do not let water touch gelatin), then top with serving plate and invert.

5. Garnish with greens, a dollop of mayonnaise, and a dash of cinnamon.
Serves 8.

ITALIAN-STYLE TURKEY PIE

2 tbsp. olive oil or
    salad oil
½ c. chopped onion
1½ c. thinly sliced
    carrot
1 green pepper, chopped
1 clove garlic, minced
½ c. tomato juice
1 tsp. dry whole
    oregano leaves
⅛ tsp. pepper

16-oz. can sliced
    Italian tomatoes
2 tbsp. all-purpose flour
3 c. cubed cooked turkey
¼ c. drained sliced
    black olives
pastry for single crust
    pie (unrolled)
½ c. grated Parmesan
    cheese

1. In a large skillet, sauté onion, carrot, pepper, and garlic in oil until carrot is tender. Stir in tomato juice, oregano, and pepper.

2. Drain canned tomatoes, saving juice in a small bowl. Combine juice with flour. Mix until smooth. Add to sautéed mixture, stirring over low heat until thickened.

3. Remove pan from heat. Add turkey, olives, and drained tomatoes. Refrigerate 15 minutes.

4. Roll pastry into a 12″ square. Cut into one-inch strips. Grease a 9″ × 13″ baking dish.

5. Spoon cooled turkey mixture into the prepared pan. Place pastry strips in a diagonal lattice across top. Sprinkle with Parmesan cheese.

6. Bake in a preheated 375° oven for 35 minutes or until crust is golden and filling is bubbly.

⟨T⟩ Pie may be covered with plastic wrap and chilled up to 6 hours before baking at 375° for 45 minutes.

QUICK PARFAITS

Prepare a few hours before the meal or just before serving. You will need:

Parfait glasses (one per person)

2 or more of the following:

whipped cream	fruit syrup
ice cream	dessert sauce(s)
sherbet	nuts, coconut, crushed
pudding	candy
yogurt (plain or	grated chocolate
flavored	cherries
fruit (fresh, frozen,	
or canned)	

1. Select your ingredients from the list above, considering color and flavor combinations.
2. Alternate layers of ingredients in the tall glasses. Top it off decoratively with a mint leaf, a small cookie, a long-stemmed cherry.

Custom Inspection: Happy New Year!

England

Celebrating the medieval Feast of Fools, townspeople parodied the rituals of church and court on this day. Even the clergy joined in the singing and satire. The frivolity was unpopular with the ruling class and was condemned by the Council of Basil in 1431.

Argentina

The New Year is welcomed with feasting and gift exchanges—a marked contrast to the reverent worship of Christmas Day.

France

New Year's Day is a favorite feast day, the grownups' equivalent to the gift exchanges and activities enjoyed by children on Christmas Day. Family members traditionally come together to exchange gifts and share their hopes for the New Year.

Scotland

"Should old acquaintance be forgot . . ." The great Scottish poet Robbie Burns gave the day its own song, and that "cup of kindness" has inspired party-goers ever since.

> The midnight bells are ringing
>   The Old Year's solemn knell,
> What is the New-Year bringing?
>   Alas, we cannot tell.
>   —"The Passing of the Old Year"
>   a German carol by J. H. Voss

NEW YEAR'S IN OR OUT

New Year's Day may seem a bit anticlimactic after the wonder (and chaos) of Christmas *and* the late-night festivities of New Year's Eve. Televised parades and football games provide easy entertainment for many; still new games and puzzles are enjoyed by others.

The freshness of a New Year may inspire you to take a drive—perhaps visit friends or just tour the countryside. With few travelers on the back roads and no deadlines to meet, it is a fun day for an adventure.

This menu can be enjoyed at home or on the road.

⟨*⟩ Mimosas
Hearty stew (homemade or purchased)
Hot bread or crackers
⟨*⟩ Grand Finale Cake

If you choose to have a picnic, sew tiny bells to the edge

of your picnic tablecloth. They'll add a merry "jingle" to your meal and keep the cloth in place.

This menu can be enjoyed at home or on the road.

⟨P⟩ To pack stew for a picnic: Put boiling-hot stew in a Dutch oven or soup pot with a tight-fitting lid. Wrap in three layers of foil, then several layers of newspaper. Secure paper with masking tape.

MIMOSAS

Pour equal amounts of champagne and orange juice in tall glasses. Serve immediately.

You may prefer ⅓ champagne and ⅔ orange juice—or use sparkling white grape juice instead of champagne. Freshly squeezed orange juice is best—and be sure both beverages are *very* cold.

In medieval days, Dom Perignon was given the job of caring for the wines of a certain monastery. He discovered a forgotten supply of wine and found the bottles filled with tiny bubbles. After one sip of the unusual beverage, he ran outside; exclaiming, "O, come quickly, I am drinking stars!"

Dom Perignon's discovery became known as champagne, a festively effervescent wine named for an area in northern France that has become famous for its production of superb champagne.

In southern Europe, January 1 marks the Commemoration of the Circumcision. First celebrated in Byzantine and Gallican churches, a three-day fast was observed to keep the faithful from the pagan celebrations of the calends. In the fourth century, the day became known as St. Basil's Day, and it is still remembered as such in Greece, Rumania, and Albania.

The St. Basil's cake traditionally has the New Year written in nuts across the top. Containing a single coin that brings good luck to the finder, the cake is a fun and delicious dessert.

GRAND FINALE CAKE

4 c. grated, peeled apple	1 c. sugar
	3 eggs

1 tbsp. white vinegar   ½ tsp nutmeg
1 c. salad oil   ½ tsp. cloves
3 c. flour   1 c. chopped nuts
2 tsp. baking soda   1 c. raisins or chopped
1 tsp. salt   dates
2 tsp. cinnamon   slivered almonds
1 tsp. allspice

1. Combine apples and sugar. Set aside for 15 minutes. (Mixture will brown slightly.)

2. Beat eggs with electric mixer until frothy, about 5 minutes. Add vinegar and oil and stir until combined.

3. Combine or sift flour with salt and spices in a separate bowl. Add all at once to egg mixture. Stir gently just until blended.

4. Fold in apple mixture, then nuts and raisins or dates.

5. Pour batter into a greased and floured 10″ tube pan or two 9″ × 5″ × 3″ loaf pans. (Add a foil-wrapped coin if you'd like to share the Eastern European custom.) Bake at 325° 1¼ hours or until cake tests done.

6. Let stand 10 minutes on a wire rack before removing from pan.

A Christmas toast (which also applies to packing a picnic):

A Christmas wish—
   May you never forget what is worth remembering
      or remember what is best forgotten.

                    —Paul Dickson
                      Toasts

These celebrations are just a sampling of the possibilities for entertaining during the holiday weeks. Extending our hospitality gives us an opportunity to say, "I care" in a tangible and personal way. Jesus' promise to be with us "whenever two or more are gathered" is evidenced by the joy of our celebrations. Caught up in the fellowship of the season, the spirit of Christmas comes alive when we gather with those we care about the most.

I wonder as I wander out under the sky
how Jesus the Savior did come for to die.
—Appalachian carol

Christmas is a wonder-filled season. The decorations, gifts, and parties mark the beginning, not the ending, of an amazing event: the life of a Savior who has changed the world. Christmas calls us to a new faith, a new joy.

Into a frenetic, financially strained holiday we can bring an enthusiasm worthy of its Founder, the Prince of Peace. Let us "go over to Bethlehem" and return home to celebrate the wonder of Christmas.

BIBLIOGRAPHY

CHRISTMAS FACTS, TRADITIONS & CUSTOMS

Anderson, Raymond, and Anderson, Georgene. *The Jesse Tree*. Philadelphia: Fortress Press, 1966.

Auld, William Muir. *Christmas Traditions*. New York: The Macmillan Co., 1933.

Biddle, Dorothy, and Blum, Dorothea. *Christmas Idea Book*. New York: M. Barrows & Co., 1953.

Bishop, Claire Huchet. *Here Is France*. New York: Farrar, Straus, & Giroux, 1969.

Blanco, Tomás. *The Child's Gifts: A Twelfth Night Tale*. Philadelphia: Westminster Press, 1976.

Brewster, H. Pomeroy. *Saints and Festivals of the Christian Church*. New York: Frederick A. Stokes Co., 1904.

Burnett, Bernice. *The First Book of Holidays*. Rev. ed. New York: Franklin Watts, 1974.

Cagner, Ewert, compiled and issued by. *Swedish Christmas*. Gothenburg: Tre Tryckare, 1955.

Cole, Ruth. *America's Christmas Heritage*. New York: Kainen, Funk & Wagnalls, 1969.

Cooke, Gillian, ed. *A Celebration of Christmas*. New York: G. P. Putnam's Sons, 1980.

Count, Earl W. *4000 Years of Christmas*. New York: Henry Schuman, 1948.

Couzyn, Jeni. *Christmas in Africa*. London: Heinemann; Vancouver: J. J. Douglas, 1975.

Csicsery-Rónay, István. *The First Book of Hungary*. New York: Franklin Watts, 1967.

Cure, Karen. "The Great Austrian True-Blue, Down-on-the-Farm Epiphany Celebrations." *Holiday*, vol. 57, no. 6 (November/December 1976), pp. 22–23.

Del Re, Gerard, and Del Re, Patricia. *The Christmas Almanack*. Garden City, New York: Doubleday & Co., 1979.

Dickson, Paul. *Toasts*. New York: Delacorte Press, 1981.

Editors of Time–Life Books. *The Life Book of Christmas* Vol. I: *The Glory and Pageantry of Christmas*. Maplewood, New Jersey: Hammond Inc., 1963.

Editors of Time–Life Books. *The Life Book of Christmas* Vol. III: *The Merriment of Christmas*. New York: Time Inc., 1963.

Ehrlich, Henry. "A Compulsive Traveler's Christmas." *Travel and Leisure*, vol. 6, no. 12 (December 1976), pp. 24–28.

Fodor, Eugene. *Belgium and Luxembourg*. New York: David McKay, 1966.

Gaer, Joseph. *Holidays Around the World*. Boston: Little, Brown & Co., 1953.

Gardner, Horace J. *Let's Celebrate Christmas*. New York: A. S. Barnes & Co., 1940.

Gebhard, Anna Laura, and Gebhard, Edward W. *Come to Christmas!* New York and Nashville: Abingdon Press, 1960.

Hadfield, John, ed. *The Christmas Companion*. New York: E. P. Dutton & Co., 1939.

Herman, Judith, and Herman, Marguerite Shalett. *The Cornucopia*. New York: Harper & Row, 1973.

Hole, Christina. *Christmas and Its Customs*. New York: M. Barrows & Co., 1958.

Hole, Christina. *Saints in Folklore*. New York: M. Barrows & Co., 1965.

Hornung, Clarence P. *An Old-Fashioned Christmas in Illustration and Decoration*. New York: Dover Publications, 1970.

Hottes, Alfred Carl. *1001 Christmas Facts and Fancies*. New York: A. T. De La Mare Co., 1937.

House & Garden Magazine, vol. 151, no. 12 (December 1979).

Jarrett, Lauren. "Lift High the Wassail Bowl." *The Conservationist*, January–February 1978.

Kainen, Ruth Cole. *America's Christmas Heritage*. New York: Funk & Wagnalls, 1969.

Krythe, Maymie R. *All About Christmas*. New York: Harper & Brothers, 1954.

Kuhn, Irene Corbally. "Christmas in Lexington & Concord." *Gourmet*, vol. 36, no. 12 (December 1976), pp. 17–20, 110–120.

Langseth-Christensen, Lillian. *The Holiday Book*. New York: The Lion Press, 1969.

Link, Mark (S.J.). *The Merriest Christmas Book*. Niles, Illinois: Argus Communications, 1974.

McKnight, George H. *St. Nicholas—His Legend and His Rôle in the Christmas Celebration and Other Popular Customs*. New York and London: G. P. Putnam's Sons, 1917.

McSpadden, J. Walker. *The Book of Holidays*. New York: Thomas Y. Crowell, 1958.

Metcalfe, Edna. *The Trees of Christmas*. Nashville: Abingdon Press, 1969.

Miles, Clement A. *Christmas in Ritual and Tradition Christian and Pagan*. London: T. Fisher Unwin, 1912.

Milne, Jean. *Fiesta Time in Latin America*. Los Angeles: The Ward Ritchie Press, 1965.

Muir, Frank. *Christmas Customs and Traditions*. New York: Taplinger Publishing Co., 1977.

Newsom-Brighton, Maryanne. "Six Charming Myths of Christmas." *Good Housekeeping*, vol. 191, no. 6 (December 1980), p. 90.

Reeves, James, ed. *The Christmas Book*. New York: E. P. Dutton & Co., 1968.

Response magazine, December 1979.

Response magazine, December 1981.

Revoir, Trudie West. *Legends and Traditions of Christmas*. Valley Forge, Pennsylvania: Judson Press, 1985.

Rinkoff, Barbara. *The Family Christmas Book*. New York: Doubleday & Co., 1969.

Rosenthal, Barbara, and Rosenthal, Nadia. *Christmas—New Ideas for an Old-Fashioned Celebration*. New York: Clarkson N. Potter, 1980.

Sechrist, Elizabeth Hough. *Christmas Everywhere*. Philadelphia: Macrae-Smith Co., 1936.

Sechrist, Elizabeth Hough, and Woolsey, Janette. *It's Time for Christmas*. Philadelphia: Macrae-Smith Co., 1959.

Seiden, Allen. "A Yosemite Christmas." *Travel*, vol. 146, no. 6 (December 1976), pp. 52–55, 66.

Sheraton, Mimi. *Visions of Sugarplums*. New York: Harper & Row, 1981.

Snyder, Phillip. *December 25th*. New York: Dodd, Mead & Co., 1985.

Thurston, Herbert, and Attwater, Donald, eds. *Butler's Lives of the Saints*, Vol. IV. New York: P. J. Kennedy & Sons, 1956.

Watts, Franklin, ed. *The Complete Christmas Book*. New York: Franklin Watts, 1958.

Weiser, Francis X. *The Christmas Book*. New York: Harcourt, Brace & Co., 1952.

Wernecke, Herbert H., ed. *Celebrating Christmas Around the World*. Philadelphia: The Westminster Press, 1962.

Wyon, Olive. *The World of Christmas: Stories from Many Lands*. Philadelphia: Fortress Press, 1964.

CONSUMER INFORMATION

Council of Better Business Bureau. "Consumer Tips on Buying by Mail." Better Business Bureau Consumer Information Series, 1979.

George, Richard. *The New Consumer Survival Kit*. Boston and Toronto: Little, Brown & Co., 1968.

Hoge Sr., Cecil C. *Mail Order Moonlighting*. Berkeley, California: Ten Speed Press, 1976.

Joffe, Gerardo. *How You Too Can Make at Least $1 Million (but probably much more) In the Mail-Order Business*. San Francisco: Advance Books, 1978.

Marcus, Stanley. *Quest for the Best*. New York: Viking Press, 1979.

Matthews, Douglas et al. *Secondhand is Better*. New York: Arbor House, 1975.

Oregon Poison Control and Drug Information Center. "Common House Plants." Portland, OR: February 1980.

Oregon Recycling Information and Organizing Network. "There's no such thing as GARBAGE," (pamphlet) 1973.

Oregon State University Extension Service. "Poisonous Plants Encountered in Oregon." Extension Circular 801, September 1981.

Rogers, Maggie, and Hawkins, Judith. *The Glass Christmas Ornament: Old and New—A Collector's Compendium and Price Guide*. Forest Grove, Oregon: Timber Press, 1977.

Young, Jean, and Young, Jim. "Salvaged and Recycled." *The Garage Sale Manual*. New York: Praeger Publishers, 1973.

Young, Michael. "Critters." *The Garage Sale Manual*. New York: Praeger Publishers, 1973.

COOKING AND ENTERTAINING

Beard, James, and Aaron, Sam. *How to Eat Better for Less Money*. New York: Simon & Schuster, 1970.

Beard, James. *James Beard's Theory and Practice of Good Cooking*. New York: Alfred A. Knopf, 1977.

Beard, James. *Menus for Entertaining*. New York: Delacorte Press, 1965.

Blanchard, Marjorie P. *Cater from your Kitchen*. Indianapolis, New York: Bobbs-Merrill Co., 1981.

Brooks, Karen. *The Forget-About-Meat Cookbook*. Emmaus, Pennsylvania: Rodale Press, 1974.

Cantrell, Rose. *Polish Cooking*. Baltimore, Maryland: Ottenheimer Publishers, 1978.

Capon, Robert Farrar. *Party Spirit*. New York: William Morrow & Co., 1979.

Catanzaro, Angela. *Mama Mia Italian Cookbook*. New York: Liveright Publishing Corporation, 1955.

Clairborne, Craig. *An Herb and Spice Cookbook*. New York, Evanston and London: Harper & Row, 1963.

Cooper, Jane. *Love at First Bite*. New York: Alfred A. Knopf, 1977.

Cornell, Jane. *The Art of Table Decoration*. New York: Warner Publishers, 1980.

Cox, Harvey. *The Feast of Fools*. Cambridge, Massachusetts: Harvard Univesity Press, 1969.

Cross, Kate. *Cooking Round the World*. London: Blandford Press, 1964.

Dariaux, Genevieve Antoine. *Entertaining with Elegance*. Garden City, New York: Doubleday & Co., 1965.

de Andrade, Margarette. *Brazilian Cookery*. Rutland, Vermont: Charles E. Tuttle Co., 1965.

de Groot, Roy Andries. *Esquire's Handbook for Hosts*. New York: Grosset & Dunlap, 1973.

Dyer, Ceil. *The After Work Entertaining Cookbook*. New York: Ceil Dyer Publications, 1976.

Editors of *Better Homes & Gardens*. *Creative Table Settings*. Des Moines, Iowa: Meredith Corporation, 1973.

Editors of *Better Homes & Gardens*. *Holiday Cook Book: Special Foods for all Special Occasions*. Des Moines, Iowa: Meredith Corporation, 1959.

Editors of *Better Homes & Gardens*. "How to Produce a Party." *Christmas Ideas*, 1975.

Editors of *Better Homes & Gardens*. *Mexican Cook Book*. Des Moines, Iowa: Meredith Corporation, 1977.

Editors of *Better Homes & Gardens*. "Timesaving, Worksaving Cooking Tips." *Better Homes & Gardens*, January 1982.

Editors of *Family Health*. "Indulging Without Bulging." *Family Health*, vol. 9, no. 12 (December 1977), pp. 30–35.

Editors of *House & Garden*. *The Art of Carving*. New York: Simon & Schuster, 1963.

Editors of Sunset Books and *Sunset* magazine. *Sunset Cook Book for Entertaining*. Menlo Park, California: Lane Magazine & Book Co., 1968.

Editors of Sunset Books and *Sunset* magazine. *Sunset Menu Cook Book*. Menlo Park, California: Lane Magazine & Book Co., 1975.

Editors of Sunset Books and *Sunset* magazine. *Sunset Mexican Cook Book*. Menlo Park, California: Lane Magazine & Book Co., 1975.

Editors of Time–Life Books. *Pasta—The Good Cook/Techniques and Recipes*. Alexandria, Virginia: Time–Life Books, 1981.

Editors of Time–Life Books. *The Time–Life Holiday Cookbook*. New York: Time–Life Books, 1976.

Frank, Beryl. *Scandinavian Cooking*. Baltimore, Maryland: Ottenheimer Publishers, 1977.

Geise, Judie. *The Northwest Kitchen*. Seattle: B. Wright & Co., 1978.

Gordon, Pearl Sgutt. *Simply Elegant*. Winnetka, Illinois: Simply Elegant Co., 1975.

Hazelton, Nika Standen. *The Art of Danish Cooking*. Garden City, New York: Doubleday & Co., 1964.

Heller, Edna Eby. *The Art of Pennsylvania Dutch Cooking*. Garden City, New York: Doubleday & Co., 1968.

Hodgson, Moira. *The Quick and Easy Raw Food Cookbook*. New York: Grosset & Dunlap, 1973.

House Beautiful, vol. 119, no. 12 (December 1977).

Kershner, Ruth. *Greek Cooking*. Baltimore, Maryland: Ottenheimer Publishers, 1977.

Kershner, Ruth Bauder. *Italian Cooking*. Baltimore, Maryland: Ottenheimer Publishers, 1978.

Lee, Nata. *The Complete Book of Entertaining*. New York: Hawthorn Books, 1961.

Leonard, Jonathan Norton. *American Cooking: New England*. New York: Time–Life Inc., 1970.

Longacre, Doris Janzen. *More with Less Cookbook*. Scottdale, Pennsylvania: Herald Press, 1976.

Malinowski, Ruth et al. *German Cooking*. Baltimore, Maryland: Ottenheimer Publishers, 1978.

Manning, Elise W., ed. *Farm Journal's Best-Ever Recipes*. Philadelphia: Countryside Press, 1977.

Manning, Elise W., ed. "Make-aheads for a Merry Christmas." *Farm Journal*, vol. 96, no. 12, December 1972, pp. 36–38.

Mark, Theonie. *Greek Islands Cooking*. Boston and Toronto: Little, Brown & Co., 1972.

Martens, Rachel, ed. *Christmas with a Country Flavor*. Philadelphia: Countryside Press, 1973.

McCall's, vol. 105, no. 3, December 1977.

McCall's, vol. 106, no. 3, December 1978.

Muffoletto, Anna. *The Art of Sicilian Cooking*. Garden City, New York: Doubleday & Co., 1971.

Mullen, Tom. *Where 2 or 3 are gathered together, Someone Spills His Milk*. Waco, Texas: Word Books, 1973.

Ojakangas, Beatrice. "Open House, Scandinavian Style". *Woman's Day*, December 1976, pp. 96–97, 104–106.

Poole, Shana Crawford, *The Christmas Cookbook*. New York: Atheneum, 1979.

Post, Elizabeth, and Staffieri, Anthony. *The Complete Book of Entertaining*. New York: Harper & Row, 1981.

Romagnoli, Margaret, and Romagnoli, G. Franco. *The Romagnolis' Table: Italian Family Recipes*. Boston and Toronto: Little, Brown & Co., 1974, 1975.

Rombauer, Irma S., and Becker, Marion Rombauer. *Joy of Cooking*. Indianapolis, Indiana: Bobbs–Merrill Co., 1964.

Sarvis, Shirley. *Woman's Day Home Cooking Around the World*. New York: Simon & Schuster, 1978.

Seafood Cookbook. Fishermen's Wives, Newport, Oregon.

Smith, Michael. *The Duchess of Duke Street Entertains*. New York: Coward, McCann & Geoghegan, 1977.

Thomas, Anna. *The Vegetarian Epicure*. New York: Vintage Books, 1972.

Travers, P. L. *Mary Poppins in the Kitchen*. New York and London: Harcourt Brace Jovanovich, 1975.

Van der Tuuk, Marianne Grönwall. *The Best of Swedish Cooking and Baking*. Chicago: Rand McNally, 1960.

Wolfsohn, Reeta Bochner. *Successful Children's Parties*. Provo, Utah: Arco Publishing Co., 1979.

CREATIVE ACTIVITIES AND CRAFTS
(Including Christmas Decorations)

Aldrich, Dot. *Creating with Cattails, Cones and Pods*. Great Neck, New York: Hearthside Press, 1971.

Alternate Celebrations Catalog. 3rd ed. Greensboro, North Carolina: Alternatives, 1975.

Anderson, Mildred. *Papier-Mâché and How To Use It*. New York: Sterling Publishing Co., 1966.

Ashton, Pearl F. *Everyone Can Paint Fabrics*. New York: Studio Publications, 1952.

Bauer, Caroline Feller. *Storytelling*. Oregon Educational and Public Broadcasting Service "Campus of the Air," 1974.

Burke, Linda, and Kallen, Mary, eds. *Time Out for Children*. Pullman, Washington: Creative Child Care, 1969.

Callandine, Carole, and Callandine, Andrew. "Ten Tips for the Merriest Christmas Your Family Ever Had." *Family Circle*, vol. 92, no. 17, 11 December 1979, p. 56.

Caney, Steven. *Playbook*. New York: Workman Publishing Co., 1975.

Chrisman, Irma Brown. *Christmas Trees, Decorations and Ornaments*. New York: Hearthside Press, 1956.

Coffey, Ernestine Sabrina, and Minton, Dorothy Fitch. *Designs for a Family Christmas*. New York: Hearthside Press, 1964.

Comstock, Nanina et al. *The McCall's Book of Handcrafts*. New York: The McCall Pattern Co. (Random House), 1972.

Creekmore, Betsey B. *Making Gifts from Oddments and Outdoor Materials*. New York: Hearthside Press, 1970.

Crockett, James Underwood, and Tanner, Ogden. *Herbs*. Alexandria, Virginia: Time–Life Books, 1977.

Dörner, Gerd. *Mexican Folk Art*. Munich and Vienna: Wilhelm Andermann Verlagg, 1962.

Duvall, Evelyn Millis. *Faith in Families*. Chicago, New York, and San Francisco: Rand McNally & Co., 1970.

Editors of *Better Homes & Gardens*. *Country Crafts*. Des Moines, Iowa: Meredith Corporation, 1982.

Editors of *Better Homes & Gardens*. *Treasury of Christmas Crafts and Foods*. Des Moines, Iowa: Meredith Corporation, 1980.

Editors of *Parents'* Magazine. *Christmas Holiday Book*. New York: Parents' Magazine Press, 1972.

Family Circle, vol. 95, no. 17, 7 December 1982.

Fiarotta, Phyllis. *Snips and Snails and Walnut Whales*. New York: Workman Publishing Co., 1975.

Field News Service. "SCROOGE puts cash in its place." *The Oregonian*, 18 December 1980, p. C7.

Fink, Ed. *Look, Mom, It's Growing*. Barrington, Illinois: Countryside Books, 1976.

Fitch, Charles Marden. *The Complete Book of Houseplants*. New York: Hawthorn Books, 1972.

Foster, Gertrude B. *Herbs for Every Garden*. New York: A Sunrise Book, E. P. Dutton & Co., 1973.

Froman, Robert. *The Many Human Senses*. Boston and Toronto: Little, Brown & Co., 1966.

Gillies, Jean, "Family Traditions Give Christmas Special Meaning." *Farm Journal*, vol. 96, no. 12, December 1972, p. 30.

Goddard, Helen Snow Wilson. *The Gardener's Christmas Book*. New York: The Macmillan Co., 1968.

Gramet, Charles. *Sound and Hearing*. London, New York and Toronto: Abelard-Schuman, 1965.

Handbook on Herbs and Their Ornamental Uses. Brooklyn Botanic Garden Record Plants and Gardens, vol. 28, no. 1, 1972.

Hatfield, Audrey Wynne, *Pleasures of Herbs*. New York: St. Martin's Press, 1965.

Hein, Lucille E. *Entertaining Your Child*. New York: Harper & Row, 1971.

Hemingway, Beth. *A Second Treasury of Christmas Decorations*. New York: Hearthside Press, 1961.

House & Garden, vol. 142, no. 6 (December 1972).

Howard, Jane. *Families*. New York: Simon & Schuster, 1978.

Hume, H. Harold. *Hollies*. New York: The Macmillan Co., 1953.

Ickis, Marguerite. *The Book of Christmas*. New York: Dodd, Mead, & Co., 1960.

Kelley, Marguerite, and Parsons, Elia. *The Mother's Almanac*. New York: Doubleday & Co., 1975.

Ketcham, Howard. *How to Use Color and Decorating Design in the Home*. New York: Greystone Press, 1949.

Krech, David, and Crutchfield, Richard S. *Elements of Psychology*. New York: Alfred A. Knopf, 1969.

McCall's Magazine, vol. 108, no. 3 (December 1980).

Meyer, Carolyn. *Christmas Crafts*. New York, Evanston, San Francisco, London: Harper & Row, 1974.

Montagu, Ashley. *Touching—The Human Significance of the Skin*. New York and London: Columbia University Press, 1971.

Mulac, Margaret E. *Family Fun and Activities*. New York: Harper & Brothers, 1958.

Newsome, Arden J. *Spoolcraft*. New York: Lothrop, Lee & Shepard Co., 1970.

Parents'. December issues of 1972, 1973, 1974, 1976, 1979, 1980.

Rosenthal, Barbara, and Rosenthal, Nadia. *Christmas—New Ideas for an Old-Fashioned Celebration*. New York: Clarkson N. Potter, 1980.

Rossi, Alice S. et al, eds. *The Family*. New York: W. W. Norton & Co., 1978.

Saros, Theodore A. *Christmas Lighting and Decorating: Outdoors and Indoors*. Toronto, New York, London: D. Van Nostrand Co., 1954.

Schafer, Violet. *Herbcraft*. San Francisco: Yerba Buena Press, 1971.

Schulke, Zelda Wyatt. *A Treasury of Christmas Decorations*. New York: Hearthside Press, 1957.

Shoemaker, Kathryn E. *Creative Christmas*. Minneapolis, Minnesota: Winston Press, 1978.

Simmons, Adelma Grenier. *A Merry Christmas Herbal.* New York: William Morrow & Co., 1968.

Staley, Lucy. *New Trends in Table Settings . . . and Period Designs Too*. New York: Hearthside Press, 1968.

Sunset magazine. December issues from 1970 to 1982.

Taylor, Norman, ed. *Taylor's Encyclopedia of Gardening*. Cambridge, Massachusetts: The Riverside Press, 1956.

Waller, Willard. *The Family: A Dynamic Interpretation*. New York: Holt, Rinehart & Winston, 1951.

Warring, Ron. *Modelling with Balsa*. London: Stanley Paul, 1958.

Waugh, Dorothy. *A Handbook of Christmas Decoration*. New York: The Macmillan Co., 1958.

Wertsner, Anne. *Make Your Own Merry Christmas*. New York: M. Barrows & Co., 1946–47.

Zweybruck, Emmy. *The New Stencil Book*. Sandusky, Ohio: Prang Company Publishers, 1953.

HISTORY

Baur, John E. *Christmas on the American Frontier 1800–1900*. Caldwell, Idaho: The Caxton Printers, 1961.

Clark, Ella E. *Indian Legends of the Pacific Northwest*. Berkeley: University of California Press, 1971.

Day, Donald, ed. *The Autobiography of Will Rogers*. Boston: Houghton Mifflin Co., 1926.

Egan, Ferol. *Fremont: Explorer for a Restless Nation*. Garden City, New York: Doubleday & Co., 1977.

Eisenhower, John S. D., ed. *Letters to Mamie* (by Dwight D. Eisenhower). Garden City, New York: Doubleday & Co., 1978.

Foley, Winifred. *As the Twig is Bent*. New York: Taplinger Publishing Co., 1978.

Jordan, Mildred. *The Distelfink Country of the Pennsylvania Dutch*. New York: Crown Publishers, 1978.

A Journal of Thos: Hughes (1778–1789). New York: Cambridge University Press, 1947.

Lehner, Ernest, and Lehner, Johanna. *Folklore and Symbolism of Flowers, Plants and Trees*. New York: Tudor Publishing Co., 1960.

Loschiavo, LindaAnn. "Pretzel Power!" *Seventeen*, May 1981, p. 84.

Mead, Margaret. *Letters from the Field 1925–1975*. New York: Harper & Row, 1977.

Moulton, Phillips P., ed. *The Journal and Major Essays of John Woolman*. New York: Oxford University Press, 1971.

Munford, James Kenneth, ed. *John Ledyard's Journal of Captain Cook's Last Voyage*. Corvallis, Oregon: Oregon State University Press, 1963.

Sabine, Ellen S. *American Folk Art*. Princeton, New Jersey: D. Van Nostrand Co., 1958.

Schaefer, Herwin. *Nineteenth Century Modern*. New York and Washington: Praeger Publishers, 1970.

Skinner, Charles M. *Myths and Legends of Flowers, Trees, Fruits, and Plants*. Philadelphia and London: J. B. Lippincott Co., 1911.

Truman, Margaret, ed. *Letters from Father*. New York: Arbor House, 1981.

Von Kardorff, Ursula. *Diary of a Nightmare: Berlin 1942–1945*. New York: The John Day Co., 1966.

Wilson, Dorothy Clarke. *Lone Woman: The Story of Elizabeth Blackwell The First Woman Doctor*. Boston and Toronto: Little, Brown & Co., 1970.

LITERATURE & RELIGION

Carr, Jo. *Touch the Wind*. Nashville: The Upper Room, 1975.

Dickens, Charles. *A Christmas Carol*. New York: The Macmillan Co., 1963.

Dunn, David. *Try Giving Yourself Away: A Tonic for These Troubled Times*. New Jersey: Prentice-Hall, 1970.

Frost, Lesley, ed. *Come Christmas—A Selection of Christmas Poetry, Song, Drama and Prose*. New York: Coward-McCann, 1929.

Garland, Henry, and Garland, Mary, eds. *The Oxford Companion to German Literature*. Oxford: Clarendon Press, 1976.

Garland, Henry, and Garland, Mary, eds. *The Oxford Companion to German Literature*. New York: Oxford University Press, 1986.

The Holy Bible, Revised Standard Version. Grand Rapids, Michigan: Zondervan Bible Publishers, 1952 (Old Testament Section) and 1971 (New Testament Section, Second Edition).

Irving, Washington. *Old Christmas*. Boston and New York: Houghton Mifflin Co., 1919.

Jones, Elizabeth Orton. *How Far Is It to Bethlehem?* Boston: The Horn Book, 1955.

McGinley, Phyllis. *A Wreath of Christmas Legends*. New York: The Macmillan Co., 1964.

Rollins, Charlemae, ed. *Christmas Gif'*. Chicago: Follet Publishing Co., 1963.

Rosenthal, Lois. *Living Better*. Cincinnati, Ohio: Writer's Digest Books, 1978.

Schaeffer, Edith. *Hidden Art*. Wheaton, Illinois: Tyndale House Publishers, 1971.

Schauffler, Robert Haven, ed. *Christmas: Its Origin, Celebration and Significance as Related in Prose and Verse*. New York: Moffat, Yard & Co., 1916.

Shakespeare, William. *Twelfth Night; or, What You Will*. In *The Complete Works of Shakespeare*. Edited by David Bevington. Glenview, Illinois: Scott, Foresman & Co., 1980.

Shea, Father John. "Does Jesus Believe in Santa Claus?" *US Catholic*, December 1980.

Thomas, Dylan. *A Child's Christmas in Wales*. New York: New Directions, 1954.

Woods, Ralph L., ed. *A Second Treasury of the Familiar*. New York: The Macmillan Co., 1959.

Zumthor, Paul. *Daily Life in Rembrandt's Holland*. New York: The Macmillan Co., 1963.

MUSIC

Agay, Dense, arranger. *The Joy of Christmas*. New York: Yorktown Music Press, 1965.

Ambrosio, W. F., arranger. *Christmas Joys in Verse and Song*. New York: Carl Fischer, 1908.

Coleman, Satis N., and Jörgensen, Elin K., arrangers. *Christmas Carols from Many Countries*. New York: G. Schirmer, 1934.

Duncan, Edmondstoune. *The Story of The Carol*. Detroit: Singing Tree Press, 1968.

Ehret, Walter, and Evans, George K. *The International Book of Christmas Carols*. New Jersey, Prentice-Hall, 1963.

Guenthere, Felix. *Round-the-World Christmas Album*. New York: Edward B. Marks Music Corporation, 1943.

Hawkinson, John, and Faulhaber, Martha. *Rhythms, Music and Instruments To Make*. Chicago: Albert Whitman & Co., 1970.

Heller, Ruth, arranger. *Christmas: Its Carols, Customs and Legends*. Minneapolis: Schmitt, Hall & McCreary Co., 1948.

Hopkins, John H. "Gather Around the Christmas Tree." In *170 Christmas Songs and Carols*, arranged by David Nelson. New York: The Big 3 Music Corporation, 1972.

Hopkins, Lee Bennett, ed. *Sing Hey for Christmas Day!* New York and London: Harcourt Brace Jovanovich, 1975.

Machlis, Joseph. *The Enjoyment of Music*. New York: W. W. Norton & Co., 1955.

The Methodist Hymnal. Nashville: The Methodist Publishing House, 1966.

Myers, Robert Manson. *Handel's Messiah—A Touchstone of Taste*. New York: The Macmillan Co., 1948.

Nelson, David, arranger. *170 Christmas Songs and Carols*. New York: The Big 3 Music Corporation, 1972.

Reed, W. L., ed. *The Second Treasury of Christmas Music*. New York: Emerson Books, 1968.

Roeder, Ann E., arranger. *Folksongs and Games of Holland*. New York: G. Schirmer, 1956.

Routley, Erik. *The Musical Wesleys*. New York: Oxford University Press, 1968.

Spaeth, Sigmund. *A History of Popular Music in America*. New York: Random House, 1948.

Sylvestre, Joshua. *Christmas Carols: Ancient and Modern*. New York: A. Wessels Company, 1905.

Young, Percy M. *Masters of Music, Tchaikovsky*. New York: David White, 1968.

Zanzig, Augustus D., ed. *Singing America Song and Chorus Book*. Boston: C. C. Birchard & Co., 1941.

INDEX

ABOUT THE AUTHORS

Kristin Tucker has enjoyed studying and experimenting with foods as long as she can remember. She earned her B.A. in community nutrition (Oregon State University, 1977) and has worked as a dietary technician, camp cook, and substitute teacher. Now self-employed as a free-lance writer, she specializes in writing on topics related to health, food, and education. Kristin has a special love for church camping and youth ministries programs, and is active in numerous church and community projects.

Kristin lives in Twin Falls, Idaho, with her husband, Tom, pastor of Twin Falls United Methodist Church, and their two children, Nicole and Michael. Together, they work to maintain a home environment that is comfortable and caring, and a place where all are welcome.

Rebecca Lowe Warren is active in the American Association of University Women, the United Methodist Church, and the KBPS Public Radio Advisory Council. When she is not leading Parenting for Peace and Justice workshops or writing histories of houses, Rebecca is planning get-togethers with friends or is running. Having completed one marathon, she is now thinking of training for another. Other interests include gardening, hiking, handcrafts, and travel.

Born and raised in Oregon, Rebecca lives in Portland, Oregon, with her husband, Roger, a salesman, and daughter, Holly.

12/30/89
12/21/91
12/1/94